The Person
of the Therapist

The Person of the Therapist

Edward W. L. Smith

McFarland & Company, Inc., Publishers

Jefferson, North Carolina, and London

ISBN 0-7864-1645-9 (softcover : 50# alkaline paper)

Library of Congress cataloguing data are available

British Library cataloguing data are available

Cover image ©2003 PhotoSpin

Manufactured in the United States of America

*McFarland & Company, Inc., Publishers
Box 611, Jefferson, North Carolina 28640
www.mcfarlandpub.com*

Contents

Preface *On a Personal Note* 1

Chapter 1 A Contextual Note 5

Chapter 2 A Theoretical Note 23

Chapter 3 A Research Note 51

Chapter 4 A Philosophical and Spiritual Note 67

Chapter 5 A Note on the Development of Personhood ... 105

Chapter 6 A Political Note 147

Chapter 7 A Concluding Note 173

References 177

Index 189

On a Personal Note

Intrigued by a certain mystique, I was drawn to membership in the American Academy of Psychotherapists early in the decade of the 1970s. Several of my colleagues, senior to me, were active members. Their eager participation and their enthusiastic discussions about the Academy invited my serious interest and, upon completing the membership requirement of personal therapy, my seeking membership.

In the late 1960s, I had participated in the pre-doctoral Veterans Administration Psychology Traineeship Program. On the wall of the office of one of my supervisors, David Johnson, hung a certificate of membership in the American Academy of Psychotherapists, signed by the president at the time of his joining, Carl Rogers. I often gazed wistfully at that certificate, and upon hearing about the journal published by the Academy, I soon subscribed. *Voices: The Art and Science of Psychotherapy* was the first journal which I read with any regularity, and it is the journal which has best held my loyal interest for more than 30 years of subscription. I was attracted to this journal, imbued as it is with the subjectivity of its authors. Eschewing the reports of statistics-laden objective research, it dared to invite open and personal discussion of the experience of psychotherapy from therapists and clients alike.

I have forgotten the details of the requirements for membership at the time I joined the Academy. I do remember, however, that in addition to a terminal degree in one of the mental health fields which qualified one for license for autonomous practice in one's state, province, or country of residence, a certain number of hours of supervised practice in psychotherapy following the academic degree, and two or three letters of recommendation (some of which were to be from Academy members), there was a requirement of personal therapy. Coming from a traditional clinical psychology program at the University of Kentucky, I had had no encouragement to seek personal therapy. (In fact, the few students who did seek therapy were regarded as afflicted, and at best they received a condescending wish for recovery before their disturbed mental health might disqualify them from further study. The exception to this was my brief experience of group therapy with Charles Truax as part of his psychotherapy course. The requirement of personal therapy for membership in the Academy surprised me, and at the same time appealed to the rebel within me.

So there was much about the Academy that attracted me. There it was, a professional organization requiring its members to have been in personal therapy, and publishing a professional journal that gloried in subjective writing! The mystique was summarized and at the same time enhanced by the credo which I heard spoken: "The Academy is dedicated to the continued development of the person of the therapist." This credo was given radical and bald expression by John Warkentin, one of the founding editors of *Voices*, when he wrote in the inaugural issue in 1965 (1[1], p. 4), "Any sincere therapist should be in continuous therapy for himself during his entire professional life!" This credo, this perdurable theme, has maintained its central place in the Academy as reflected in the types of workshops and peer therapy groups which take place at the meetings. And this theme is in evidence in over 35 years of *Voices*. Fred Klein, in the introduction to the spring 2000 (36[1], p.4) issue, wrote, "The American Academy of Psychotherapists (AAP) is unique among the professional organizations that deal with the field of psychotherapy. AAP explicitly highlights its focus on *the person of the therapist*" (italics added).

Lest one begin to form the opinion that interest in the person of the therapist is confined to the Academy and its members, take note that the concept, if not the phrase itself, can be found more broadly in the literature. Just a few examples will, I believe, suffice. John

Norcross has used the phrase "the person of the therapist" in his presidential column in the *Psychotherapy Bulletin* (2000, 35[2], p. 3), the official publication of the Division of Psychotherapy of the American Psychological Association. Donald Kerr wrote of the person of the therapist in his *Becoming a Therapist: A Workbook for Personal Exploration* (2000, Waveland Press, p.v). Finally, there was a special issue of the *Journal of Couples Therapy* (2000, 9[3/4]) which Barbara Jo Brothers, editor, dedicated to "The Personhood of the Therapist."

I wish to tell an anecdote concerning my initiation into the mystery of the person of the therapist. Just a few years out of graduate school, a young assistant professor and fledgling psychotherapist, I was seeking a theoretical affiliation and identity. In graduate school, I was focused on what was then termed Client Centered therapy, on existential phenomenology, and on Kaiserian therapy. I had the usual broad but somewhat superficial exposure to the panorama of the psychotherapies of the time, typical of the graduate school survey, but it was these three approaches in which I was offered greater depth — Client Centered therapy by Charles Truax; existential phenomenology by Erwin Straus, Richard Griffith, Erling Eng, and Joseph Lyons; and the Kaiserian approach by Juris Berzins. Nevertheless, my identity remained inchoate at best.

In search of a psychotherapeutic identity, I participated in as many training workshops as I could afford during my first years out of graduate school, and I enrolled, serially, in three ongoing post-degree training seminars, two of them lasting a year each and one going on for several years. Sometime during this search, I was invited by John Warkentin to take part in his supervision group. Eager to learn from his supervision, I yet felt a bit of guilt, for I was not an "experiential psychotherapist." One day while sitting with him and the others of our small group, I was feeling, in addition to a twinge of guilt, an especially strong surfeit of theories and techniques. Being thus cloyed only added to my crisis of theoretical identity.

John Warkentin listened patiently and most attentively as I spoke: "I don't know what to call myself as a therapist. I am confused. I like Gestalt, Transactional Analysis, Bioenergetics, Jungian analysis, Satir, Psychomotor therapy, existential therapy, Client Centered therapy ... and experiential therapy," I was quick to add. He waited for me to complete my list, looked at me kindly yet intensely, and said calmly, "I don't see anything wrong with that."

This was an epiphany. I felt teary with relief. He did not explain. He spoke only of how each of these psychotherapies had much that was worthwhile to offer. The irony was that Warkentin called his supervision group his "technique seminar." But, with him, all techniques were subordinated to the person of the therapist.

This phrase — this concept — and the mystique surrounding it still fascinate me. And the idea begs for expatiation. To that end I offer what follows.

Chapter 1

A Contextual Note

Before attempting to understand the person of the therapist, we must first understand the context of psychotherapy, for it is in that context that the person exists *as therapist*. Psychotherapy is, of course, an interpersonal event, an event in which, depending on the format, one or more persons who are therapists encounter one or more persons who are in therapy. The format may be individual, couple, or family therapy. Although individual therapy is usually one-on-one, there may be more than one therapist; in the case of work with a couple or a family, more than one therapist is quite common. In the case of couple and family therapy, and depending on the theoretical orientation of the therapist, the therapist may look upon the couple or the family as the client, or may seek a balance of attention to the couple or family unit and the individuals who constitute that unit. The mode of interaction is verbal in the case of most therapies, although the body psychotherapies involve body interventions (sometimes even direct manipulation of the body of the person in therapy by the therapist) as a formal mode of interaction. Although there are brief models of psychotherapy, therapy usually involves a more or less prolonged interaction between the therapist and the person in therapy. And, finally, there is an agreed-upon agenda of growth or healing for the person in therapy.

As a graduate student and neophyte psychotherapist, I read Robert Harper's (1959) classic *Psychoanalysis & Psychotherapy: 36 Systems,* feeling nearly overwhelmed by this plethora of psychotherapies. Further reading only added to this feeling as I discovered more and more therapies.

Fascinated, yet adrift in a sea of psychotherapies, I began to find my bearings when I learned that each therapy has several elements. First, there is a philosophical underpinning. This may be explicit, as in the case of existential therapies, or it may be implicit, requiring some ferreting out by the student. This philosophical base may address issues of how we can know what we know, including the nature of evidence; what constitutes a good life, and how we as people ought to conduct ourselves; the nature of right thinking; the role and definition of beauty in one's life; and the place of spirituality. These issues of epistemology, ethics, logic, esthetics, and metaphysics (in its more recent meaning, not its original meaning) are the foundation upon which any psychotherapy system is built.

Next, each therapy system has a body of theory. This may include a theory of healthy personality functioning, a theory of normal development, a theory of psychopathology and what leads to pathological development, and a theory of what leads to cure or psychological growth. Again, as is the case with the philosophical underpinnings, therapy systems differ as to how explicit they are in dealing with each of these theoretical areas.

Thirdly, a therapy system contains a body of techniques. Each therapy offers certain methods or procedures to be followed by the therapist in order to encourage growth or healing on the part of the person in therapy. This is, then, a growth or healing technology. Compared to the philosophical or the theoretical aspects of a therapy system, the body of techniques is the aspect most easily recognized. To hear a therapist reflect back to a person in therapy a feeling expressed by the latter may identify the therapy as client centered; an invitation to imagine someone sitting in a designated empty chair and to talk to that person as if he or she were there would be recognized as Gestalt therapy, and so forth. But as accurate as the identification of a technique may be as pertains to its origin, this lends only a superficial understanding of the therapy system itself. Consider for a moment how much is left out when the technique in question is not understood in the fullness of the system from which it comes, including its basic philosophy and its more or less elaborate theory.

In navigating this sea of psychotherapies, I have come to recognize that each system also has a socio-cultural identity. By this I mean that therapies to a greater or lesser extent create their own subcultures. Elements of such a subculture may include a journal or journals dedicated to the particular therapy in question, membership organizations, dedicated meetings or conventions, and perhaps even a jargon and style of dress. Business suits, jump suits, or clothes of purple give visual evidence of membership, as specialized quasi-technical phrases give verbal evidence. Such socio-cultural identity is most likely the least temporally stable aspect of a therapy system. I suggest that the philosophical, theoretical, and technical elements evolve slowly, but as the socio-cultural identity is part of a larger cultural matrix, it may change both more frequently and more noticeably.

To summarize, in order to explicate a system of psychotherapy, one must understand its philosophical underpinnings, its theory, its techniques, and the relationship among these. For full explication, the socio-cultural element in relation to these other elements may have to be added.

For the psychotherapy scholar, there is a natural penchant to compare and contrast the systems as an aid in understanding them. In this process, one may want to form therapies into groups, with respect to some dimension deemed important. Several writers have done such grouping, in the process creating formal models of classification. An early example, offered almost inadvertently in his discussion of the treatment of schizophrenia, appeared in Colby's (1951) *A Primer for Psychotherapists*. Therein, he defined *covering therapy* as defense adding and strengthening, and *uncovering therapy* as dissolving of ego defenses.

A further example of classification can be found in the work of Jung, who, in 1954, drew a distinction between *minor psychotherapy* and *major psychotherapy*. The former consists of "suggestion, good advice, or an apt explanation," whereas the latter consists of a much longer and more elaborate "dialectical procedure" (1966, p. 117). Jung saw psychotherapy as consisting of many layers, each layer being appropriate to a particular patient. There are patients who need only good advice and common sense. Then there are those who are in need of confession or abreaction. For a patient with a more severe neurosis, advice, common sense, confession and abreaction are not sufficient; what is needed is a reductive analysis of their symptoms. Such analysis, according to Jung, should proceed along the lines of Freud if the patient's issues involve infantile pleasure seeking. For those patients who have difficulty in adapting themselves socially, Jung recommended Adler's approach to analysis. "But when the thing becomes monotonous and you begin to get repetitions, ... or when mythological or archetypal contents appear, then is the time to give up the analytical-reductive method and to treat the symbols ana-gogically or synthetically, which is equivalent to the dialectical pro-cedure and the way of individuation" (p. 20). It is in this realm of the dialectic that Jung was clearly most interested. Writing of this dialectic, Jung emphasized that the therapist "must for better or worse give up all pretensions to superior knowledge, all authority and desire to influence. I must perforce adopt a dialectical procedure consist-ing in a comparison of our mutual findings.... My reaction is the only thing with which I as an individual can legitimately confront my patient" (p. 5). Furthermore, Jung indicated that it would not be too great an exaggeration to say that "a good half of every treatment that probes at all deeply consists in the doctor's examining himself, for only what he can put right in himself can he hope to put right in the patient.... It is his own hurt that gives the measure of his power to heal" (p. 116). This, then, is Jung's *major psychotherapy*. We may note that major psychotherapy underscores the importance of the person of the therapist. "As I am, so will I proceed" (p. 329).

Another relatively early example of a model of classification is that of Robert Harper (1959). "Let us make a broad division of the various schools into two main categories: A. the emotionally ori-ented, or affective, therapies and B. the intellectually oriented, or cognitive, therapies" (p. 143). This is a distinction whose use and rel-evance have persisted.

John Warkentin (personal communication, May, 15, 1974) dis-tinguished *rational therapy* from *non-rational therapy*. He described rational therapy as intellectual, fact oriented, problem solving, insight oriented, and adjustment oriented. The therapist is a teacher who prescribes what is to be learned. In contrast, Warkentin described non-rational therapy as emphasizing the emotional rela-tionship of the therapist and the patient. In this relationship, there is respect for the unconscious qua unconscious. The person in ther-apy is more like a disciple and the therapist works to help her or him to find greater freedom of choice and freedom of action on those choices, to become greater. This distinction was highly relevant to Warkentin's work insofar as non-rationality is a salient feature of the Experiential Psychotherapy which he pioneered along with Richard Felder, Tom Malone, and Carl Whitaker. (To clarify, this is the Atlanta Psychiatric Clinic Experiential Psychotherapy. There are at least two other instances of the use of the name. Alvin Mahrer uses it for his therapeutic approach, and the term is sometimes used more generically for therapies in which the focus is on the experience of the person in the therapy session, an experience which goes beyond just intellectual understanding and is centered in the therapeutic relationship.)

In *The Triumph of the Therapeutic*, Philip Rieff (1966) wrote that two therapies may oppose each other, one claiming to be the more scientific. He continued, then, to describe *religious therapies* and *scientific therapies* in the following recondite manner: "The critical difference between religious and scientific therapies is in the locus of control and in the criterion of assessment. In religious therapies, the sense of well-being is measured against the commitment, which is said to 'transcend' it. In scientific therapies, the commitment is measured against the sense of well-being, which is said to be 'immanent' in the commitment" (p. 201).

As useful as these several dichotomous models of classifications may be in understanding psychotherapy, I have found yet another to be even more so. This is the one offered by Perry London (1964). It is closely related to that of Jerome Frank (1961), and was perhaps even inspired by Frank's work. First, then, let us look at Frank's model. Frank differentiated *directive therapy* from *evocative therapy*. In the former, the therapist tries to alleviate specific symptoms or to bring about limited behavioral change through direct interventions. In the latter, the therapist tries to evoke and then explore a wide range of the person's attitudes and feelings as a means of increasing both the extent and the accuracy of self knowledge.

In *The Modes and Morals of Psychotherapy*, London (1964) divided therapies into *action therapy* and *insight therapy*. The goal of action therapy (behavior therapy) is the cure of symptoms, whereas the goal of insight therapy is the expansion of consciousness. With differing goals, the two modes of therapy are therefore appropriate in different situations. That is, circumscribed symptoms call for action therapy, and problems of meaning call for insight therapy. In a form rhetorical and most poetic, London acknowledges the deeper meaning which is approached by insight therapy: "May not men leap from cliffs for other reasons than those for which dogs salivate to bells? Are there not meanings, goals, and fears, and aspirations which, subject to words, to understanding and appraisal, dictate some pains and balms alike, rooting themselves more firmly as they settle into consciousness and intertwine with all man's myriad thoughts of self?" (pp. 38-39).

Had London been writing a few years later than he did, he perhaps would have included a third mode of therapy. In the interest of a more complete and current system of formal classification of psychotherapy systems, he would have had to include the *expressive* therapies. This mode includes Reichian Orgonomy, Alexander Lowen's Bioenergetics and other Neo-Reichian therapies (e.g., John Pierrakos' Core Energetics, Ron Kurtz's Hakomi Method of Body-Centered Psychotherapy, Malcolm Brown's Organismic Psychotherapy, Charles Kelley's Radix therapy, and so forth), Gestalt therapy, Pesso System Psychomotor therapy, and Jacob Moreno's Psychodrama. In describing this expressive mode of therapy, I have written as follows. "At the risk of oversimplification, I would characterize this mode as focusing on facilitating the person in therapy to open to creative and spontaneous expression of feelings" (Smith, 2001, p. 108).

Moving beyond the inherent limitations of dichotomous classifications, Richard Erskine (personal communication, May 6, 1975), in a professional workshop, offered a dynamic model for comparing systems of psychotherapy. His starting place was to acknowledge that there have been three traditional models of therapy, namely, cognitive, affective, and behavioral. (He thereby added the behavioral model to the cognitive and affective models discussed much earlier by Harper.) Placing these three labels at the angles of an equilateral triangle, each therapy system can be located within the triangle, its position suggesting how closely it tends to cognition, affect, and behavior. A therapy that is truly balanced with respect to these three dimensions would, for instance, be placed in the very center of the triangle. This model is dynamic in the sense that it allows for the graphic placement of a given therapy in a manner that reflects the relative strengths and the interaction of the three dimensions.

Erskine's model takes into consideration these interactions

rather than forcing a given therapy, for the purpose of classification, into one of three static compartments. This is important for understanding, for even those therapists whose biases run strongly to one or another of these three dimensions would not deny the existence of the other two. It is rather that the perennial cognitive therapist views cognition as primary, and therefore the best focus of intervention: Change the way of thinking and emotions and action will in turn change. An example of this is the Rational Emotive Therapy, or RET, of Albert Ellis. Even though in recent years he has changed the name to Rational Emotive Behavior Therapy, or REBT, the emphasis clearly remains on the rational, i.e., cognitive aspect. Likewise, the therapist whose bias runs to affect sees the emotions as primary. If the feeling state can be changed, then thinking and action will follow. Perhaps the most extreme example of this view is Primal Therapy, developed by Arthur Janov. And, the therapist given to focus on behavior sees emotion and thought as secondary, and changing in response to changes in action. Joseph Wolpe's Systematic Desensitization is a prime example. The bias as to what is considered primary can be reflected using Erskine's model, while not leaving out the other two aspects.

Interestingly, the interplay of cognition, affect, and conation was addressed at length as early as in the thought of both Plato and Aristotle. Plato divided the soul into three elements, reason, appetites, and a spirited element. Aristotle agreed with Plato that the soul has both a rational and an irrational part, and saw practical activity as arising from reason (rational part) and appetite (an aspect of the irrational part).

Each of the models discussed thus far can be considered an overlay, a template through which to view psychotherapy and by which to compare different therapies in order to understand them better. Each model offers a different perspective, focusing as it does along some particular dimension. In addition to such formalized models, psychotherapies can be viewed along various informal dimensions.

One interesting dimension on which therapies can be compared is that of degree of reliance on technique. The poles of that dimension may be labeled *technique* and *relationship*. An example of a therapy that would fall at or near the technique pole is Systematic Desensitization, developed by Joseph Wolpe. A therapy such as this lends itself to manualization. That is, since a set technique is said to carry the day, that technique can be written down as a step by step procedure. The important thing is for the therapist to follow the procedure precisely. At the other pole are those therapies that feature the relationship between the therapist and the person in therapy. It is the relationship, per se, which is valued as the arena and as the vehicle for growth and healing. Examples of therapies at this pole are the approach of Hellmuth Kaiser and that of Experiential Psychotherapy as associated with the early Atlanta Psychiatric Clinic.

At the technique pole, the emphasis is on action, on what the therapist is *doing*; at the relationship pole, the emphasis is on presence, on the therapist's *being*. The therapist who commits to either extreme may fail to appreciate what the other pole offers. The "technique-ful" therapist may underestimate the power of the relationship which forms the context in which the technique is delivered. And at the other pole, the therapist may overvalue the therapist-patient relationship as *the* necessary and sufficient condition for growth and healing.

In order to form a nexus between my central theme of the person of the therapist and this technique-relationship dimension, I want to emphasize that personhood is important along the entire dimension. However, personhood is of increasing importance as we move from the therapies closer to the technique pole to those therapies closer to the relationship pole. Or, I may state in terms of London's more formal and dichotomous model, personhood is of increasing importance as we move from more action-oriented to more insight-oriented therapies. Action-oriented therapies tend to be more technique based, the focus being on *what* is done by the therapist. Insight-oriented therapies tend to be less technique based, the focus being more on *how* the therapist does what he or she does. This focus on the how shifts the emphasis from technique to relationship. Once stated, these points may seem obvious.

Let us explore further the continuum of technique and relationship. It is a truism that in any meeting of a therapist and a person in therapy there is formed a context of relationship. So, relationship is ubiquitous in psychotherapy. Now the question becomes, To what extent are techniques explicitly added to this mix of therapist and person in therapy? Here we move through the dimension of mere presence (in the sense of presence without prescribed activity, albeit perhaps profound and efficacious presence) to method, to procedure, to specific technique, a dimension of increasingly specifically prescribed activity on the part of the therapist. The more specifically prescribed the activity of the therapist is, the more "technique-ful" is that therapy, the more the technique becomes the interface between the therapist and the person in therapy. With that said, and for economy of language, I will use just the word "technique" to include method and procedure.

Each therapy system, then, through its body of techniques, offers particular ways for the therapist to be with the person in therapy. Here, then, we have arrived at a particular perspective on technique. *A technique is a way of being-with.* I hyphenate *being-with* in order to emphasize the particular quality inherent in the relationship between therapist and person in therapy, in all its uniqueness. Some ways of being-with reveal more of the person of the therapist than do others. But even the very way of being-with chosen by the therapist, regardless of what is revealed within the context of that choice, carries a revelation of the therapist's person at a meta-level. To conceive of a therapy technique as a way of being-with is to create, then, a new perspective on the technique-relationship continuum wherein relationship is seen in its primacy. And, once again, we are back to our focus on the person of the therapist.

There is, I believe, an ethical implication to this view of technique. If we conceive of a technique as a way of being-with, and not as a disembodied thing which is applied to the person in therapy, then to be genuine a therapist must embody only techniques which are consistent with who the therapist is as a person. That is, the technique must be ego-syntonic: It must emanate from the personhood of that therapist. Or, as I have previously written,

> The first ethical duty which I see is what I term the *ego-syntonic imperative.* By this term I mean that in order for one to function optimally in the therapeutic role it is essential that he or she relate to the patient only in ways that are congruent with who that therapist is. Techniques, as I have emphasized, are given life and meaning through the person of the therapist. It is imperative, then, that the therapist only interact with the patient through techniques which are consistent with the therapist's person. To use ego-dystonic techniques is to be mechanical and inauthentic. So, if a

> therapist feels like herself or himself in using a technique, if
> that technique seems to flow out of her or him, then it is an
> appropriate technique to keep in one's repertoire [Smith,
> 1985, p. 148].

The choice of a psychotherapy orientation is, then, in part an ethical choice. One is well advised to choose a system which offers an ego-syntonic way of being with persons in therapy. In addition, the choice of one's psychotherapy orientation is an esthetic one. That is, the system chosen is better if it is pleasing, if it holds a certain beauty in the eye of the therapist. A study of the current status of research in psychotherapy leads one to conclude that, by and large, all of the psychotherapies work. The bulk of the evidence points to this conclusion. So, one cannot simply choose a therapy because it is, overall, more efficacious. Rather, one must choose a therapy because one likes how it looks, sounds, and feels, and because it fits one's person. I believe that if the therapist is honest with herself or himself that therapist will recognize this view as valid.

To speak of the esthetic dimension of psychotherapy is to acknowledge, at least tacitly, that it is an art. Certainly science is close at hand. The development of theory surely is heavily laden with scientific criteria and considerations. And research on psychotherapy is a quintessential scientific enterprise. Nevertheless, being with a person in therapy in a way which facilitates growth and healing is an art form. It is a performing art in the most noble and most profound sense of the term. Tom Leland (1965), one of the founding editors of *Voices*, in his inaugural editorial used the phrase "the art of psychotherapy and therapy as an art form" in describing the emphasis of this new journal, subtitled *The Art and Science of Psychotherapy* (p. 5). A score and more years later, James Bugental (1987) reiterated that psychotherapy is an art form when he titled one of his books *The Art of the Psychotherapist*.

Sue Galler Rosenthal (1999) has written eloquently about the esthetic experience of psychotherapy. "Just as much of modern art is self-reflexive, revealing the process of the focal medium, so the *message* of diverse systems of therapy is clearly heard through the *medium*, the personhood of the therapist. It is the mediating style, the perception and sensitivity of the therapist which may ultimately make of the therapeutic encounter an aesthetic experience, rather than a merely functional communication mode" (p. 7).

Thus, one may say correctly that psychotherapy is both art and science. To theorize about it and to conduct research on it is science; to do it is art. But society is reluctant to pay for art, to lend strong support to its artists. So, to appease the industry which pays for psychotherapy, some psychotherapists themselves downplay their art qua art and emphasize the scientific aspects of it. And so a language of diagnosis, therapy, treatment, cure, and patient, randomized trials, meta-analysis, and statistical significance is reinforced by economics, to the neglect of the acknowledgment of another aspect, the artistic.

Just as the term "patient" sets a certain mood for psychotherapy, so too do all of the other terms that may take its place. Such terms as "client," "counselee," "consumer," and "person in psychotherapy" bring with them not only denotations but connotations as well. And, in a more poetic vein, what about terms like "pilgrim," "seeker," "fellow traveler," and others which may occasionally be used? It may be interesting to contemplate for a few minutes the ramifications even of these various terms used for persons who are seen in psychotherapy. Not only do they have implications for the psychotherapy setting itself, but they also have implications for the image and place of psychotherapy in the larger societal context.

To recognize psychotherapy as an art form and the therapist as an artist is, once again, to come back to the person of the therapist, for art is *personal* creativity. The *how* is once more figural and the *what* has receded to background. The style is dominant, the content secondary.

Another dimension, interesting to consider, is that of the degree to which a given psychotherapy relies on an altered state of consciousness. Some therapies do so explicitly, reflecting this in the names used. Examples of this are Ericksonian hypnosis, hypnoanalysis, hypnotherapy, or simply clinical hypnosis. In such cases, with the exception sometimes of Ericksonian hypnosis, a formal hypnotic trance induction is used, this being the defining technique. Whatever else is done, the basic technique is trance induction. It should be remembered that if a therapy is called hypnosis, or variations with hypno- as a prefix, it is to this technique that reference is made, and that the underlying theory and philosophical underpinning may be quite varied. Ericksonian hypnosis, of course, has considerable theory contained in the system. Hypnoanalysis, too, has such, in the form of psychoanalytic theory.

Other therapies may rely on the use of an altered state of consciousness other than hypnosis. One example is the Holotropic Breath Work pioneered by Stanislav Grof. Another is the integration of shamanic journeying into psychotherapy. Mediated by a prescribed drumming or rattling, a shamanic state of consciousness is believed by such therapists to be evoked.

Still other therapies may at times be attended by an altered state of consciousness, even though this may not be made explicit in all of the literature or discussions of these therapies. I have made a case for such in the situation of the psychodramatic acting out (e.g., the empty chair dialogue) which is often a part of Gestalt therapy (Smith, 1975, 1978). (Notable for extensive use of formal trance induction within the theoretical and philosophical framework of Gestalt therapy is the work of Abraham Levitsky [1997]). Pesso System Psychomotor, PSP, seems often to involve an altered state of unconsciousness, brought about through the ritual, often age-regressive, of creating the role-play situation known as a *structure*. Based on my limited experience with Psychodrama, the therapy system created by Jacob Moreno, my opinion is that an altered state of consciousness sometimes attends this as well. In the cases of Gestalt psychodramatic acting out, the Psychomotor structure, and the Psychodrama, role play is involved. Perhaps the effectiveness of role-play depends to a greater or lesser degree on the establishment of an altered state of consciousness whereby the enacted role is endowed with a quality of psychological reality. If so, then even behavioral rehearsal, a technique of behavior therapy, may rely on a degree of altered consciousness.

So, for benefit of understanding, psychotherapy systems may be viewed along a dimension of use of altered consciousness, whether or not a system is explicit about the alteration of consciousness in its theory or in its techniques.

Earlier, I alluded to the conclusion, supported by research, that in general, psychotherapy works. This conclusion is important as part of the broader context of psychotherapy in which the person of the therapist is explored. Because of the importance of this aspect of the context of psychotherapy, I want to elaborate. Michael Lambert and Allen Bergin (1994) wrote an erudite summary of research on psychotherapy outcomes, making several compelling points, including the following:

> Many psychotherapies that have been subjected to empirical study have been shown to have demonstrable effects on a variety of clients. These effects are not only statistically significant but also clinically meaningful.... Data support the use of brief therapies for some problems and cast doubt on their value for other problems.... The effects of therapy tend to be lasting.... Not only is there clear evidence for the effectiveness of therapy relative to untreated patients, but psychotherapy patients show gains that surpass those resulting from pseudotherapies and placebo controls.... Differences in outcome between various forms of therapy are not as pronounced as might have been expected.... Average positive effects mask considerable variability in outcomes. Wide variations exist in therapists. The therapist factor, as a contributor to outcome, is looming large in the assessment of outcomes [pp. 180-181].

In November of 1995, *Consumer Reports* published an article based on the reactions that persons in therapy had to their therapy experience. This approach, psychotherapy *effectiveness* based on consumer satisfaction, contrasted with the usual research in psychotherapy which came to be labeled psychotherapy *efficacy*. Martin Seligman (1995) summarized the *Consumer Reports* study, stating, among other things, that "patients benefited very substantially from psychotherapy, that long-term treatment did considerably better than short-term treatment, and that psychotherapy alone did not differ in effectiveness from medication plus psychotherapy. Furthermore, no specific modality of psychotherapy did better than any other for any disorder.... Patients whose length of therapy or choice of therapist was limited by insurance or managed care did worse" (p. 965).

To include research which was reported after the publication of the chapter that he and Bergin wrote and after the publication of the *Consumer Reports* study, Michael Lambert (2001) offered an updated summary. The impact of the further research was to reinforce what had been stated earlier. His conclusions were that

> psychotherapy is effective.... Hundreds of studies have now
> been conducted on the effects of psychotherapy including
> research on psychodynamic, humanistic, behavioral, cogni-
> tive, and variations and combinations of these approaches.
> Reviews of this research, both qualitative and quantitative,
> have shown that about 75 percent of those who enter treat-
> ment show some benefit.... For the most part, psychological
> interventions surpass the effects of medication for psychologi-
> cal disorders.... The effects of psychotherapy are more power-
> ful than informal support systems and placebo controls....
> The outcomes of psychotherapy are substantial.... The out-
> comes of therapy tend to be maintained.... Psychotherapy is
> relatively efficient [pp. 9-10].

It is not surprising, then, with the plethora of therapies extant,
and with research supporting their efficacy, that many therapists do
not hold allegiance to only one, but may claim several, or aspects of
several, as their therapeutic focus. In fact, according to the
cognoscenti, eclectic approaches are very popular. Richard Sharf
(2000) reports in his *Theories of Psychotherapy and Counseling* that
in a recent survey 27 percent of clinical psychologists, 40 percent of
counseling psychologists, 53 percent of psychiatrists, 34 percent of
social workers, and 37 percent of counselors identified themselves as
eclectic or integrative when asked their primary theoretical orientation. In another study reported by Sharf, 68 percent of the therapists
identified themselves as eclectics, and when asked to indicate which
therapies they integrated into their eclectic positions, they listed an
average of 4.4 theories.

By considering the various aspects of a psychotherapy system,
we can see the possibility of different levels of integration. One level
is a *technical eclecticism*, in which a therapist of a particular theoretical persuasion may integrate techniques from one or more other systems into her or his work. This is made feasible by the fact that
techniques, themselves, are often only tenuously connected with
their underlying theory. Additionally, a given technique may well be
understood in terms of more than one theory and thus be found
compatible with more than one psychotherapy system. This makes
it possible, then, to take techniques which are identified with other
theoretical systems and combine them without doing violence to the
underlying theoretical system of the therapist.

Another level is the integration of theories themselves, along with their respective techniques. In order to appreciate the appeal of such *theoretical eclecticism,* it may be helpful to think of theories as analogous to languages. A language contains a vocabulary and a syntax or grammar. So, too, with a theory. Each theory presents us with particular words for the labeling of phenomena and with rules whereby these words can be related to other words, that is, rules whereby one phenomenon can be related to other phenomena. This vocabulary reveals, particularly in the case of words and phrases that are peculiar to a given theory, the phenomena which are invested with the greatest importance by that theory. *Noogenic neuroses, Oedipus complex, being-in-the-world, enantiodromia, cognitive schemas, reciprocal inhibition, tele,* and *Gemeinschaftsgeful,* are examples of such terms, terms which carry the burden of meaning writ large. These tightly packed words and phrases serve as a summary, and when unpacked present major theoretical concepts. The size of the vocabulary of a particular psychotherapy system is a clue to the breadth of phenomena addressed by that system and to the degree of precision with which these phenomena are addressed. Just as a desired nuance of expression may dictate which language a polyglot may choose to use in a particular situation, being able to speak several theoretical languages may give the therapist greater range and depth of understanding and expression. The therapist who has accomplished a theoretical eclecticism is in the position of choosing from a greater base of descriptive and explanatory constructs and attending techniques.

In the interest of thoroughness, a third level of integration must be mentioned, *transtheoretical integration.* Using the model described by Prochaska and Norcross as his example, Sharf (2000) describes the transtheoretical approach as one which "examines many theories, selecting concepts, techniques, and other factors that effective psychotherapeutic approaches have in common" (p. 629). The goal of this approach is, then, to enucleate various therapies, to recognize what they hold in common, and to combine those commonalities, allowing an approach to emerge, new in its Gestalt.

Early in my education as a psychotherapist, I noted that oftentimes the therapists who identified themselves as eclectic lacked a deep understanding of the systems which they purported to integrate. Theoretical incompatibilities were in evidence, or techniques were employed without benefit of convincing theoretical rationale. At its worst, I saw a theoretical hodgepodge and bags of technical tricks, a psychotherapy of *omnium-gatherum*. The caveat with respect to eclecticism is to not move to integration too quickly, before becoming intimate with the individual systems in their own right; the danger with respect to eclecticism is dilettantism.

Turning now to yet another topic, I have been fascinated by seeing that psychotherapy systems are sometimes endued with a religious mien. Perhaps this is a manifestation of Jung's religious archetype, invited by the social structure and social position of psychotherapy, at a time when psychotherapists do not find their spiritual needs satisfied by more traditional religion. My statement seems to me to be consonant with Philip Rieff's (1966) lengthy and scholarly exploration of the place of psychotherapy in our post-religious society. Seeing psychotherapy as a contemporary answer to the religious question, he stated the following: "The religious question: How are we to be consoled for the misery of living? may be answered by a culture, thus defined, in various ways.... The prophet in all three of Freud's most powerful successor-critics was much stronger than the scientist" (p. 29). Much of his view is reflected in the titles that he chose for the chapters of his book, as well as in the book title itself: *The Triumph of the Therapeutic: Uses of Faith After Freud*. Consider these chapters devoted to "Freud's most powerful successor-critics": "The Therapeutic as Theologian: Jung's Psychology as a Language of Faith," "The Therapeutic as Martyr: Reich's Religion of Energy," and "The Therapeutic as Mythmaker: Lawrence's True Christian Philosophy."

One of the strongest cases for seeing a psychotherapy in religious terms has been made by Richard Noll (1997) in *The Jung Cult: Origins of a Charismatic Movement*. After lengthy analysis, he concludes that "in Weberian terms, Jung was indeed a prophet who, through his 'personal call,' was both a 'renewer of religion' and a 'founder of religion'" (p. 277).

On a less lofty level, we can ponder the following points, relevant to many of the psychotherapies. Master therapists, those pioneers who have developed psychotherapy systems, often are regarded as high priests by a following of disciples. The disciples often witness for them, and proselytize for them. If there is any doubt about this, it should be dispelled by a reading of Orson Bean's (1971) *Me and the Orgone*, to cite just one example. These disciples, led by their high priests, sometimes conduct psychotherapy "holy wars" on the field of debate. It is not at all uncommon to hear leaders and disciples alike proclaiming the superiority of their systems over all others, particularly at professional conventions. The selection of a system of psychotherapy by a therapist is often based primarily on belief. The person in therapy may go to a therapist to confess (a term used by therapists as different as Jung and O. H. Mowrer), to be absolved, and perhaps be given penance in the form of homework to be practiced before the next psychotherapy session. And just as, according to William James, religious experience is justified on experiential grounds and needs no justification outside that experience, so too, is psychotherapy for many. For better or for worse, I think that this religious overtone is worth considering as part of the broad context of psychotherapy.

My limning of psychotherapy as a necessary context for the person of the therapist has been perforce brief and biased. Whole books could be developed around several of the core topics that I have chosen. Furthermore, my choice of topics just as much reveals my ignorance and lack of interest as it does my knowledge and passionate interest. Hopefully, my portrayal of the context will serve its purpose. I have invoked a paradox. Psychotherapy exists only as it is given life through the person of a particular therapist, yet psychotherapy exists, like a Platonic Form, apart from the practitioner. So far, our discussion has been mostly of psychotherapy. Let us now delve into the person of the therapist.

Chapter 2

A Theoretical Note

"When the wrong man uses the right means, the right means work in the wrong way." Barry Stevens (1970, p. 7), wrote this. She had a knack for stating wisdom in such down-to-earth terms, in terms so simple and so clear, that the truth shone through and illuminated. I stood with her one clear, cool morning at daybreak. We stood in silence as we watched the sun emerge over the peak of a Colorado mountain and flood the valley with light. This is how she was. Within a few hours, I watched her as she worked with a volunteer in a seminar. She worked slowly, gently, respectfully. As she demonstrated her way of Gestalt, her way of body work, I was certain that she was, in her phrase, the "right man."

Beyond the system of psychotherapy, with its underlying philosophy, its theories, and its methods, there is something more, something of a different plane. Earlier, I wrote that "techniques, as well as philosophies and theories, are abstractions. As abstractions, techniques are made concrete only through the work of the therapist. That is, technique is given life through the person of the therapist. The technique only becomes a lived event as it is brought to life through the therapist's personal expression" (Smith, 2000, p.44). In addition, "I suggest that no given technique, however objectively pure it seems in the abstract, when read about or talked about, is ever the same when given life by different persons. The *personal* is, here, vital. It is the individual, personally mediated expression of the technique which is real and present for the person in therapy" (Smith, 2001, p. 73). There is a plane of abstractions and there is a plane of lived events. On this latter plane the abstract technique is brought to life by a breathing, living therapist.

Again, putting methods into the personal context, Michael Lambert and Allen Bergin (1994) wrote, "The complexity and subtlety of psychotherapeutic processes cannot be reduced to a set of disembodied techniques because techniques gain their meaning and, in turn, their effectiveness from the particular interaction of the individuals involved" (p. 167). Although they referred to the interaction of the individuals involved, inclusive of therapist and person in therapy, the focus I want to keep is on the therapist. With respect to the therapist, and with reference to research evidence, they continued, reporting that "despite careful selection, training, monitoring, and supervision, therapists offering the same treatments can have highly divergent results" (p. 174). The research suggests strongly, then, that the same method may have very different results when manifested through different, but equally trained and supervised psychotherapists! Lambert and Bergin stated further that "the therapist factor, as a contributor to outcome, is looming large in the assessment of outcomes" (p. 182).

It is, I believe, important to emphasize that the therapist factor prevails even when therapists are following an explicit protocol. As Lambert and Bergin (1994) expressed this, "The individual therapist can play a surprisingly large role in treatment outcome even when treatment is being offered within the stipulations of manual-guided therapy" (p. 181). Different therapists evidence different levels of efficacy, even when they do therapy "by the book," as reflected in training, supervision, and monitoring.

Implicit in the finding that different therapists employing the same method have different results is the suggestion that some therapists may not be very efficacious. Or, stated more bluntly, some therapists may not be very good at what they do! I learned of this when I took my first psychotherapy course, taught by Charles Truax, who had been one of Carl Rogers' students. His course was heavily imbued with the research which he and his associates had conducted in what was then known as Client Centered Therapy. One of the papers distributed to us students was a chapter which he and Robert Carkhuff had authored for a 1964 book published by McGill University Press, the chapter being titled "For Better or for Worse...The Process of Psychotherapeutic Personality Change." In this chapter, and in several other publications, Truax and Carkhuff presented a model for psychotherapy based on the work of Carl Rogers. The model indicated *Constructive Personality Change* (CPC) to be a function of *Accurate Empathy* (AE), *Unconditional Positive Regard* (UPR), *Therapist Self-Congruence* (TSC), and *Depth of Intrapersonal Exploration* (DX). The model was written in mathematical format as follows:

$$CPC = K + (AE)B1 + (UPR)B2 + (TSC)B3 + (DX)B4 + e$$

This mathematical model is, more specifically, a regression equation, in which K stands for a constant, B1, B2, B3, and B4 for beta weights (to be derived empirically), and e a residual error term. What the model suggests, stripped of its sophisticated mathematical cloak, is that therapeutic change is a function of certain therapeutic conditions and those therapeutic conditions can assume different amounts of relative importance. Truax referred to these conditions as *core conditions*. The first three, being under the control of the therapist, were seen as therapist variables, whereas the fourth, Depth of Intrapersonal Exploration, being under the control of the client, was seen as a client variable. The three therapist variables—or, more properly stated, the three therapist behaviors—of accurate empathy, unconditional positive regard, and self-congruence or genuineness were seen by Rogers as both necessary and sufficient conditions for personality growth.

Truax refined scales for the measurement of these core conditions for use with tape recorded therapy sessions, a nine-point scale for AE, a five-point scale for UPR, a seven-point scale for TSC, and a ten-point scale for DX. Using the ratings of therapy sessions generated by trained raters, and an array of pre-therapy and post-therapy personality measures, Truax and his associates not only investigated therapy outcome but also conducted therapy process research. That is, they investigated the relationship between the therapist variables and therapy outcome, the process of psychotherapy and its effects. Truax and Carkhuff reported in their paper that their research suggested not only that constructive personality change was in evidence when the core conditions were at high levels, but also that, when the core conditions were at low levels, clients actually showed negative personality change. They reported what they termed a very

sober finding: *psychotherapy can be for better or for worse!* Additionally, they found evidence that the greater the degree of depth at which
the client engaged in intrapersonal exploration, the greater the degree
of constructive personality change.

I have dwelt on the work of Truax because of two very important implications. These implications emerge from the conceptual
model, and should not be missed by virtue of taking issue with the
use of a mathematical regression equation, with its promise of a high
degree of precision. Whether one likes or does not like the implication of precision, or any meta-message which the regression equation carries, the implications of the conceptual model endure. The
first implication is that therapists, because of personal characteristics, may contribute to deterioration in the persons who are in therapy with them. Based on a considerable body of research since that
of Truax, and consistent with his findings, Lambert and Bergin (1994)
state that a portion of those whom psychotherapy is intended to help
are harmed; and, as cited above, therapists using the same methods
can have very different results. A corollary to this point is that when
psychotherapy outcome research is conducted without assessing the
efficacy of the individual therapists involved, the work of the "good"
therapists and the work of the "poor" therapists may cancel each other
out statistically, yielding a less than convincing net result as to the
efficacy of psychotherapy. This corollary, too, is addressed by Lambert and Bergin in their review of the research literature: "Evidence
was presented ... of some rather large differences in outcome rates
when they were estimated therapist by therapist.... Negative change
appeared in some cases and was associated more with some therapists than with others. To the extent that negative changes occur,
they obviously subtract from overall therapeutic effect sizes" (p. 176).

The second implication of Truax's work that I want to emphasize is that his model can account for the efficacy of different personal
styles of therapy. If constructive personality change is a function of
these several variables, each having a weighting, then two different
therapists could have different levels of each of the variables, as long
as the summation reached the cutoff point for constructive personality change. In other words, one efficacious therapist may exhibit
less empathy, but be more genuine, than another. A great deal of self-
congruence on the part of this therapist may compensate for somewhat less empathy, and together with the other variables reach the

minimal level for constructive personality change. While there may be a minimal level of each of the variables that is *necessary*, it is the sum of the levels relative to some cutoff point that is the *sufficient* condition for positive therapy outcome.

Returning to Barry Stevens, and paraphrasing her, when a poor therapist uses a good method, the results will be poor. But she said more, with reference to psychotherapy technique: "Quite often, good things happen when these tools are used by people of good will who don't understand them or don't completely understand them" (Stevens, 1970, p. 7). Not only did she recognize the deterioration effect, but she recognized that some quality of the person of the therapist may be more important than technical understanding in the determination of outcome. The message is the same, whether it is stated more poetically or in a mathematical model, whether it is discovered in the psychotherapy workshop or in formal research on the process of psychotherapy. And the message is the same whether the characteristic is summarized by the phrase "good will," or that phrase is expanded into accurate empathy, unconditional positive regard, and therapist self-congruence.

Earlier, I considered the placement of different therapies on a continuum of relationship and technique. At the extremes, the therapist at one pole would espouse the belief that relationship is everything. The therapist at the anti-pole would espouse the belief that technique is everything. Even if these antipodes are somewhat forced, they call attention to the fact that therapists do disagree as to the relative importance of personal interaction and technical manipulation. With respect to personhood, those therapists at the pole of relationship would embrace belief in its importance. Those therapists at the opposite pole may need reminders of the research evidence concerning the importance of personal qualities in therapy outcome. A useful perspective, and one which fully acknowledges the importance of the person of the therapist, regardless of the theoretical orientation of the therapist, is this: Most therapists locate themselves somewhere between the antipodes, reflecting the fact that no matter what the therapy, there cannot be disembodied technique in the consulting room, nor can there be a therapist present who does not occupy that time and space with her or his level of consciousness. These temporal and extensional dimensions pale in comparison with the third, the dimension of aware presence.

My onetime mentor and longtime colleague, Irma Lee Shepherd (1992), has expressed her doubt that psychotherapy can be taught. Perhaps shocking in its terseness, let us see what this means. Shepherd explained that being a psychotherapist may not be able to be taught in the same sense that being an artist may not be able to be taught. (She used the term artist in its more specific meaning, but she would certainly agree that the psychotherapist is, in the broader sense of the word, an artist.) In order for a therapist to transcend the artificial application of techniques, it is personal resources which are crucial. It is these personal resources which must be developed. As I see the parallel, just as with an artist, talent may be recognized, but that talent must be accessed and it must be developed in order for the person in question to become a psychotherapist. Continuing with the parallel, there are art historians, there are art critics, there are those who do art; and there are those who research psychotherapy, there are those who teach about it, and there those who do psychotherapy. Then there are those who *are* artists, taken either in the narrower or the wider sense of the word. Shepherd drew this distinction, writing that it is the "power and authenticity of the person" which is needed for one to *be* a therapist and not just *do* therapy (p. 239). Consider this phrase — power and authenticity of the person.

Perhaps it would be useful at this point to see how the emphasis on personal resources can articulate an underlying theory. Although there was hint of this in my allusion to Rogers and the discussion of Truax's work earlier, I would now like to give a more complete example by means of a sojourn in the system of Hellmuth Kaiser. Kaiser's position is not well known, and yet, for me, is attended by a certain elegant simplicity, as well as being a prime example of trust in the therapeutic power of the person of the therapist. And if the importance of personhood reaches its zenith where technique is least in evidence, perhaps Kaiser has much to teach us.

In the Afterword of his editing of Kaiser's works, *Effective Psychotherapy: The Contribution of Hellmuth Kaiser*, Louis Fierman (1965) wrote that Kaiser "identifies the essential ingredient of effective psychotherapy as being the authentic communicative relationship offered to the patient by the therapist. A model for effective psychotherapy can thus be conceptualized as one in which the sole and exclusive concern and interest of the therapist is to maintain a communicative intimacy" (p. 203). Fierman then offered a remarkably tightly packed summary of Kaiser's model: "The *universal triad* consists of the *universal psychopathology*, the *universal symptom*, and the *universal therapy*. The universal psychopathology is the attempt to create in real life the illusion of the universal fantasy of fusion. The universal symptom is duplicity in communication. The universal therapy is the communicative intimacy offered by the psychotherapist" (p. 207).

My task, now, will be to unpack this tightly wrapped package, allowing its meaning to emerge in greater fullness. In discussing the universal psychopathology, Kaiser used the term *neurotic*, but at the time of his writing this term was used somewhat more broadly than is now the case. Using his term, the neurotic is one who cannot tolerate the fact of her or his fundamental aloneness, and therefore seeks to deny this existential fact. Three mental activities seem especially conducive to the production of this inner experience of aloneness (Enelow & Adler, 1965). Whenever one reaches a conviction which is not supported by authority, or wants something which others do not value, or makes a decision that is not widely approved, the basic fact of individuality, or existential aloneness, is poignantly emphasized. (One may note here the similarity to Jean-Paul Sartre's description of the human condition. In Sartre's view, the human condition is constituted of *anguish*, created by the imperative to choose, the angst which comes with choice and responsibility. It is constituted of *despair* over our inability to make the world, including other people, do as we would will, leaving us to deal with only probabilities as to what may happen. It is constituted, also, of a sense of *abandonment*, the situation in which there is no ultimate authority to tell us what to choose. I find no reference to Sartre in Fierman's definitive volume on Kaiser. However, it is interesting to note that Kaiser, having fled Germany, did live in Paris during the late 1930s.)

In the attempt to deny the existential fact of her or his aloneness, the neurotic tries to avoid personal, that is, individual, responsibility for her or his life. There is an *illusion of fusion*, an illusion that we are not alone, that may be experienced by belonging to a club, an interest group, or a religion, by playing on a team, playing in a musical group, or marching in a parade. In joint activities and in memberships, we create an illusion of fusing with others. But with the neurotic, there is an attempt to create in real life this illusion, making of it a *delusion of fusion*.

The way that the neurotic avoids individual responsibility for her or his life, the way that the delusion of fusion is created, is through *duplicitous communication*. The neurotic is not behind her or his words. It is this duplicity in communication that is the common thread running through all neuroses, the universal symptom. (Here, again, one may sense an affinity between Kaiser's ideas and those of Sartre. For Kaiser, it is that the neurotic is duplicitous in her or his communication, trying to avoid personal responsibility for her or his life; for Sartre, this is a matter of *mauvaise foi, bad faith.*)

If duplicitous communication is the universal symptom, then the universal treatment is straightforward, that is, non-duplicitous, communication on the part of the therapist. The goal of therapy is quite simply the establishment of straightforward communication. When the person in therapy experiences non-duplicity on the part of the therapist, and finds that this is safe, he or she can then move to be more behind his or her words.

In his discussion of Kaiser's approach, Hans Welling (2000) traced the evolution of the process of analysis from Freud to Kaiser. Whereas Freud began with the *analysis of content* early in his psychoanalytic work, he mentioned by 1914 the idea of *analysis of resistance* in the analysand. Welling suggested that it was an elaboration of resistance analysis which became Wilhelm Reich's *character analysis*. Reich recognized that it is not *what* the patient says, but *how* the patient says it that must be interpreted. "Reich argued that character resistance can hinder the classic content analysis, as every content interpretation is distorted by the typical rigid cognitive functioning of the patient's character structure" (p. 58). Kaiser became an advocate of consistent resistance analysis. But as he allowed his theory to evolve, he came to focus on the *analysis of duplicity*. The purpose of interventions, according to Kaiser in 1934, was to eliminate resistance; in 1955 it was to increase the sense of responsibility in the patient; and in 1965 to diminish duplicity. According to Allen Enelow and Leta McKinney Adler (1965), what Kaiser referred to as *resistance analysis* early in his work he later called *defense analysis*, before finally coming to settle on *duplicity analysis*.

Kaiser's work evolved, then, from that of resistance analysis to defense analysis to duplicity analysis. It focuses radically on the *how* of the communication, rather than the *what*, the *style* rather than the *content*, a focus derived from his work with Reich (Enelow & Adler,

1965). Duplicity is, of course, revealed in *how* one communicates, in one's *style*.

Kaiser's (1965) guideline for the psychotherapist is "don't withdraw, neither physically nor psychologically!" (p. 155). This guideline comes in the context "that the conditions for effective psychotherapy can be expressed only in terms of personality characteristics of the therapist, and *not* in rules of what he should do" (p. 160). What are these personality characteristics, according to Kaiser? He articulated them as follows: First, the therapist must be interested in establishing straightforward communication with relatively uncommunicative persons, uncommunicative because of their neurosis. This interest must be genuine in that it is an end in itself. Second, the therapist is free to have her or his communications determined by the above named interest and not restricted by theoretical restraints. Third, the therapist must be relatively free from neurosis, that is, free from the symptom of duplicitous communication, herself or himself. And fourth, the therapist must be sensitive to recognizing duplicity in the other (p. 159).

Implicit in the above guidelines is the central importance of personhood. Kaiser was relationship-oriented rather than technique-oriented, and defined a therapeutic process which depends on the personal qualities of the therapist, those being clearly articulated, with the goal being, paradoxically, the communicative process itself.

Considering that the Atlanta Psychiatric Clinic model of experiential psychotherapy is also an approach which emphasizes the relationship between the therapist and the person in therapy, one would predict that this group has offered something in the way of elucidation of the person of the therapist. As early as in their first formal articulation of their approach in *The Roots of Psychotherapy*, Carl Whitaker and Tom Malone (1953) indicated their basic position, saying "there is an emotional exchange (process) in interpersonal relationships, which, when it occurs successfully, speeds up the growth experience of one or both participants in that relationship. This appears to be true regardless of the specific content of the relationship, the techniques utilized in it, whether it be professional or occurring in the everyday human relationships, or whether it be consciously or intuitively understood" (p. xiii). Read this carefully, for this contains the basis for experiential psychotherapy. (I have dropped the capitalization in recognition of their statement, "We are not interested in developing a 'new school' of psychotherapy" [p. vii]). Emphasis on the importance of the relationship was added by Kareen Malone, Tom Malone, Ray Kuckleberg, Ross Cox, John Barnett, and David Barstow (1982) as they stated that "the single most important component of therapeutic change, the greatest tool therapists possess, is the relationship which the therapist and client develop" (p. 154). In further elaboration concerning this therapeutic relationship, they wrote the following:

> Each person, in the expanding context of their relationship, presents and transforms the forms of life made available by the other; most of this process occurs unconsciously and is only articulated at an affective level. Affect organizes, as a general mode or orientation, what may later be known explicitly. However, there is no guarantee that the expressive relationships of therapy will ever congeal into conscious thought. Chances are that they will, instead, be lived as another form of life, as new connections, as an artistic creation in the making [p. 167].

Furthermore, "psychotherapy is a private affair between the client and therapist, difficult to describe from a third-party perspective without stripping it of its essentially personal nature" (p. 153).

Given this nature of psychotherapy, what, then, are the implications for the nature of the therapist? Frederick Klein (2001) has stated that, in experiential psychotherapy,

> The person of the therapist is expected to be more revealed than hidden, more present than remote and removed.... Experiential psychotherapy calls on the therapist to be[come] as fully mindful as possible of his/her interior goings-on while with the patient. This means everything and anything—stray musical tunes, boredom, sleepiness, sexual urges, anger, sadness, curiosity, longing, energizing surges, etc. The therapist is expected to appreciate active countertransference reactions as they occur, and to fashion a response—including the possibility of making a no-response response—likely to be of real value or use to the patient and/or to the relationship [pp. 13–14].

The point made by Klein is one of utmost importance. First, the call is for the therapist to be as aware as he or she can be of *all* that goes on inside himself or herself while with the person in therapy. Second, the call is for the therapist to *decide whether and how* to act on such awareness. As Klein clarified, "it is imperative that we as therapists expect ourselves to model ways to struggle that avoid exploitation, ruthlessness and self-serving behavior at our patients' expense" (p. 14).

In a similar vein, and using a simple phrase, Malone et al. (1982) wrote that "for therapy to succeed, therapists must be scrupulously honest with themselves about the nature of their participation in the therapeutic relationship" (p. 164). Consider that phrase, *scrupulously honest.* The focus requested of the therapist is inward, an honest look inside to evaluate within oneself how one is being in the relationship with the person in therapy. Additionally, Malone et al. stated that "in order for therapeutic change to occur, both the therapist and client must give up being special" (p. 164). It is only by such rescinding of the position of specialness that the therapist can be open to encountering fully the experience of the person in therapy.

The above theme has also been explored by Earl Brown (1982):

> Experiential Psychotherapy has been defined more by personal values and attitude toward life than by professional codes and techniques. Experientialists tend to esteem life itself, humankind, simple and natural events, living in relationship, intra- and interpersonal process, health, and growth towards joyful play. In their work with patients, they are likely to begin with a high degree of personal presence, an appreciation of the potential range of the human condition, a disposition to have faith and trust in the patient, a willingness to be open and honest, a readiness to confront in the context of caring, and the courage to risk themselves and be vulnerable in the venture [p. 26].

With this, Brown has limned a portrait of the person of the experiential psychotherapist.

The experiential psychotherapist must be willing to engage the person in therapy through the therapist's self. It is, as Richard Felder and Avrum Weiss (1991) wrote, "the therapist's subjective involvement in the therapeutic relationship [that] is so central as to be the primary determinant of the dynamics of the psychotherapy" (p. 25). This statement reflects the concept of the *therapist's use of self,* a concept which has become one of the most identifiable features of experiential psychotherapy (Weiss, 2001). Weiss, in exploring this concept, pointed out that, inherent in the therapeutic use of one's self, a balance must be reached between remaining enigmatically aloof, as in Freud's likening the analyst to a tabula rasa, and in being completely and uncritically self-revealing as in Jourard's transparent self. This understanding of the therapist's use of self seems completely consistent with Klein's view, discussed above.

One rather specific feature of the person of the therapist, unique to experiential psychotherapy in its prominence, is the *patient vector in the therapist*. Acknowledging that there are both patient-vectors and therapist-vectors in both the therapist and the person in therapy, experiential therapists take the position that therapy is effective when the therapist is primarily in her or his therapist-vector and the person in therapy is mostly able to be in her or his patient-vector (Weiss, 2001). Note carefully the definitions given by Whitaker and Malone (1953) for the two vectors. "*Patient-vectors*— Immature transference needs expressed in an interpersonal relationship which offers some possibility of their satisfaction and resolution" (p. 232). (When thinking of the patient-vector in the therapist, "countertransference" should be substituted for "transference" in this definition.) "*Therapist-vector*— Mature affect expressed in an interpersonal relationship in response to the immature needs of the other participant" (p. 233). Whitaker and Malone took the position that the person in therapy will improve if the patient-vectors of the therapist do not make excessive demands on the therapist-vectors of the person in therapy. When something goes wrong with the therapy, they saw this as due to the therapist's patient-vectors. However, they added, the therapist does not have to be, in their words, "a completely adequate therapist" in order for therapy to be effective (p. 164). In fact,

> in the best therapeutic relationship, the therapist recurrently brings his own patient-vectors to the patient. The resolving of these factors materially advances the process of treating the patient-vectors of the real patient, probably because the relationship is thereby bilateral.... This we term a "sliver type" of involvement on the part of the therapist.... The acceptance of such limitations in therapy provides, in fact, a realistic basis for growth. Moreover, the therapist's patient-vectors are, in

themselves, an effective dynamic element in the process of good therapy. Indeed, a therapeutic impasse can often be resolved only by the therapist's willingness to bring his patient-vectors to the patient quite overtly. This principle implies that were the therapist free of all patient-vectors, he would be no therapist at all [p. 165].

Weiss (2001) reported a personal communication with Carl Whitaker in which Whitaker stated paradoxically about being a therapist, "I'm here for me. If you can get anything out of it, so much the better" (p. 7). This can be understood from the experiential perspective; as Whitaker and Malone (1953) explained it, "the patient demands the total participation of the therapist, including even the latter's immaturities" (p. 164).

Weiss (2001) noted that the phrase "use of the self" was introduced for the first time by Felder in 1967 in an article titled "The Use of the Self in Psychotherapy." Interestingly, Virginia Satir (2000) employed a close alternative in her writing in 1975: "To be useful, any technique must emanate from what is going on at that moment in time because it seems to fit, and it is effective only within a context of trust.... This is why I cannot teach people techniques, I can only teach them some ways in which they can *use themselves* when certain thing [*sic*] happen" (p. 1). The italics used for emphasis were hers. In an annotation in this article, Barbara Jo Brothers wrote an expansion on Satir's statement: "She worked on helping her student therapist to become a fine instrument.... Her goal was to teach use of the self of the therapist. This meant developing enough self-awareness and self-worth awareness to be able to communicate therapeutically with self (internally) as well as the other" (p. 2).

In explaining how psychotherapy works, Satir (2000) wrote that "the whole therapeutic process must be aimed at opening up the healing potential within the patient or the client" (p. 2). *Nota bene:* Satir is identifying the person in therapy as the agent of change. The potential to heal is located within that person. From this it follows that the task of the therapist, in broadest terms, is to open up that healing potential. She continued, "The way is through the meeting of the deepest self of the therapist with the deepest self of the person, patient, or client. When this occurs, it creates a context of vulnerability — of openness to change" (p. 2).

In another annotation in Satir's (2000) article, Brothers credited

Satir with inventing the word "personhood." Brothers stated that Satir was not interested in creating an academic definition of personhood, but rather in "drawing forth the actuality of personhood — the real experience" in the therapists whom she taught (p. 10). We see, then, in the work of Satir an emphasis on the personhood of the therapist, and, at the same time, a reluctance to try to define it in words. She was a master, however, in inviting forth this unique essence. It is this essential personhood which allows being fully present with the person in therapy. Quoting Satir, Brothers (1991) wrote, "When I am in touch with myself, my feelings, my thoughts, with what I see and hear, I am growing toward becoming a more integrated self. I am more congruent, I am more 'whole,' and I am able to make greater contact with the other person" (p. 5).

In reading the above material, one may discern a paradox. This paradox is one of equality within non-equality. Equality has been suggested in many of the phrases introduced. Consider, for instance, unconditional positive regard and therapist self-congruence; good will; authenticity; communicative intimacy through non-duplicitous communication and neither withdrawing physically nor psychologically; emotional exchange which speeds up growth in one or both participants; a private affair which is essentially personal; being more present than remote and removed, more revealed than hidden; without self-serving behaviors; willingness to be open and honest with the courage to risk oneself and to be vulnerable; meeting with the deepest self. With this conceptual collection comes the implication that the efficacious therapist is not to be "one-up," but is to meet the person in therapy on the equal plane of humanity.

The theme of growth in both participants, therapist and person in therapy alike, is one which was addressed by Carl Jung. Jung discussed four stages in the development of analytic therapy, namely, *confession*, *elucidation*, *education*, and *transformation*. With regard to the first stage, Jung wrote that the prototype of all analytic treatment is in the institution of the confessional. With the invention of the idea of sin came the need for psychic concealment, or secrets. Secrets are for Jung like a psychic poison. Although, in small doses, this poison is necessary for individual differentiation, too much alienates the possessor from her or his community. A secret when shared with someone can be beneficial, but a private secret works like a burden of guilt, thus cutting the person off from her or his community. When conscious of the secret, the situation is less severe, but when the secret is repressed, the hidden content splits off into an independent complex. The secret is then hidden even from oneself. The act of holding back emotions also constitutes concealment. The affect which is held back is a type of secret. This is not to be confused with socially appropriate self-restraint, of course. Jung concluded that "the respective predominance of secrets or of inhibited emotions is probably responsible for the different forms of neurosis.... To cherish secrets and hold back emotion is a psychic misdemeanour for which nature finally visits us with sickness" (1966, p. 58). It follows that the goal of the confessional stage of therapy is catharsis, or cleansing. This meant, for Jung, "full confession — not merely the intellectual recognition of the facts with the head, but their confirmation by the heart and the actual release of suppressed emotion" (p. 59).

Explaining that even though the effects of confession can be very great, often even leading to astonishing results, Jung went on to write that it is not a panacea. For some persons in therapy a further type of analysis is necessary, that being an analysis of transference. This phase of therapy Jung termed elucidation. The cardinal distinction between confession and elucidation is that confession, with its catharsis, brings into ego consciousness material which should normally be in the conscious mind, whereas elucidation of transference involves material which would hardly ever become conscious in its original form of parent-child incest fantasies.

The third phase of therapy has as its focus the social education of the person in therapy. Unlike the second phase, which relies on reductive explanations and leads backward to childhood and downward into the unconscious, Jung saw this third phase as drawing the person out into the world and on new paths of social involvement and adaptation.

It is useful to think of confession as the pre–Freudian stage in the development of therapy, elucidation as the Freudian stage, and education as the Adlerian stage. "Whereas Freud is the investigator and interpreter, Adler is primarily the educator" (Jung, 1966, p. 67). As I read Jung, I believe that he saw these not only as three stages in the development of psychotherapy, but also as stages which a given person in therapy may traverse in the course of a complete analysis. Clearly, he expressed appreciation for the value of each, emphasizing that each one may be the most important for a given person in therapy. The catharsis of the confessional stage makes one feel, the elucidation of transference frees one from childhood illusions about how life is, and education brings one to realize that confession and explanation do not by themselves lead to normal adaptation. They each address an aspect of the same problem (Jung, 1966).

The fourth stage is the contribution of Jung, the stage of transformation. Using the metaphor of a chemical reaction, Jung explained that when the therapist and the person in therapy come together both are transformed. The therapist cannot influence without being herself or himself influenced. The therapist must live up to everything which he or she expects of the person in therapy, no matter how painful this may be. This calls for self-examination and self-criticism on the part of the therapist. It also argues strongly for the therapist's personal therapy. In fact Jung stated that he, based on Freud's invaluable discovery that analysts have their own complexes, was the first to demand that the analyst should be analyzed!

If we think of these not just as historical-theoretical stages, but as stages in a parallel personal-therapeutic process, we can see that, in many instances of therapy, this final stage may not be reached. Indeed, in many instances the entire course of therapy may be restricted even within the first stage, let alone the second, third, or fourth, due to factors internal to the therapy or due to many possible outside economic or logistic factors. The experience of the profundity of the stage of transformation may be precluded by brief therapy models—those in which therapy is truncated at the point of symptomatic relief, for example. My point is that many therapists and many persons in therapy may have limited or no experience with the stage of transformation. Unfortunately, such lack of experience on the part of a therapist may result in not just a misunderstanding of what happens between therapist and person in therapy during this phase, but in the denial, based on ignorance, that such a stage even exists.

Fritz Perls, too, emphasized personal equality between the therapist and the person in therapy in his development of the Gestalt approach. He did so by adopting Martin Buber's concept of the *I-Thou* as the appropriate relationship for the therapist and the person in therapy, as opposed to the *I-It* relationship. In "The Rules and Games of Gestalt Therapy" (Levitsky & Perls, 1970), the I-Thou was listed along with the principle of the now, "it" language and "I" language, use of the awareness continuum, no gossiping, and non-response to questions which are not genuine, as the basic rules in conducting Gestalt therapy. Although this discussion of the I-Thou relationship did not strive for the philosophical depth of that of Buber, it clearly put this mode of relationship in a central role. Consistent with this, James Simkin defined Gestalt therapy with the pithy phrase, "I and Thou, here and now" (personal communication, March, 1975). It was this definition which I heard Irma Lee Shepherd echo many times over the years. In order to give a brief exposure to the meaning of the I-Thou relationship within Gestalt therapy, I turn to the work of Erving and Miriam Polster (1973). In the opening of their chapter on "The Contact Boundary," a Gestalt therapy term for the contour of the meeting point of a person with another person or with her or his environment, they quoted Buber himself: "Only the being whose otherness, accepted by my being, lives and faces me in the whole compression of existence, brings the radiance of eternity to me. Only when two say to one another with all that they are, 'It is *Thou*,' is the indwelling of the Present Being between them" (p. 98). Such poesy, reflective of such depth of meaning, deserves reading and rereading, slowly and with reflection.

Let us now turn to the other side of the paradox, and one which begs for clarification, the side of inequality. Is the inequality between the therapist and the person in therapy the context in which the human equality exists? Or is the human equality the broader context within which the enterprise of psychotherapy is found? Or is it simultaneously both? Perhaps the last is the best way to see the paradox. However the paradox is viewed, there is a level of person-qua-person equality and a level of role-related inequality.

The inequality of therapist and person in therapy was addressed by Leon Levy (1963) in what I find to be a most perceptive manner. Pointing out that even though we may wish to question the desirability of it, there is none the less a *status differential* in psychotherapy. The therapy situation is fundamentally a helping situation in which the therapist is sought out with the expectation that the person in therapy will be helped. The person in therapy explicitly or implicitly acknowledges that all is not well with her or his life. In this sense, then, there is an inequality inherent in psychotherapy. I will add that this status differential is expressed and at the same time symbolized in the usual psychotherapy arrangement. That is, the person in therapy travels to the office of the therapist, goes to the therapist. In addition, it is the person in therapy who pays the therapist, and not the other way around. It is even not uncommon for persons in therapy to pay for psychotherapy appointments that they have not kept when they have not canceled them at least 24 hours in advance!

Levy (1963) identified a second, and closely related inequality, which he termed a *phoric differential*. The thoughts, feelings, and behaviors that the person in therapy reports to the therapist are less disturbing to the therapist than they are to her or him. So it is, too, with euphoric as well as dysphoric material. The person in therapy most often feels much more strongly than does the therapist, be the feelings pleasant or unpleasant.

A *cognitive* and *perceptual differential* is the third inequality which Levy (1963) identified. The therapist often has a different perspective, a different way of conceptualizing the material presented, from that of the person in therapy. This different framing is hopefully better in some significant way. But, again, this creates an inequality.

Added to the differentials between the therapist and the person in therapy which Levy (1963) described so astutely, I suggest there is yet another factor of inequality. "To wit, *psychotherapists are less afraid of doing psychotherapy than patients are of receiving it....* Those of us who belong to the psychotherapy subculture are often so ensconced in it that we fail to appreciate how threatening it can be to the outsider" (Smith, 1984, p. 49). When I use a technique over and over, I come to have comfort and ease with it. Through my experience with it, I come to trust in a certain likelihood of benign outcome. Too easily I may forget the fear and trepidation with which I first lay over a breathing stool, assumed a stress posture, or spoke to an empty chair. Different from the phoric differential of which Levy wrote, I refer to a fear engendered by the methods themselves, a fear not shared by the therapist.

This paradox of equality within inequality, or inequality within equality, is perhaps implicitly stated in the "tasks of the therapist" as laid out by Joen Fagan (1970) in the book that she and Irma Lee Shepherd edited, *Gestalt Therapy Now*. Her exploration of the tasks was written most clearly and at once compellingly. Briefly stated, the tasks, named *patterning, control, potency, humaness,* and *commitment,* refer to the following. Patterning is the task of perceiving and constructing a pattern from the symptoms reported, the request for change, the history reported, and the personal information revealed in the course of therapy, be that information verbal or non-verbal, intentionally or unintentionally given. The term *patterning* was chosen by Fagan for this task in order to get away from evoking the medical model and from implying that the purpose of the task is to arrive at a label, both of which attend the more common term *diagnosis*. Control is defined as the ability of the therapist to persuade the person in therapy to comply with whatever therapeutic procedures have been chosen. Potency has to do with the therapist's ability to intervene in a manner that accelerates and provokes change in a positive direction for the person in therapy. Humanness is Fagan's term for the therapist's *person*al contribution to the therapeutic process, including "a variety of involvements: the therapist's concern for and caring about his patient on a personal and emotional level; his willingness to share himself and bring to the patient his own direct emotional responses and/or pertinent accounts of his own experiences; his ability to recognize in the patient gropings toward deepened authenticity ... and his continued openness to his own growth, which serves as a model for the patient" (pp. 100–101). Commitment includes the therapist's commitment to the vocation of psychotherapy (with the requirement of continued personal growth), commitment to the individuals in therapy with her or him, and commitment to contributing to the field of psychotherapy through research, teaching, training, writing, and so forth.

In calling attention to the relationship among certain of the tasks, Fagan (1970) offered a perspective on the paradox of equality and inequality: "Many therapists who see authenticity as a primary task of the therapist fear those who, having stopped short in their own struggles with growing, substitute increased emphasis on control and potency" (p. 103). The caveat that we may take as implied is that to emphasize potency and control, and to neglect personal growth, is for the therapist to fail to honor the equality side of the paradox. It is to fail to honor the person qua person equality, wherein both the therapist and the person in therapy are committed to their own personal growth.

Another author in the Gestalt approach, Patricia Baumgardner (1975), also wrote about that which Fagan identified as the task of humaness. Describing the therapist, Baumgardner had this to say: The therapist, in being with someone in therapy, combines *attention* and *awareness*, attending to the awareness which the person in therapy brings and awareness of the personal process in the therapist herself or himself. Being simply available, the therapist ideally perceives whatever phenomena the person in therapy creates, and in return is authentically what he or she is. This means to respond internally as one will, being open to the experience of whatever body sensations and feeling may arise in response to the person in therapy. Speaking of herself as therapist, Baumgardner expressed this simply and clearly:

> Playing therapist to me means observing a selective economy of expression of my response. I want ideally to stay in relatively close touch with my feelings, my body, my voice, to know a lot about how I feel and change inside. I want to express outwardly only that part of my inner experience which I believe has a reasonable chance of facilitating the work of therapy. Along with this process of selective response, I want to give no false messages. For if I pretend or become unreal, try to hide or mislead, I act to block the client's authenticity as well [p. 27].

Both Baumgardner and Fagan, particularly in the former's elaboration of the task of humanness, highlight personhood, and more particularly emphasize, once again, authenticity.

Turning now to a stylistic difference in the person of the therapist, I want to call attention to some earlier work that has caught my attention. On the surface it may sound almost trivial, but, explored more deeply, there may emerge a richness of meaning that greatly enhances the understanding of personhood as it manifests in psychotherapy. Drawing on a work by Isaiah Berlin (1953) entitled *The Hedgehog and the Fox: An Essay on Tolstoy's View of History*, Berl Mendel (1964) suggested that psychotherapists may be either like a hedgehog or like a fox! In order to delve quickly into this enigmatic metaphor, I will quote Berlin. "There is a line among the fragments of the Greek poet Archilochus which says: 'The fox knows many things, but the hedgehog knows one big thing'" (p. 3). Going on to say that this could be taken as meaning no more than that the cunning fox is defeated by the hedgehog's single defense, Berlin suggests we consider a more figurative level of interpretation, to wit: "taken figuratively, the words can be made to yield a sense in which they mark one of the deepest differences which divide writers and thinkers, and, it may be, human beings in general" (p. 3). Seeing a "great chasm" between the two, Berlin wrote of those who relate everything to "a single central vision, one system ... a single, universal, organising principle in terms of which alone all that they are and say has significance," and those who "lead lives, perform acts and entertain ideas that are centrifugal rather than centripetal," whose "thought is scattered or diffused, moving on many levels, seizing upon the essence of a vast variety of experiences" (p. 3). Continuing, Berlin wrote that "the first kind of intellectual and artistic personality belongs to the hedgehogs, the second to the foxes" (p. 3). We may leave Berlin at this point, for he then, after giving long lists of hedgehog and fox types of philosophers and literary figures, turned to his analysis of Tolstoy's view of history as reflected in Tolstoy's being by nature a fox, but trying to be a hedgehog.

Applying Berlin's metaphor to psychotherapists, Mendel (1964) elaborated the core concept of knowing one big thing versus knowing many things. "Hedgehoggery," he suggested, is characterized by a problem solving mind, a mind both reasonable and logical, having a central vision from which to relate everything, and thus a clearly fixed position. "Foxiness," in contrast, is characterized by an abstracting mind, guided by intuition and "knowing," thus having no central vision. Either, Mendel claimed, may be a good or a poor therapist.

The distinction that Berlin drew using philosophers and writers as examples seems to apply in the realm of religion as well. The priest may be likened to the hedgehog and the shaman to the fox. As viewed by Sheldon Kopp (1971) we may have both gained something and lost something in the transition from the paradigm of the hunter-gatherer to that of the planter, a paradigm shift that replaced the shaman with the priest. The shaman was spawned by the setting of the hunter, one where "self-reliance, personal initiative, imagination, and daring" were important virtues (p. 26). The priesthood arose in the planter society where "stability, order, and the sacrifice of individuality and self-determination for the good of the group" came to be of value (p. 26). Along with this change in values, the shift from hunting and gathering to an agricultural base brought larger societal units, and a greater complexity of societal structure with greater specialization of individual activities. Reflected in the roles of the religious leader, then, "the Priest qualified by learning ritual acts and words verbatim, while the Shaman was required to demonstrate a talent for improvisation, for creative adaptation to new situations" (p. 28).

The shaman has learned through long and often arduous apprenticeship to enter an ecstatic state, and, while on this "shamanic journey," to confer with those of the upper and lower spirit worlds. Returning from the journey, he or she conveys the message for healing and guidance, as given by the spirits. In contrast, the priest has studied the liturgy and learned prescribed ceremonial forms. He or she can perform the rites, in the manner of the doctrine. The priest's activity is, therefore, more predictable. Continuing to explore the role of the shaman, Kopp (1971) explained that the shaman

> liberates the other members of his hunting community by turning them on, each to his own personal vision. By freeing each to get with himself, the Shaman opens each hunter to a wellspring of wonder and an inner source of power. He cannot help to heal any particular hunter without experiencing all that the other endures, experiencing it within himself with full intensity. For the Shaman the healing is a repetition or a renewal of the healing of himself through a creative act with the other.... Thus the Shaman ... holds office by virtue of personal spiritual attainment. According to the needs of the moment, he can deal individually with others in personal ways, improvising to meet them in the everyday world with all of its shifting perplexities [p. 30].

Kopp (1971) offered shaman and priest as one of his several metaphors to use in exploring the role of the psychotherapist. By analogy, the shaman is to the fox as the priest is to the hedgehog. As I sit with this metaphor and that of the fox and the hedgehog, I see them merge then separate, as two streams, leaving a rich alluvium of meaning.

In the work of Wilhelm Reich, I find yet more material that helps to elucidate the person of the therapist. As much as his theories are neglected by contemporary psychotherapists, there is a concept within his body of work that is even more neglected. Terming it *emotional plague*, Reich (1949) devoted an entire chapter to this concept in one of his major works, *Character-Analysis*. In addition, emotional plague is a central and unifying thread which weaves throughout and binds together Reich's (1974) most political work, *Listen, Little Man!* In Reich's (1949) words, "an individual moves through life by the means of the emotional plague if ... his natural, self-regulatory life manifestations have been suppressed. The individual afflicted with the emotional plague *limps, characterologically speaking. The emotional plague is a chronic biopathy of the organism*" (p. 248). Continuing with a definition of his concept, Reich stated that "*the emotional plague is that human behavior which, on the basis of a biopathic character structure, makes itself felt in interpersonal, that is, social relationships and which becomes organized in corresponding institutions*" (p. 252). It is the contradiction between the intense longing for life and the inability to find a corresponding fulfillment in life that characterizes the plagued individual.

Looking at the resulting manifestations of the emotional plague, Reich (1949), and later Elsworth Baker (1967), suggested that it appears in numerous and important sectors of life, such as in destructive forms of mysticism, moralism, sadistic child rearing, gossip and defamation, cruelty, authoritarian bureaucracies, imperialistic war ideologies, pornography, criminal antisociality, race hatred, and resentment of others' good fortune. At times through history, the plague has become pandemic, as witnessed in the Inquisition and in the various forms of Fascism of the twentieth century. Distilled through the alembic of Baker's mind, the essence, then, of emotional plague behavior is the attempt to tear down others or to control their lives. The plagued individual is intolerant of natural expression because it engenders, within, an intolerable longing for aliveness. This leads to the wish to kill such aliveness wherever it is seen. Plagued individuals, unfortunately for society, often form organizations to support their work of suppressing aliveness in others, organizations whose platforms are intolerant of natural aliveness.

Reich (1949) maintained that his term was meant to carry no defamatory connotation, and did not refer to any conscious malice. My understanding, as I have previously expressed it in *The Body in Psychotherapy* (Smith, 1985), is as follows:

> A person is a victim of the plague to the extent that her or his natural, self-regulatory life manifestations have been suppressed. So, to the extent that one does not live her or

his body, does not embody organismic aliveness, he or she is manifesting some degree of the emotional plague.... Out of the fear of one's own organismic aliveness, the plagued individual is threatened by aliveness in others. So, the plagued individual won't endure free and natural expressions of life either in herself or himself or in others [p. 167].

The relevance of the concept of emotional plague to the functioning of the psychotherapist is surely by now apodictic. The clarion message is that for the psychotherapist to be able to facilitate growth in another, the therapist *must* be relatively free from any desire to suppress the natural aliveness of that other. That is to say, a therapist *must* be relatively free from emotional plague. The antidote to a predisposition to emotional plague, Reich (1974) told us, is one's "own feeling for true life. The life-force does not seek power but demands only to play its full and acknowledged part in human affairs. It manifests itself through love, work, and knowledge" (pp. xi–xii). And, waxing more poetic, Reich added, "Only one thing matters: live a good, happy life. Do your heart's bidding, even when it leads you on paths that timid souls would avoid. Even when life is a torment, don't let it harden you" (p. 127).

I find myself lingering with that phrase, "on paths that timid souls would avoid." Put in the context of the psychotherapeutic encounter, the avoidance of a path, born of timidness, would be a sin of omission, as surely as an active suppression of aliveness in the person in therapy by the therapist would be a sin of commission. The former sin may be more subtle, thus not as easily recognized; it is a sin nevertheless. If one may be seduced into such subtle emotional-plague behavior by and through timorousness, then the resistance is by and through courage. Seeing it as a quality contributing to an optimal experientially based therapeutic attitude, Ken Bradford (2001) emphasized the inestimable importance of courage: "It is not enough to have insight into and empathy with a person's predicament; I must also have the courage to engage that predicament" (p. 5). Yes, "engage that predicament," take the path that timid souls would avoid. For, as he wrote, "*therapeutic courage* [is] *the capacity to be open and responsive in the places of unsettledness, uncertainty, fear and anxiety that inevitably arise in the exchange of therapeutic intimacy*" (p. 5). To do otherwise is, to quote Bradford again, "therapeutic cowardice" (p. 6). Echoed, here, are the words of Plato, when he recommended that those who treat the mind possess knowledge, benevolence, and *boldness* (Colby, 1951, p. 23).

A final theoretical note, I offer here. This has to do with the motives to be a psychotherapist, and draws heavily upon the work of Joseph Rychlak (1965) and James Dublin (1971). In his now-classic article, "The Motives to Psychotherapy," Rychlak delineated three, namely the *scholarly*, the *ethical*, and the *curative*. These motives he saw as underlying three respective definitions of psychotherapy. The first is *insight*, second is *self-determined growth*, and the third is *cure*. Rychlak suggested Sigmund Freud as the prime example of a therapist having a scholarly motive and an insight therapy built upon that motive. His prime example of a therapist of the ethical motive and a corresponding therapy of self-determined growth was Carl Rogers. And, finally, he named Joseph Wolpe as the prime example of a therapist whose work reflected a curative motive and whose therapy was defined by cure. Psychoanalysis, for Freud, was first and foremost a scientific method for exploring, in depth, the human psyche. Its effectiveness in alleviating psychoneuroses was secondary. For Rogers, the ethic of self-determination was predominant, and his client-centered approach to therapy was to create an atmosphere that supported and nurtured the unfoldment of growth as guided by the self-determination of the client. Finally, with Wolpe, the eradication of unwanted symptoms was the cynosure, and the method was to be judged pragmatically. Any given psychotherapist, then, may be considered as tending to one of these motives, as being biased in one of these directions.

Building on the work of Rychlak, Dublin (1971) suggested a fourth motive. This is the motive, he wrote, that corresponds to another basic approach to psychotherapy, that which is often referred to as *existential*. (I would add the term *experiential* to that.) The motive itself Dublin termed *communicative intimacy*. Prior to any technique, and more essential than the technique, communicative intimacy is also a particular stance taken by the therapist. In this stance, "the therapist, deeply and genuinely himself, is engaged as a person with a person" (p. 402). Dublin noted that this relationship has been called "I-Thou" by Martin Buber, "intimate" by Arthur Kovaks, "shared encounter" by Ludwig Binswanger and by Medard Boss, "experiential encounter" by Walter Kempler, "congruent encounter" by Richard Johnson, "authentic being" by Hendrik

Ruitenbeek, and "authenticity" by James Bugental (p. 402). Dublin's own words reveal a corollary of such person-to-person engagement:

> If the therapist is to behave as a person–that is, if he is to avoid behaving as if some psychotherapeutic technique or the psychotherapeutic situation were responsible for his actions and words–he must at times use the first person pronoun, and he must at times include productive and germane self-disclosure [p. 408].

Communicative intimacy as a motive-cum-stance does not preclude the scholarly, ethical, or curative motives, but adumbrates these in its primacy. For no combination of these first three, as Dublin instructed, adequately describes or encompasses the motivation for a psychotherapy defined as existential.

Coming full circle, we can ask, then, what constitutes Barry Stevens' "*right* man," the person who can make the right means work in "*the right way*"? We can inquire of the several theorists discussed above and thereby create a response that is an agglutination of perspectives, each contributing its own nuance. Beginning with Barry Stevens herself, we can name good will, then add empathic ability; positive regard that is unconditional; genuineness; power and authenticity; non-duplicity combined with a sensitivity to duplicity in others and the desire to establish straightforward communication with relatively uncommunicative persons; a willingness to be totally and subjectively involved and thus risk vulnerability and the revelation of one's own "patient vectors"; full presence; willingness to be transformed, willingness to enter the encounter of the I with the Thou; acceptance of responsibility for control and potency within a context of humaness and commitment; self-awareness leading to selective response but without any false messages; freedom from emotional plague; courage to engage the predicament; and the desire for communicative intimacy as at least part of one's motivation.

As I read these words and phrases of summary, I gain a felt sense of the person of the therapist, and yet wish not to force a reduction to a few prime factors. As neat and convenient as that might be, such a reduction would fail as a distillation of a pure essence, for each of the nuances implied by the above words and phrases may itself be essential in its individual presence. Overlapping in places, nearly synonymous in others, these words and phrases nevertheless deserve honor for whatever degree of uniqueness each holds, as their con-notations are carefully considered. I trust that the men and women who chose these did so very thoughtfully, reflecting carefully on their experiences in working with persons in therapy. (Certainly my choice of theorists who have addressed the personhood of the therapist is not exhaustive. Hopefully, it is representative, and not misleadingly biased.) Eschewing the oversimplification that I see as inherent in a reduction to a prime factor or two, I choose to marvel at the ubiq-uitous yet elusive quality of the person of the therapist. And, in keep-ing with the advice of Rilke, I have chosen to love the very question of the person of the therapist.

Chapter 3

A Research Note

In moving beyond the broad question of whether psychotherapy works, a question which by now can, I believe, be laid to rest with an affirmative answer, more specific research questions beg to be answered. One such question is, of course, in psychotherapy the role of the person of the therapist. The importance of this question was highlighted by Michael Lambert and Allen Bergin (1994), with their characteristic attention to research evidence, when they reported that "despite careful selection, training, monitoring, and supervision, therapists offering the same treatments can have highly divergent results" (p. 174). It is not only that in the context of such technical uniformity different therapists can be demonstrated to have different degrees of ameliorative effect. It is also the case that the persons in therapy with some therapists not only do not improve, but are worsened by the experience. Returning to the words of Lambert and Bergin, based on compelling evidence, a portion of those whom therapy "is intended to help are actually harmed by ... negative therapist characteristics" (p. 182). They went on to state that "the therapist factor, as a contributor to outcome, is looming large in the assessment of outcomes" (p. 182).

These conclusions, reached by current research, were deemed sufficiently established by Donald Kerr (2000) that he stated in the preface to *Becoming a Therapist: A Workbook for Personal Exploration* his conviction that "the person of the therapist is a powerful variable in the therapy process" (p. v). Based on this conviction, he posed the increasing of self-awareness as a major element of the goals of the workbook.

With the importance of the role of the person of the therapist established, perhaps the next appropriate research question is the nature of the person of the therapist. This question, central though it is, has proven to be extremely hard to answer. Larry Beutler, Paulo Machado, and Susan Neufeldt (1994) have performed the impressive task of reviewing the relevant research, concentrating on that reported since 1985. With more than 340 references cited, it would be not only redundant but unmanageable (to say nothing of masochistic) to try to duplicate their thoroughness in the present chapter. What I will try to do is to summarize their conclusions, leaving it to the interested reader to go to their chapter for elaboration and for the citations themselves.

Beutler et al. (1994) began their review of therapist variables by establishing the following foundation: "(1) In statistical analyses, magnitude of benefit is more closely associated with the identity of the therapist than with the type of psychotherapy that the therapist practices ...; (2) some therapists in all therapeutic approaches produce consistently more positive effects than others ...; and (3) some therapists produce consistently negative effects ..." (p. 229). Acknowledging that much of the effort to identify the therapist characteristics which account for these general findings has been fruitless, they offered a plausible explanation. "This is probably because therapist characteristics interact in complex ways with characteristics of the client, the situation, and the type of therapy practiced" (p. 229).

In their attempt to organize this mass of research findings, Beutler et al. (1994) created the following schema. The schema is two dimensional, one axis distinguishing objective and subjective therapist characteristics, the other distinguishing cross-situational therapist traits and therapy-specific states. These dimensions thus define four cells in a 2 × 2 arrangement, each of which I will discuss in turn.

Objective, Cross-Situational Traits

Beutler et al. (1994) addressed age, sex, and ethnicity in this cell. With respect to age, the studies indicate that neither the age of the therapist nor the age of the therapist in interaction with the age of the client seems to influence therapy outcome. (I add, however, that due to educational and training requirements there tends to be a minimal age at which one would be able to be a therapist.)

Interest in gender has been a focus of research particularly because of the concern on the part of some that a male-oriented therapy bias would victimize and dis-empower female clients. Most of the research has failed to provide evidence for this concern, however. The studies reviewed did not support the sex of the therapist or the sex of therapist and sex of client matching as a significant factor in therapy outcome.

Also having socio-political implications is the topic of ethnicity. The research reviewed concerning the effect of therapist-client ethnicity is equivocal, at best.

Age, sex, and ethnicity seem not to be important variables in understanding therapy outcome, and, in turn, not to be important variables for understanding the person of the therapist.

Subjective, Cross-Situational Traits

This cell contains a large number of traits, including personality patterns (the A-B therapist typology, based on interest patterns reflected in performance on the Strong Vocational Interest Blank; and performance on the Myers-Briggs Type Indicator, purporting to assess the Jungian dimensions of extroversion-introversion, thinking-feeling, sensing-intuiting, and a derived dimension of perceiving-sensing), dominance and related concepts (dogmatism, open-mindedness, flexibility), locus of control, emotional well-being, conceptual level (abstract and complex —concrete and nondiscriminating), personal therapy, values, attitudes (lifestyle, views of gender, socioeconomic background), and religious beliefs.

Although the A-B therapist typology was promising in the 1960s and 1970s, with reliable and robust predictions of efficacious treatment of schizophrenics, the wider use of medications and therefore less interest in psychotherapy as a treatment for this patient population has halted this line of research. An additional factor that may have deterred the continuation of this line of research was the lack of a coherent theory. The A-B research remained but a body of empirical findings, and without a theory to relate these findings, there was a limit to both its credibility and its ability to be generalized.

Unfortunately, I believe, the full impact and complete ramifications of the A-B variable have not been explored. Intriguing, for instance, are some of the findings of my program of research on the communication styles of A and B persons who were not therapists. One of my early investigations was a therapy analogue study in which interviews were conducted between A and B type interviewers and A and B type interviewees (Smith, 1972). The focus of the investigation was on the non-verbal communication between interviewers and interviewees, specifically the channels of postural and gestural communication. Consistent with predictions, A types, as a group, were more variable in their postural and gestural behavior than were B types, as a group. In addition, B types, as a group, reflected greater interpersonal approach and affiliation in their postural and gestural behavior than did A types, as a group. Consistent with this latter finding, Charles Conway (1974), in an unpublished master's thesis that I directed, found evidence that B type male college students scored more in the extroverted direction on the Myers-Briggs Type Indicator than did A type male college students. (It was A type therapists that had been found to be more effective in working with schizophrenic persons, and B type therapists who had been found to be more effective in working with persons experiencing neurotic symptoms.) In another unpublished master's thesis that I directed, that of Diana Dupont (1976), results suggested that A type male college students were better able to interpret graphic communication on the expressive portion of Bell's Graphic Emotions Index and better able to interpret emotional messages presented visually on the Film Tactile Communications Index than were B type male college students. When compared on their ability to interpret non-verbal communication through touch on the Tactile Communications Index, however, no differences were in evidence, as was also the case on the receptive portion of Bell's Graphic Emotions Index. Another entry in my research program was the doctoral dissertation of Joel Heffler (1973). The responses of A and B type male college students to tape-recorded schizophrenic and neurotic communications were studied after they had been trained on the Carkhuff Accurate Empathy Scale. Consistent with predictions, the A students evidenced higher levels of accurate empathy when responding to schizophrenic communications than when responding to neurotic communications, and their level of empathy when responding to schizophrenic communication exceeded that of B students responding to that same communication. Surely, there is more that could be mined from the A-B variable in coming to understand the person of the therapist.

The A-B therapist typology research did lead, however, to investigations of the dimension of autonomy — dependency and to the finding that dependent clients were more likely to improve if treated by autonomy-oriented therapists while independent clients responded best to attachment-oriented therapists. It appears, then, that persons improve more in therapy when working with a therapist who can open their consciousness to the realm of autonomous functioning or the realm of attachment, whichever is the lesser known for that person.

Work with the Myers-Briggs Type Indicator has not supported the initial enthusiasm for attempting to match therapists and clients on the bases of the Jungian dimensions which it purports to measure. Neither matching on the basis of orientation, that is, extroversion and introversion, nor on the basis of the ectopsychic functions of thinking-feeling and sensing-intuiting, or of their derivatives perceiving-judging, has been shown to illuminate the person of the therapist in a meaningful manner. Is it that these dimensions are not significant in understanding the therapy process, or is it that the instrument is not really tapping the crucial level of those dimensions?

The research suggests that therapist dogmatism, dominance, flexibility, and openness are extremely complex variables, and may interact with other as yet unresearched variables such as type of therapy offered. Their value as factors in therapy remains, therefore, unknown.

With respect to locus of control, findings seem meager and at this point not very instructive for the therapist.

There is suggestion from the research that similarities in level and style of cognition, as assessed by the Interpersonal Discrimination Test, may be related to retention in therapy and faster improvement in early therapy sessions.

In contrast to the above findings, there is consistent evidence that the level of adjustment of the therapist is related to positive therapy outcome. Likewise, there is evidence that therapists with high levels of distress or disturbance may induce negative changes in clients.

A conservative conclusion, based in part on the inconsistent studies reported, is that the adjustment of the therapist is an important but not necessary condition for improvement in high-functioning clients, but at the same time, emotional problems on the part of the therapist may negatively affect clients.

Unfortunately, given the importance of therapist well-being in the outcome of therapy, the research on the outcome rates of therapists with different amounts of personal therapy are equivocal. However, critical thinking surely suggests that the diversity of reasons for entering therapy, coupled with the varied effects of that therapy for the therapist, may render it meaningless to research amount of therapy as a unitary variable. Regarding the amount of personal therapy as a unitary variable may be much too simplistic to be of use.

Therapeutic outcome has been shown to be related to both therapist-client similarity and dissimilarity in religious values. Thus, the evidence is contradictory and inconclusive.

In terms of general values and attitudes, there is evidence offered that therapists who value intellectual pursuits and hard work are more effective than those whose values run to social and economic status. Furthermore, therapist-client similarities in valuing wisdom, knowledge, intellectual pursuits, and honesty have been shown to be related to treatment success. In contrast, therapist-client dissimilarities in values of personal safety, interpersonal goals of treatment, social status and friendships have been shown to facilitate positive therapy outcome. Beutler et al. (1994) concluded that therapy improvement is associated with therapist-client similarities with regard to humanistic values that are involved with maintaining social order. Similarities of philosophy may enhance therapeutic engagement, while dissimilarity concerning social attachment and intimacy may facilitate therapy outcome and "value convergence" between therapist and client.

The research suggests that the ability of the therapist to communicate within the value framework of the client may contribute more to positive treatment outcome than the particular values held.

Research supports the position that therapists who hold nontraditional views of female roles rather than traditional gender views promote not only more positive change, but also greater satisfaction with women clients. This maintains regardless of gender orientation or the biological sex of the therapist.

Finally, the research is equivocal concerning the influence of therapist socio-economic background on treatment outcome. So, no conclusion can be reached based on the evidence.

Subjective, Therapy-Specific States

The evidence seems quite strong that the necessary and sufficient conditions for positive therapy outcome which Rogers posited so long ago do, indeed, prevail. Thus, we find compelling evidence for the value of accurate empathy, warmth, and genuineness on the part of the therapist. (I personally like the terms *accurate empathy, unconditional positive regard*, and *therapist self-congruence*, which were the terms used by Charles Truax in my graduate school training.) It should be noted that these therapist facilitated conditions are now seen as qualities of the client and of the therapist-client relationship, as well as of the therapist. Research suggests that facilitative therapist skills and the therapeutic alliance are closely related. Furthermore, the quality of the therapeutic relationship, or therapeutic alliance, has consistently been found to be a major factor in therapy outcome, across types of therapy.

Although a few studies have failed to demonstrate the following relationships, several studies have shown that perceived expertness, attractiveness and trustworthiness of the therapist were related to client satisfaction, changes in client self-concept, symptomatic changes, and retention in therapy.

The research is mixed when looking at the effects of therapist expectancies on therapy outcome. However, some studies have shown therapist expectancies or therapist intentions (the latter being a more specific process variable closely related to the therapist variable of expectancy) to be related to client satisfaction and positive therapeutic change.

Beutler et al. (1994) concluded, having reviewed a considerable research literature, that the therapist's theoretical orientation is *not* strongly related to therapy outcome. There is, however, suggestive evidence that those who adopt an insight orientation are more effective with clients with internalizing coping styles, while behaviorally oriented therapists may have greater impact on clients who rely on externalizing coping styles. Once again, the research confirms the observation that therapist efficacy varies widely within any given theoretical orientation.

Objective, Therapy-Specific States

This fourth cell in the Beutler et al. (1994) schema contains professional background, therapeutic styles, and therapist interventions. Research on professional background has been inconsistent and difficult to interpret because of a confounding of level of professional training, amount of experience, and professional discipline. Even when these have not been confounded an inconsistent picture still has emerged. However, when only the most rigorously controlled studies are considered, outcome differences do favor more experienced therapists. More experienced therapists seem to have a higher proportion of clients who improve and a lower proportion of clients who deteriorate when compared with less experienced therapists; to be more effective in retaining clients; and to have greater impact on more disturbed clients than do less experienced therapists. Baldly stated, experience seems important.

In terms of therapeutic style, evidence suggests poorer outcome when the therapist is hostile. Studies of therapist formality, as reflected in office furnishings and personal attire, like those of therapist formality assessed through verbal style (i.e., "chats" versus client-centered interventions) have shown little. Formality seems irrelevant, whereas therapist hostility is a negative stylistic dimension.

Turning to therapist interventions, the empirical literature is inconsistent in showing the importance of supervision in the development of therapeutic skills. Beutler et al. (1994) did, however, offer several tentative conclusions based on studies utilizing manual-guided therapies and competency-based criteria: "(1) common or nonspecific skills of therapists are manifested differently in different therapies … (2) skillfulness generally is associated with effectiveness in different treatment models … (3) therapist skill is relatively distinct from both experience level and compliance with a therapy model … (4) criteria-based training in specific procedures tends to increase levels of compliance and skill" (p. 255).

In terms of therapist directiveness, studies have shown not only that therapist directiveness is generally counterproductive in psychodynamic therapy, but also that this may maintain for other therapies as well. Other studies offer contrary evidence concerning the value of directiveness for therapy outcome.

Although limited, the research evidence seems to support the value of therapist self-disclosure in symptomatic improvement in clients. I believe that further research is clearly needed that would distinguish among types of therapist self-disclosure.

Accumulating evidence suggests that the value of interpretation depends on several factors, including the degree to which the interpretations correspond to independently derived clinical formulations and the client's history with respect to object relations. That is, clients with a history of good object relationships tended to do poorly with transference interpretations, whereas those with a history of poor object relationships benefitted. Several studies have demonstrated that frequency of interpretations (by therapists of diverse theoretical orientations) have correlated with perceived helpfulness and benefit on the part of a mixed sample of clients.

From this plethora of data, what did Beutler et al. (1994) conclude about the person of the therapist? Their most unequivocal conclusion was this: "Among the therapist subjective traits and states, consistent evidence exists to support the assertion (now nearly a 'truism') that a warm and supportive therapeutic relationship facilitates therapeutic success" (p. 259). Clearly, there are many questions left unanswered by the research data.

Some might argue that the unanswered questions concerning the person of the therapist are best sidestepped by placing greater emphasis on manual-guided therapy. They would argue, perhaps from a position of self-righteous scientism, that as more of the outcome can be controlled by increased uniformity of therapeutic procedure, we can reduce the contribution of the individual therapist to a negligible level. To counter such an assertion, we need only turn once again to the research summarized by Lambert and Bergin (1994): "The individual therapist can play a surprisingly large role in treatment outcome even when treatment is being offered within the stipulations of manual-guided therapy" (p. 181).

As president of the Division of Psychotherapy of the American Psychological Association, John Norcross (2000) recently highlighted the importance of the role of the person of the therapist in the context of the ethical and professional commitment to conduct evidence-based psychotherapy. Wryly noting that although "efficacy research has gone to considerable lengths to eliminate the individual therapist as a variable that might account for patient improvement, the inescapable fact is that the therapist as a person is a central agent of change" (p. 2–3). Citing the work of Crits-Christoph and colleagues in 1991 and that of Lambert and Okiishi in 1997 to support this claim, Norcross then goes on to proclaim that the "curative power of the person of the therapist is, arguably, as empirically validated as manualized treatments or psychotherapy methods," citing Hubble, Duncan, and Miller, 1999, and Orlinsky, Graw, and Parks, 1994 (Norcross, 2000, p. 3). Citing Lambert in 1992, he informs us that techniques account for "only 12–15 percent of the variance across therapies" (Norcross, 2000, p. 3). *Nota bene: 12–15 percent!*

Pondering these research-based conclusions in conjunction with the research based conclusions mentioned earlier, I come to the following position. *Even when therapy is conducted "by the book" through training, supervision, and monitoring, different therapists demonstrate different levels of efficacy. Many of the therapist variables studied did not really seem to address the person of the therapist in the full depth of the meaning of the phrase. The portrait of the effective therapist that the research does paint is one of an experienced therapist with a high level of functioning, that is, an absence of high levels of distress or personality disturbance, an ability to communicate within the value framework of the person in therapy, an absence of hostility, and a willingness to self-disclose appropriately. What can be said with the greatest degree of certainty is that the effective therapist is one who is warm, genuine, and expressive of accurate empathy.*

Although not addressing efficacy directly, another body of research has focused on the relationship between personal attributes of the therapist and the quality of the therapeutic alliance. Steven Ackerman and Mark Hilsenroth (2001) have reviewed this literature, with special attention to the therapist characteristics and the in-session activities that negatively influence that alliance. Including investigations that reported a quantifiable relationship between the alliance and some index of therapist variables, and that specifically examined personal attributes or technical activities of the therapist that related to the disruption or the deterioration of the alliance, the reviewers summarized 14 studies. Their review of these studies revealed evidence that "therapists who exhibited disregard for their patients, were less involved in the treatment process, and were more self-focused were less likely to form a positive connection with their patients" (p. 173). Furthermore, the studies were in agreement that poor alliances were in evidence with therapists who were not confident in their ability to be of help, who were tense, tired, bored, defensive, blaming, or unable to provide a supportive therapeutic environment. From this evidence, Ackerman and Hilsenroth concluded that "whether or not therapists can be taught to be empathic and warm, it is of critical importance that they vigilantly work toward conveying a respectful, flexible, accepting, and responsive attitude" in their therapeutic work (p. 173).

While the in-session activities are not attributes of the therapist per se, they are interesting insofar as they may be a reflection of certain underlying attitudes or characteristics. Those found to contribute negatively to the alliance included either overstructuring or the failure to structure the therapy, inappropriate use of self-disclosure, managing, unyielding transference interpretations, inappropriate use of silence, superficial interpretations, and belittling of the person in therapy (Ackerman & Hilsenroth, 2001). A careful consideration of the summary terms used by Ackerman and Hilsenroth to identify the therapist attributes associated with negative impact on the therapeutic alliance — rigid, uncertain, exploitive, critical, distant, tense, aloof, distracted — allows an alignment with the above mentioned therapist behaviors. It is not difficult, in so doing, to understand those in-session behaviors as expressions of those personal qualities of the therapist. Interestingly, the studies summarized involved a broad range of therapeutic orientations, once again highlighting the trans-theoretical ubiquity and the power of the *person of the therapist*. Furthermore, the conclusions based on this body of research are consistent with those based on the efficacy research.

So much has been done, yet so little is known. I marvel at the prevailing situation that we have as little research based knowledge of the person of the therapist as we do, considering the plethoric corpus of research. As I write this I hear the echo of Rainer Maria Rilke once more saying, "be patient toward all that is unsolved in your heart and try to love the *questions themselves*" (Schoen, 1994, p. 47). The *person of the therapist* is the question.

Painfully aware of the limitations of the existing research, and with the question of the person of the therapist indwelling, I conceived of some opportunistic research. I had scheduled within a period of a few months four separate continuing education workshops for professional psychotherapists. They were sponsored by the

American Academy of Psychotherapists (Summer Workshop), the Georgia Psychological Association (Mid-Winter Conference), the continuing education division of a Veterans Administration Medical Center, and the Tressler Centers of Delaware. The focal topic for each of these workshops was the person of the therapist, and each workshop was announced to be largely experiential. The length varied from three hours to five days. In toto, the workshops were attended by psychotherapists from the subcultures of clinical psychology, counseling psychology, pastoral counseling, clinical social work, marriage and family therapy, and alcohol and drug counseling. Although certainly not a stratified random sample by any means, the therapists were from many states from California to Pennsylvania and New York to Georgia. In conducting opportunistic research, I had no way of selecting participants with regard to any demographic variables. Additionally, the participants were all self-selected, all choosing to attend a workshop led by me and having a title and description that clearly identified the focus as being on the person of the therapist, the format being largely experiential. With the unanimous consent of the participants, I recorded in writing, or volunteers recorded in writing, the anonymous responses to a question that I posed, which is elaborated below. (Their consent included my reporting of these data.) Therefore, there is no guarantee that the words recorded are completely accurate, but must be accepted as approximate. Not all participants in all of the workshops chose to disclose their responses to the question, so another self-selection factor is part of the context of these data. Inelegant as this research is with regard to design and conduct, the spontaneous nature of it lends it, I believe, a certain interest. Although but a crudely conducted example, and therefore perhaps best considered only a pilot study, it does add a qualitative note to a literature that is overwhelmingly quantitative. I have no illusions that this is in any way the *experimentum crucis* with regard to the person of the therapist. That acknowledged, let us proceed to the question, and the context in which it was posed.

    In the experiential portion of the workshops, under dimmed lights, I invited the participants to assume a comfortable position, sitting or lying on the floor. Having explained that my intention was to ask a question to be answered while in a state of trance, I invited a trance via a few minutes of directed progressive relaxation followed by suggestions for deepening the experienced state. I then requested that participants allow the answer to my question to come from deep within, with as little editing or censorship as they could apply.

The question that I posed was, "*Who am I, that I may heal?*" I repeated this question several times over a period of fifteen or twenty minutes, at times varying it slightly, as in "Who am I, that I am a healer?" I also stated that if the question seemed spontaneously to change as they heard it within, they were then to allow an answer to come forward in response to their new question. Most of this period of time was, then, in silence. At the end of the fifteen or twenty minute period, I invited the participants to "come back to the room slowly," and then take a few minutes to review what had emerged from within, perhaps writing down what they had heard or seen, much as one might do if keeping a dream journal and having just awakened from a dream. We came back together as a group, and I invited anyone who wanted to do so to share what he or she had experienced. Forty-six people from the four workshops elected to speak.

Reading the records of what people said, I looked for clusters of themes, reflected by common words or synonyms thereof. Keep in mind that many participants reported hearing and/or seeing multiple responses to the posed question. Following is a summary of what I found.

One-third of those who spoke responded to the question with a theme of the wounded healer. For example, one person heard, "I am wounded and I heal. Heal me and heal others." Another heard the word "Suffering." Other responses on the same theme were as follows: "Gone through pain and came back on my feet." "I can greatly experience great suffering." "I have hurt and I understand hurt. Still need to work on hurt." "Chose to be a healer to heal myself." "Wounded healer." "I have suffered and come through it." "A healing one that is healing and that helps others to heal."

The next most frequent theme, expressed by about 17 percent of those who shared their experience, was one of love: "I laugh, I sing, and I love." "A lover, a sufferer, a vessel, a wayfarer." "I'm loving." "I can be loving." "Loving acceptance." "Love." "I am loved and I can love." These are examples of the expressions of the theme of love.

Somewhat less clearly defined than the first two themes were three themes that were the third most frequent, expressed by approximately 13 percent of those who spoke. One was a theme of being an instrument, vehicle, or container, as indicated by the following examples: "Instrument of peace." "A vehicle, a vessel." "I am an instrument of God." "Conduit for the creator." "A vessel." "Passing on God's healing." "Container." "I am the servant of I am [sic]."

The second of these three themes involved being blessed or a child of God. Here are some examples: "Spirits blessed me." "Grandmother's granddaughter" (expressed by a Native American). "God's child." "A child of God; a child of the King." "Child of God."

The third of these three themes is constituted of two sub-themes, those being of a journey and of being a guide on the way. Given their affinity, I think it justified to consider them together. Consider these. "Fellow traveler with another." "A wayfarer." "One of four or five women going to a shopping center." Perhaps the following can be seen as a bridge from the one sub-theme to the next. "I am a stop on the other people's journey." And then, consider these. "A taxi driver; a tourist guide who knows many languages." "Flashlight." (Having seen a flashlight, this person then heard the question, "How are you a flashlight?" The response was, "The reconciliation is leading people back to where they need to go.") "A channel of radiant light." "A lighthouse." "I hold a lantern to our way."

It may be noteworthy that there was a paucity of themes reflecting technical skill. Only a couple of responses, about 4 percent, were about skills. "Good problem solver." "Mr. Skillful." Likewise, negative statements were rare, about 6 percent. "Mr. Bluffer." "... arrogant." "I know nothing."

The participants saw images and heard things said, as if summoned by my question. Many indicated that they had experienced an altered state of consciousness. One, for instance, said, "I didn't feel like I was here. Fire hot. Felt somewhere else." Some of the reported verbal or visual images themselves suggested strongly that an altered state had been entered. As with dreams, some of the images and words seemed to come with face validity, others emerged with an air of enigma, if not mystery. And so themes emerged. By virtue of frequency, a dominant primary theme of the *wounded healer* unfolded, followed by a secondary and much less frequent theme of *love*, then by three tertiary themes of *instrument, vessel, vehicle, or conduit of God*, of being *blessed, or a child of God*, and of *guide or fellow traveler*.

If one is of strong phenomenological bent, the responses in and of themselves may hold greatest interest. Those mentioned above can be considered, and may engender the wish for the opportunity to ask the persons involved to elaborate. Perhaps even more intriguing are some of the responses that did not go gently into any of the thematic categories that were developed. Ponder these. "A jewel on the ocean only seen as the sun sets and its rays touch the ocean." Another related seeing a bowl in front of him, which he took and placed behind himself. "Shadow puppets dance around in a circle at a religious school." "A Woody Allen scenario in which there is a focus on his heel." "I am the fool with a cup of water for the thirsty." "Flock of geese coming to us, dropped out of the sky and seemed dead. Took them and dipped them in water and they came alive."

The person of the therapist is at once ubiquitous and yet elusive, as we have seen. But in spite of its elusiveness-cum-mysteriousness, and because of its ubiquity-cum-vitality, we must honor it with our attention. With practical concern, Lambert and Bergin (1994) stated their opinion "that training programs should emphasize the *development of the therapist as a person* in parity with the acquisition of therapeutic techniques"(italics mine) (p.181). Or, recalling the bold words that John Warkentin (1965) wrote in the inaugural issue of *Voices*, "Any sincere therapist should be in continuous therapy for himself during his entire professional life" (p. 4). If we do not dismiss the data that I gathered as mere artifact of one opportunistic qualitative study, defined by a particular question, then there is more than a hint therein of relevance of the philosophical and spiritual in the development of the person of the therapist.

Chapter 4

A Philosophical and Spiritual Note

As we have seen, both theory and research suggest characteristics of the person of the therapist that qualify her or him to be effective. Reflecting on the relevant theory, one can portray the person of the effective therapist as of good will, empathic, showing positive regard that is unconditional, genuine (authentic, non-duplicitous, willing to be fully present and involved, thus vulnerable to revealing one's own patient vectors); powerful, sensitive to recognizing duplicity in others and interested in establishing communication with those who are duplicitous; willing to be transformed in the crucible of the I-Thou encounter; accepting of responsibility for control and potency within a context of humaness and commitment; having a self-awareness that allows for selective responses; free from emotional plague, desirous of communicative intimacy, and courageous enough to engage the predicament of the person in therapy.

From the research, we are directed to an experienced therapist with a high level of functioning (absence of high levels of distress or personality disturbance), an ability to communicate within the value framework of the person in therapy, absence of hostility, and a willingness to self-disclose appropriately. But of greatest certainty based on the research data are the qualities of warmth, genuineness, and empathy, accurately expressed. Interestingly, in 1967 Allen Bergin

(Raskin, 1974), having reviewed the research available at that time, concluded that "therapeutic progress varies with therapist warmth, empathy, adjustment and experience" (p. 43). It seems that a quarter of a century of further research is but a footnote, albeit an important footnote, to Bergin's conclusion in 1967.

The overlap that is evident between the theory and the research is comforting and not surprising, as ideally theory gives direction to research, and research findings lead to theory revision. Theories suggest relationships to be explored empirically. As the empirical evidence accrues, theories are then altered to account for the evidence that has emerged, and once again, to suggest further relationships. This is the aspired-to cycle of reciprocity between theory and research. But, true to the respectively more speculative and more cautious natures of theory and research, the above theory-driven list is the longer and, I may say, the richer. The latter sacrifices richness for a more secure certitude.

Beyond the realm of the pragmatic, with its focus on the question of effectiveness, some of these qualities of the person of the therapist segue into yet another realm, a realm of the philosophical-cum-anagogical. In this realm of the spirit, the question is more of ethics or esthetics than of efficacy. On this spiritual plane, the question of whether this or that personal quality contributes to the growth and healing of the person in therapy is not asked. That is the practical question. Rather, the questions asked concern the moral or virtuous implications of a personal quality, and the beauty or pleasingness, in a high minded sense, of that quality.

The I-Thou relationship, explicit in the literature of the Gestalt approach and at least implicit, if not so named, in several other approaches, has obvious spiritual dimension. Actually using the term I-Thou, L. M. Leitner (2001) wrote of its essence, connecting it with *reverence*. Defined as "the awareness that one is validating the core ... process of the other," and known to be experienced "when I am aware that I am affirming your most central processes of being ..., reverence is experienced when I am aware that I am in the presence of your 'soul'" (p. 150). Leitner is explicit in his belief that the experience of reverence for the person in therapy, on the part of the therapist, can transform. I understand this as something that is not fully captured by the usual meaning of the terms healing and growth, but something more spiritual. In this reverential experience, he wrote, "there is the integration of profound intimacy with a sense of separateness" or optimal therapeutic distance (p. 152). Leitner suggested, too, that this reverence can be extended to all persons, based upon our shared humanity. This may develop out of multiple experiences with more person-specific interpersonal reverence and take us, then, to an experience of transpersonal reverence. In the transpersonal sphere, an awareness develops that to limit or deprive any person is an injury not only to that person, but to ourselves, and to the entire human race.

Self-disclosure, too, not only emerges as a relevant facet in both the theory and the research on the person of the therapist, but also has spiritual implications. Self-disclosure, as an act, is an expression of genuineness, authenticity, non-duplicity, and willingness to be fully present and involved. It is also an act that flows from the encounter of the I and Thou. Sidney Jourard (1964) referred to the person who self-discloses as a *transparent self*. Believing that to a large extent behavior begets its own kind, Jourard wrote emphatically that "*the closest I can come to eliciting and reinforcing real-self behavior in my patient is by manifesting it myself*" (italics his) (p. 64).

When I met O. H. Mowrer in the mid–1960s, he was espousing a radical view, one that formed a rather solid nexus between psychotherapy and the spiritual. He used a language mixed of the vocabularies of both psychotherapy and religion, labeling those aspects of oneself that are known to oneself but unknown to others as *sins of the flesh*, whereas those aspects of oneself that are known to others but unknown to oneself are *sins of the spirit*. What is needed for these sins, he said, is *confession*. Mowrer related his idea of confession to the Christian apostolic movement led by Paul, a movement in which confession in small groups and group-dictated penance were used. It followed for him, then, that *private treatment* is an anachronism, for, as he declared, *privatism is the disease*. In his therapy, Mowrer said, he tried to establish a true *fellowship* in which he would reveal his true self, and then the person in therapy with him would confess.

Nedra Lander and Danielle Nahon have furthered Mowrer's Integrity Therapy. Thirty-some years after listening to Mowrer, I listened to them as they presented a workshop at a meeting of the American Psychological Association. Their title, interestingly, was "Personhood of the Therapist: An Integrity Therapy Perspective." They explained that the two lynchpins of Integrity Therapy are *therapist self-disclosure* and *scrupulous honesty in self-examination of counter-transference.* When these two lynchpins are not honored, personhood is diminished. Furthermore, any inconsistency in self-disclosure on the part of the therapist may call that therapist's integrity into question. Better it is, therefore, not to self-disclose than to be inconsistent in self-disclosure. It is, in their view, this *real human encounter* that is needed for the reclaiming of personhood. Although not employing the more spiritual language of Mowrer, Lander and Nahon (2000) wrote that it is from a lack of personal integrity that mental illness springs. Lack of personal integrity is manifest when personal contracts and commitments are not honored, when one violates the very contracts that one has made. *Honesty, responsibility,* and *increased emotional involvement* with others are the defining elements of integrity. In their meaning, honesty involves the acknowledging of wrongdoings, be those past or present. Following in turn comes the responsibility for making amends for such wrongdoing. The full meaning of such honesty and setting things right is in "closing the psychological space," that is, in increasing the sense of community with the other through emotional involvement (p. 33). And, of course, as they cited Mowrer as having reminded us, there would be a lack of integrity inherent in asking the person in therapy to do what the therapist herself or himself would not be willing to do. Therapy, then, demands, in their words, "a real human encounter daring to nakedly meet the other on equal terms" (p. 40).

The concept of authenticity recurs with remarkable frequency throughout the psychotherapy literature. This should come as no surprise, given its position in the cultural and spiritual values of the West. The profound importance of authenticity in Western culture is reflected in the Grail legend as it has been interpreted by Joseph Campbell. In *Transformations of Myth Through Time,* Campbell (1990) addressed the meaning of the Grail legend. First, to set the context, the period of the Arthurian and Grail romances was the beginning of the second great phase of Western culture, the first having been the Greco-Roman period from the time of the Homeric epics. Campbell further instructed us that it was then that the main themes of Western culture were stated and elaborated as cultural and spiritual values. The four powerful European mythological traditions—that is, the Classic Greek, the Classical Italic or Roman, the Celtic, and the Germanic—that preceded the Arthurian and Grail legends all placed particular emphasis on respect for the individual and the individual path in life. Beginning with the Classic Greek tradition, the person came to be seen as a citizen rather than as a subject. During the Gothic (Germanic) period, this view was enhanced by recognizing the individual path in life. With the advent of Christianity and its introduction to the European people, the two traditions met. On the one hand was the heroic tradition drawing directly on the Germanic Celtic spirit with its emphasis on the individual path. On the other hand was the Near Eastern tradition with its emphasis on membership in community, and in turn its emphasis on ritual, rules, and law. Campbell continued, writing that the Arthurian and Grail legends represent the assimilation of the Near Eastern tradition of Christianity with the heroic tradition, a process that Europe was not ready for until A.D. 1150–1250.

With respect to authenticity, Campbell (1990) made an intriguing point, as I read him. We can recognize the meaning of the Grail as being the vivifier of the *waste land*. And what is the meaning of the waste land? It is "the world of people living inauthentic lives— doing what they're supposed to do" (p. 214). People of the twelfth century often had to profess beliefs that they did not hold, and to behave as the Church told them to behave. Thus, lives of inauthenticity, and thus, metaphorically a waste land, a Grailess land. With the finding of the Grail could come life, authenticity, again. The Grail quest, in this interpretation, is the quest for authenticity. Both a personal characteristic and a quality to be sought, authenticity is so valued in Western culture that this canonical legend of the Germanic Celtic world formed itself around it.

There is a consistency between Campbell's interpretation of the Grail legend and the way that authenticity is viewed by many existential writers. To understand such an existentialist's view, I turn to Henri Ellenberger (1967). In his exploration of existential philosophy, he cited Kierkegaard as the first to make explicit its basic assumptions, and credited Jaspers, Heidegger, Sartre, Marcel, Berdyaev, and Tillich with elaborating the basic concepts. But it was Martin Heidegger to whom he gave the honor of designation as the main influence upon psychotherapy. Taking an idea suggested much earlier by Kierkegaard and elaborated by Heidegger, Ellenberger took as a starting point that one is not a ready-made being, but will only become that which he or she makes of himself or herself. One construes oneself through choices because one has the freedom to make vital choices. Uppermost of these is the choice towards an authentic or an inauthentic modality of existence. The inauthentic modality of existence is created when one lives under the "tyranny of the *plebs* (the crowd, i.e., the anonymous collectivity). Authentic existence is the modality in which a man assumes the responsibility of his own existence" (p. 118).

Genuineness, self-congruence, non-duplicity, willingness to be fully present, engagement in I-Thou encounter, authenticity — any of these alternative terms may give rise to some felt sense of meaning. Each term offers another nuance to this felt sense of meaning. At the very core of this felt sense I find *honesty*. It was this very word, honesty, that Everett Shostrom (1968) chose as one of the four fundamental characteristics of the actualizor, in his book *Man the Manipulator: The Inner Journey from Manipulation to Actualization*. He defined honesty in the context of the actualizor by saying that "the actualizor is able honestly to be his feelings, whatever they may be. He is characterized by candidness, *expression*, and genuinely being himself," adding as defining synonyms "Transparency, Genuineness, Authenticity" (p. 23). (In order not to leave the reader hanging, the other three fundamental characteristics of the actualizor are Awareness, Freedom [Spontaneity], and Trust.) These four are in contrast to the four respective fundamental characteristics of manipulators, namely, Deception (Phoniness, Knavery), Unawareness, Control, and Cynicism.

Polonius, in Act I, scene III of Shakespeare's *Hamlet*, revealed to us the two sides of honesty, placing them in inextricable relation one to the other. "This above all, — to thine own self be true; And it must follow, as the night the day, Thou canst not then be false to any man." Fullness of authenticity implicates both self and other. To be authentic, I must be true to myself, I must find my individual way, make my path, accept my choices in becoming and the responsibility that attends that. And I must be that in relation to the other, to Thee. For the person in therapy to witness authenticity in her or his therapist, and to see that the therapist survives, may offer invitation, support, example, perhaps even challenge. A person who was in therapy with Jung, Elizabeth Shepley Sergeant (Dunne, 2000), reported in an account of a session with him that he said the following: "Yes, all men are liars, certainly. I just let them sit in that chair and lie till they get tired of lying. Then they begin to tell the truth" (p. 80).

As an ethical aspiration, truth appears throughout the sacred literature. Let us consider several examples. Going back several thousand years, perhaps as much as four or five thousand years B.C., to the sacred literature of Egypt, we can find in *The Book of the Dead* extensive references to truth. Contained therein is The Papyrus of Ani, in which is found The Negative Confession. The Negative Confession was written for the deceased, to be recited at the time of judgement, at which time the deceased's heart would be weighed. In The Negative Confession, which contains forty-two confessional items, no fewer than five deal specifically with truth:

> 8. Hail, Neba, who comest and goest, I have not uttered lies.
>
> 15. Hail, Unem-snef, who comest forth from the execution chamber, I am not a man of deceit.
>
> 18. Hail, Tenemiu, who comest forth from Bast, I have slandered (no man).
>
> 26. Hail, Nekhenu, who comest forth from Heqat, I have not shut my ears to the words of truth.
>
> 32. Hail, Neb-abui, who comest forth from Souti, I have not multiplied my words in speaking [Budge translation, pp. 577–580].

An older source, the Papyrus of Nebseni, also contains the Negative Confession. Although somewhat different, it too contains forty-two confessional items. Of these, seven have to do with truth. In summary, they state that the confessor has not acted deceitfully (7), has not told lies (9), has not acted deceitfully (14), has not set her or his mouth in motion (slandered) (17), has not turned a deaf ear to the words of truth (24), has not multiplied speech overmuch (33), and has not worked deceit, not worked wickedness (34) (pp. 582–584).

One may question the meaning of the phrases "multiplied my words" from the Papyrus of Ani and "multiplied speech overmuch" from the Papyrus of Nebseni. Do these phrases refer to simple prolixity? If so, there remain, nevertheless, four items and six items of confession in the respective Papyri that relate to truth clearly and certainly. But these two phrases in question may, too, relate to truth, for consider the words of Michel de Montaigne (Screech translation, 1993):

> For whoever believes anything reckons that it is a work of
> charity to convince someone else of it; and to do this he is
> not at all afraid to add, out of his own invention, whatever
> his story needs to overcome the resistance and the defects
> which he thinks there are in the other man's ability to grasp
> it [pp. 353–354].

We can say with certainty, then, that in the religion of the ancient
Egyptians truth was an explicit value and moral guideline, one on
which a person would be judged at the time of the weighing of her
or his heart. Eternal life hung in the balance, with truthfulness or lack
thereof as one of the weights.

As one would expect, truth is also addressed in the *Analects of
Confucius*, for this body of writing is concerned with day-to-day rules
of conduct. Born in 551 B.C., Confucius came to be known as The
First Teacher, and has been described as the supreme editor of Chinese culture (H. Smith, 1958). He was dedicated to deliberate tradition as opposed to spontaneous tradition, and saw the main
responsibility of education as being the maintenance of the former.
The content of the tradition was summarized by Confucius under five
terms. *Jen* is the basic relationship which should maintain between
people, a quality of goodness, benevolence, or human-heartedness.
Chun-tzu is the ideal relationship between human beings, poise,
grace, and a lack of pettiness. *Li* refers first to propriety or the way
things should be done, including the Doctrine of the Mean (nothing
in excess), Rectification of Names (correctness and care in speaking),
the Five Relationships (a father loving, a son reverential; an elder
brother gentle, a younger brother respectful; a husband good, a wife
listening; an elder friend considerate, a younger friend deferential;
a ruler benevolent, a subject loyal), and respect for Age. *Li* refers secondly to ritual, or the ordering of life through intricate ceremonial
patterns. *Te* is the power by which men are ruled (the acceptance of
the will of the state). *Wen* refers to the arts of peace, or culture in its
esthetic mode, most specifically art, music, and poetry (H. Smith,
1958).

Within this matrix of deliberate tradition, and with esthetic
attention to writing style, Confucius offered specific guidance in his
Analects with regard to truth. "I daily thrice examine myself. In counseling men, have I not been wholeheartedly sincere? In associating
with friends, have I not been truthful to my word? In transmitting

something, have I not been proficient?" (Huang translation, pp. 47–48). Furthermore, he wrote,

> If a gentleman is not grave, he will not be awe-inspiring. If he learns, he will not be benighted. He keeps whole-hearted sincerity and truthfulness as his major principles and does not befriend those beneath him. When he makes a mistake, he is not afraid to correct it [p. 48].

Note the emphasis in this passage on sincerity and truthfulness as they are stated as major principles for one to follow. They are basic to a good life, for, Confucius wrote, "if a man is not truthful, I do not know how he can get along" (p. 57). And teaching by pointing to contradiction, Confucius added, "High-minded yet not straight-forward, puerile yet not honest, sincere yet not truthful — I do not understand such people" (p. 98).

Not so focused on day-to-day conduct, Lao Tsu, an older contemporary of Confucius, was concerned with a more spiritual level of being. He recorded his thoughts in eighty-one chapters of only about 5,000 words, the *Tao Te Ching* (Feng & English translation, 1972). Herein, in the major text of Taoism, he, too, wrote of truth. In chapter eighty-one can be found, in his idiom of mysterious air,

> Truthful words are not beautiful.
> Beautiful words are not truthful [no page number].

Perhaps more to the point, albeit enigmatically stated and lifted from where it was poetically ensconced, line seven of chapter eight reads "In speech, be true" (no page number). In another translation (Bynner, 1962) of the same line it is written that one, when at her or his best, loves "the pick of words that tell the truth" (p. 29).

The Taoist literature offers further understanding of truth through the work of Chuang Tsu. Chuang Tsu, living around the fourth century B.C., has been placed in relationship to Lao Tsu as St. Paul is to Jesus and Plato to Socrates. According to translators Gia-Fu Feng and Jane English, the idea of a rhythm of life, organically unfolding, that was implied in the writing of Lao Tsu finds full expression through rigorous logic in the work of Chuang Tsu (*Inner Chapters*, 1974, p. vii). He explored truth in relation to exaggeration, as follows:

> Carrying messages of delight or anger between two parties is
> the most difficult thing in the world. When they are both
> pleased, there is bound to be exaggeration of flattery; when
> they are both angry, there is bound to be exaggeration of
> criticism. Exaggeration leads away from truth. Without truth,
> there will be no trust. When there is no trust, the messengers
> will be in danger. Therefore, it is said, "Speak the truth and
> do not exaggerate; then you will not be harmed" [p. 73].

Note Chuang Tsu's use of logic in this passage. Exaggeration,
either positive as in flattery or negative as in criticism, leads away
from truth. Without truth, there will be no trust. Without trust, one
is in danger. Therefore, do not exaggerate — tell the truth. On the
surface, Chuang Tsu's point may appear as only a practical one. On
a more subtle level, he has identified exaggeration for what it is — a
lie.

Consulting the Hindu tradition offers further evidence of the
spiritual value of truth. An example of such evidence comes from the
Bhagavad-Gita (the Song of God) (Prabhavananda & Isherwood
translation, 1951), the most popular book in Hindu religious literature. Unlike the Upanishads, which are regarded as *Sruti*, or scrip-
tural teachings revealed by God, the Bhagavad-Gita is regarded as
Smriti, "the teachings of divine incarnations, saints or prophets, who
[further] explain and elaborate ... the scriptures" (pp. 27–28). Written between the fifth and second centuries B.C., "it has profoundly
influenced the spiritual, cultural, intellectual and political life of
[India] throughout the centuries" (p. 28).

For the Hindu, Brahman is the name given to the supreme reality. If thought of as personification, he is Brahma (the Creator),
Vishnu (the Preserver), and Shiva (the Destroyer) "who in the end
resolves all finite forms back into the primordial nature from which
they emerged" (H. Smith, 1958, p. 76). Sri Krishna (Lord Krishna),
as the divine incarnation of Vishnu, spoke as follows:

> A man who is born with tendencies toward the Divine, is
> fearless and pure in heart.... He is charitable. He can control
> his passions. He studies the scriptures regularly, and obeys
> their directions. He practises spiritual disciplines. He is
> straightforward, truthful, and of an even temper. He harms
> no one. He renounces the things of this world. He has a

> tranquil mind and an unmalicious tongue. He is compassion-
> ate toward all. He is not greedy. He is gentle and modest. He
> abstains from useless activity. He has faith in the strength of
> his higher nature. He can forgive and endure. He is clean in
> thought and act. He is free from hatred and from pride [Bha-
> gavad-Gita, 1951, p. 114].

Within this statement is the association of straightforwardness, truthfulness, and non-malicious speech with the tendency toward the Divine.

Lingering with religions of Asia, I now turn attention to Buddhism. The story is told that Gautama, born around 560 B.C., sat
under a fig tree, vowing not to arise until enlightened. That tree is
now referred to as the Bo tree, from the word *Bodhi* (enlightenment)
or the Immovable Spot, for it was here that he sat for forty-nine days.
Arising from the spell of rapture, he began walking to Benares, stopping to deliver his first sermon following enlightenment. In that sermon Gautama spoke of the Four Noble Truths, in which the doctrinal
core of Buddhism is revealed. At the risk of oversimplification, the
first three Noble Truths are as follows: Life is *dukkha*, suffering, the
pain that is the accompaniment to existence. Dukkha follows from
tanha, wrong desire, craving, egoistic attachment. The Third Noble
Truth follows logically from these: Overcome tanha, and dukkha is
relieved. Advice on how tanha may be overcome constitutes the
Fourth Noble Truth, known as the Eightfold Path. The Eightfold Path
consists of right knowledge, right aspiration, right speech, right
behavior, right livelihood, right effort, right mindfulness, and right
absorption. Each aspect of the Eightfold Path is, of course, explained
and elaborated. For instance, right behavior is made more specific by
way of the Five Precepts: do not kill (leading to vegetarianism for
those who make a strict interpretation of the precept); do not steal;
do not lie; do not be unchaste (continence for monks and the unmar-
ried; for the married, restraint appropriate to their distance along the
spiritual path); do not drink intoxicants (H. Smith, 1958).

As we see, truth is addressed in the third of the Five Precepts.
Therein, it is given baldly as an element of right behavior. As we have
also seen, one of the aspects of the Eightfold Path is specific to right
speech, and we would tend to guess that the reference is to truth in
speech. But, to understand the Eightfold Path, one must appreciate
that Buddhism is quite psychological. The Buddha preached a religion
devoid of authority, devoid of ritual, devoid of speculation, devoid

of tradition, devoid of the supernatural. He preached a religion of intense self-effort, of *personal practice*. As such, it is, as I said, quite psychological. In that context, we can better understand right speech. One's way of speaking not only reflects one's character, but also serves as an arena for working on one's spiritual development. It likely would be too great a step simply to resolve always to speak the truth (H. Smith, 1958). (This would be a most naive and simplistic level of cognitive-behavioral therapy. "Just stop ...," "Just don't do that ...," or "Just do it ..." seem not effective interventions even when dealing with circumscribed symptoms such as obsessions, compulsions, and phobic avoidances.) Rather than naive resolve, one can choose simply to observe, to be aware of how many times a day and in what circumstances one chooses to deviate from the truth. To the Buddhist, this is mindfulness practice. Right speech includes not only truth, but charity in speech (H. Smith, 1958). Again, the practice is mindfulness. In the process of becoming more mindful, rather than trying to change, change may come more gently and without force. In the context of mindfulness, one can choose, in the moment, toward truth and toward charity.

"The value of truth in Buddha's eyes was not moral but ontological. Deceit is bad because it reduces one's being.... The motive is almost always a fear of revealing to others or to ourselves what we really are" (H. Smith, 1958, p. 115). Speaking untruth, therefore, is an attempt to protect the ego, and thus keeps one in the realm of dukkha through the perpetuation of tanha. The Third Noble Truth can only be realized when one can choose away from lies, false witness, idle chatter, abusive language, and slander, as well as their more subtle forms such as belittling, hostile humor, and tactlessness.

What we know of the Germanic mythological tradition of Northern Europe that predated the coming of Christianity is limited because of the attempt on the part of early Christian missionaries to destroy all things deemed pagan. Surviving, however, are several collections of writing that serve as repositories of the mythology and much of the heroic lore of these Nordic people. One of the foremost collections is the *Poetic Edda* (Hollander translation, 1962), written in the West Norse language spoken in Norway, Iceland, and the Norwegian colonies in the Atlantic during Viking times, between 800 and 1050. The Eddic poems were probably written over a period of three to four centuries. These lays, like *Beowulf*, may be remnants of a flourishing poetic literature during the period of Scandinavian hegemony in the north of Europe. As a source of the ethical views and cultural life of the Viking period, the *Poetic Edda* gives us a perspective on truth.

In the "Lay of Sigrdrifa," verse twenty-five, is perhaps the clearest statement of the ethical value of truth in the Norse religion.

> This other I counsel,   That oath thou swear not
>   But thou tell the truth:
> For baleful doom   Follows breach of truce;
>   Ill fares the breaker of oaths [p. 238].

And, if the point were not sufficiently made, it is reinforced two verses later, where the word "lie" is juxtaposed with "wicked" (p. 239).

In the longest of the Eddic poems, "Havamal" ("The Sayings of Har"), we find one of the five sections devoted to a series of counsels from Odin (Har), himself. Herein is a verse, one-hundred and twenty-four, in which Odin advises on speaking the truth.

> Then love is mingled   When a man can say
>   To a bosom friend what burdens him;
> Few things are worse   Than fickle mind
>   No friend he who but speaks the fair [p. 33].

As I read this verse, I understand Odin to speak of authenticity, or genuiness, and see this as the loving thing to do. This counsel clearly precludes flattery, or trying to make another feel good at the expense of speaking the truth. Truth is valued above pleasantry.

An accurate understanding of the Viking ethos requires a consideration of the other side of truth, as well. Speaking once again, in verses forty-five and forty-six of the "Havamal," Odin proclaims the following:

> If another there be   Whom ill thou trustest,
>   Yet would'st get from him gain:
> Speak fair to him   Though false thou meanest,
>   And pay him lesing for lies.
> And eke this heed: If ill thou trust one,
>   And hollow-hearted his speech:
> Thou shalt laugh with him And lure him on,
>   And let him have tit for tat [p. 21].

It appears, thus, that in the Norse religion truth is not an absolute rule. Rather, it is contextualized in friendship, not honored with those whom one deems untrustworthy.

Using the phrase the "People of the Book," Huston Smith (1958) called attention to the fact that the Old Testament of the Bible is held in common as sacred literature in Judaism, Christianity, and Islam. In surah III of the Koran, the phrase "People of the Scripture" is employed multiple times to refer to Jews and Christians (*The Meaning of the Glorious Koran*, Pickthall translation, 1961, pp. 67–70). So, even though in Judaism the Talmud and the Midrashim stand as augmentation to the Torah (the first five books of the Old Testament in which the Law is explicated) and the rest of the Old Testament, and in Christianity the New Testament augments the Old Testament, and in Islam both the New Testament and the Koran serve as augmentation, the Old Testament remains as common and core scripture in these three religions. (In Christianity there have, of course, been further sectarian augmentations to the Bible. The Book of Mormon in the Church of Jesus Christ of the Latter-Day Saints is an example, as are several books of the Apocrypha in the Roman Catholic Church.)

In Exodus, the second book of the Old Testament, it is written that God spoke to the people saying, "I *am* the Lord thy God, which have brought thee out of the land of Egypt, out of the house of bondage" (King James version, 20:2). Therewith, it is written, God proclaimed the Ten Commandments. The ninth of these, appearing in the twentieth chapter, sixteenth verse, reads "Thou shalt not bear false witness against thy neighbor." The commandment, so stated, is echoed later in Exodus in the twenty-third chapter, first verse: "Thou shalt not raise a false report: put not thine hand with the wicked to be an unrighteous witness." In Solomon's Proverbs, written as instruction in "wisdom, justice, and judgement, and equity" (1:3), the gist of this is once again stated: "Be not a witness against thy neighbor without cause; and deceive *not* with thy lips" (24:28).

A clear reading of the Old Testament reveals an ethos of strict law and harsh punishment for transgressions of that law. Joseph Campbell (1988a), in an interview with Bill Moyers, alluded to the Old Testament conception of God as one of a lot of rules and no mercy. This context can, perhaps, be understood more fully by contrasting it with the Taoist or Buddhist perspective. Speaking from the latter, the Zen philosopher D. T. Suzuki was quoted by Campbell

(1988b) as reacting to Christianity as follows: "God against man. Man against God. Man against nature. Nature against man. Nature against God. God against nature — very funny religion!" (p. 56). (Huston Smith [1958] explained that "Indian Buddhism processed through Chinese Taoism becomes Japanese Zen" [p. 197].)

In keeping with the Christian tradition, and especially the Roman Catholic expression thereof, we can find further consideration of truth in *The Divine Comedy* of Dante (Sayers translation, 1960), first circulated about 1314. In this poem, hell is the place or condition of lost souls after death, a funnel-shaped pit. Allegorically, "it is the image of the deepening possibilities of evil within the soul.... The sinners who there remain fixed forever in the evil which they have obstinately chosen are also images of the perverted choices themselves" (p. 68). Dante, shown about by the poet Virgil (author of the *Aeneid* and looked upon as an unconscious prophet of Christianity), descended into hell. What is most instructive for us in our quest to understand the role of truth in various religious traditions is the location of people of untruth in Dante's Inferno. (I will capitalize the names because these not only identify the sins, but are the labels of the topography itself.)

In Upper Hell are, in descending order, the souls of the Lustful, the Gluttonous, the Hoarders and Spendthrifts, the Wrathful. These are the specific sins of Incontinence.

In Nether Hell, two additional major classes of sin are encountered, namely Violence and Fraud or Malice. Having descended through the loci of Incontinence in Upper Hell, and Violence in Nether Hell, we come upon Fraud also in Nether Hell. Herein, we find the sinners by Simple Fraud, namely the Panders and Seducers, Flatterers, Simoniacs (those who have trafficked in holy things, including the sale of sacraments or ecclesiastical office), Sorcerers, Barrators (who are to the City what the Simoniacs are to the Church), Hypocrites, Thieves, Counselors of Fraud (those who have counseled others to commit fraud), Sowers of Discord, and Falsifiers. Deeper still is found Complex Fraud, with its Caina (betrayers of their own kindred, after Cain), Antenora (betrayers of their country, after Antenor of Troy), Ptolomaea (betrayers of their guests, after Ptolemy, Captain of Jericho), and Judecca (betrayers of their holy lords, after Judas).

Dishonesty or deviation from the truth is involved in a number of sins, if not those of Incontinence located in Upper Hell, or those of Violence located in Nether Hell, then certainly those of Fraud located father down in Nether Hell. Particularly useful for the Panders and Seducers, the Flatterers, the Hypocrites, and the Falsifiers, inauthenticity is well represented. As punishment, the Panders and Seducers are beaten with heavy whips as they run naked around the rim of their level of Hell. Just as they " exploited the passions of others and so drove them to serve their own interests, [they] are themselves driven and scourged" (p. 185). The lot that befalls the Flatterers is to be plunged into a pit of slop and dung. Since they have corrupted language, they are now plunged into the filth that they had excreted upon the world. (A warning to all who utter, as we say, "bullshit"!) Gilded cloaks lined with lead are worn by the Hypocrites, giving fine outward show, but making a "weary mantle for eternity…. Crushed 'neath that vast load those sad folks plied" (p. 215). Falsifiers, those who had falsified things, words, money, and persons, lie stricken with hideous diseases, reflective of corrupt hearts and a society corrupted by them. Thus, the pit of disease.

It is interesting to note the order of these sins most reflective of untruth-cum-inauthenticity. As we descend with Dante and Virgil, the sins of the sufferers are increasingly serious and the punishments, therefore, more severe.

Deemed a poetic masterpiece of the high Middle Ages, Dante's *Divine Comedy* may have both reflected the beliefs of the time and served to perpetuate and maintain those beliefs. As Dante himself explained in his letter to his patron,

> The subject of the whole work, then, taken merely in the *literal* sense is "the state of the soul after death straightforwardly affirmed," for the development of the whole work hinges on and about that. But if, indeed, the work is taken *allegorically*, its subject is: "Man, as by good or ill deserts, in the exercise of his free choice, he becomes liable to rewarding or punishing Justice" [Brinton, Christopher, & Wolff, 1958, p. 308].

Sometime around 1386, Geoffrey Chaucer began to compose and to set in order his long poem, *The Canterbury Tales*. In one of these, "The Parson's Tale," Chaucer instructed, "There are seven deadly sins of which the first is pride" (Coghill translation, p. 503). He listed the sins in order as Pride, Envy, Anger, Accidie or Sloth, Avarice, Gluttony, and Lechery. Although these are not formally listed in the Bible, all can be found therein. Following a thorough explanation of each of the sins, Chaucer suggested a remedy for each. "The remedy for Pride is Humility or true knowledge.... The remedy for Envy is to love God, your neighbour, and your enemy.... The remedy for Anger is Patience.... [for Accidie] The remedy is Fortitude.... [for Avarice] The remedy is Mercy or 'pity largely taken.' ... [for Gluttony] The remedy is Abstinence, Temperance, and Sobriety.... [for Lechery] The remedy is Chastity and Continence, and not to eat or drink too much. [Adding for good measure,] When the pot boils strongly the best remedy is to withdraw the fire" (pp. 503–504).

Standing as a legacy of Dante and Chaucer, but with reference to biblical authority, we find the following in *A Catechism of Christian Doctrine for General Use* of 1866: "Pride, covetousness, lust, anger, gluttony, envy and sloth, are the seven capital sins" (Evans, 1968, p. 633). Four of the sins, namely lust, gluttony, covetousness, and anger, correspond to the levels of Incontinence in Dante's Upper Hell. The Gluttonous are worse than the Lustful, for the mutual indulgence that characterizes lust descends to solitary self-indulgence in the case of gluttony. The Hoarders and Spendthrifts represent but two sides of covetousness, in which selfish appetites are indulged with awareness of the incompatibility of such indulgence with the appetites of other people. Therefore, the Hoarders and Spendthrifts are worse than the Gluttons, covetousness (greed, avarice) worse than gluttony. Even lower are the Wrathful, who create chaos through anger toward all.

The other three sins are not as easily related to the levels of the Inferno. If they do correspond, they could relate to levels of Fraud in Nether Hell. Perhaps a case could be made that sloth would lead to making others one's tools, the sin of the Panders and Seducers. Perhaps, too, pride would lead one to join the ranks of the Hypocrites. (Chaucer, in fact, stated in "The Parson's Tale" that hypocrisy is one of the forms of pride.) And envy, the chagrin or discontent at the good fortune or excellence of another, could lead to the sins of Complex Fraud. If these correspondences are accepted, the first four with greater certainty, the last three more tentatively, the sins could be seen in the following order of severity, using Dante's Inferno as the point of reference: lust, gluttony, covetousness (greed, avarice),

anger, sloth, pride, envy. The final three would be seen as more iniq-
uitous than the first four, residing as they do in Nether Hell. Of these,
sloth and pride would be Simple Fraud, but envy would be Complex
Fraud, making it the most pernicious of all sins. (Chaucer wrote
of Envy that "it is the worst of sins as it sets itself against all other
virtues and goodness" [p. 504].) For sins of Complex Fraud, Caina,
Antenora, Ptolomaes, and Judecca have been traitors, betraying kin,
country, guests, or the Lord.

Once again, it may be useful to note that, even though not in
itself one of the Seven Capital or Deadly Sins (socalled because they
kill the soul) or a level of the Inferno, the lie-cum-inauthenticity
seems an aid in the expression of each. Considered as a complex of
motive and value, with corresponding thought and feeling, then
surely each sin in manifest form requires dishonesty. Consider each
in turn: lust, gluttony, covetousness (greed, avarice), anger, sloth,
pride, envy. To provide but one example, let us look to the Apoph-
thegms and Interludes of Friedrich Nietzsche in *Beyond Good and
Evil*: "'I did that,' says my memory. 'I could not have done that,' says
my pride, and remains inexorable. Eventually — the memory yields"
(p. 73). We may conclude that the lie-cum-inauthenticity is, in its
very ubiquity in the realms of sin, most baleful.

With no intention of, or illusion of, exhaustiveness, I have
looked to these several spiritual traditions for elucidation of truth as
core value in authenticity. Each of these sacred traditions— the
ancient Egyptian, Confucianism, Taoism, Hinduism, Buddhism, the
Norse, Judaism, Islam, Christianity — has, indeed, helped to illuminate truth, or more precisely, truthfulness.

Given that authenticity is such a core value in humanistic and
existential psychotherapy, and that existentialism in its several variations constitutes the philosophical underpinning of such psychotherapy, it is no surprise that the luminaries of existential thought
have addressed this concept-cum-value. Authenticity is explored
through both philosophical essays and fictional works beginning with
Kierkegaard and continuing through Nietzsche, Sartre, and Camus.
The theme common to these writers' "heroes of authenticity" is "their
wish to transcend their social and ethical predicaments and achieve
authentic modes of living.... They want to attain authenticity by
being faithful to scripts they have written for themselves" (Golomb,
1995, p. 3). Noting that the term *hero* suggests someone admired for

outstanding achievement and noble qualities relative to community values or the prevailing ethos, Jacob Golomb suggested that the term *anti-heroes* may be more apt. For these fictive figures are engaged in a struggle to transcend the ethos of their societies and to "attain a personal and subjective pathos (in terms of a particular experience, feeling or sentiment) which expresses their individuality as human beings who become what they singularly are" (p. 3). Often, these anti-heroes are placed in extreme conditions, for it is in personal, external, and historical crises that the quest for authenticity is particularly pronounced.

Golomb (1999) found in Nietzsche's work two models of authenticity. The first, derived from a biological metaphor, is that of a plant actualizing the potential of its seed. In this model, one is authentic insofar as he or she makes manifest his or her innate nature. It was to this Nietzsche was referring when, as quoted in Golomb, he wrote of loving one's fate. "My formula for greatness in a human being is *amor fati*: that one wants nothing to be different.... Not merely bear what is necessary, still less conceal it ... but *love* it" (1999, p. 19). The second model, using the metaphor of the artist, is that of shaping oneself through spontaneous choice from among the many options one is presented within life. In this second model, primary for Nietzsche, to be authentic is to create oneself freely. It is this creative model of authenticity that is echoed by Nietzsche through the voice of Zarathustra. "This is *my* way; where is yours? — thus I answered those who asked me 'the way.' For *the* way — that does not exist" (Golomb, 1999, p. 15).

This "tension between Nietzsche's two prescriptions for authentic life," to borrow Golomb's (1995) phrase, may be resolved in Heidegger's ontological synthesis, rephrased by Golomb. "Own your Being by creating your self and by appropriating your heritage. Return to your self and its historicality and accept them anxiously by overcoming the temptation to lose them in the distraction of everydayness" (p. 120). In *creating* oneself one is manifesting the artistic mode of authenticity, whereas in *appropriating* one's heritage one is claiming one's innate nature, thereby honoring the actualization mode of authenticity. Heidegger's caveat is not to fail to possess one's own being by falling into common activity — common both in the sense of ordinary and routine, and in the sense of going along with others without exercising discernment.

Notice that the definition of authenticity proffered by the existential writers is not simply one of congruence between what one feels or believes and what one claims to feel or believe. It is to such congruence that Lionel Trilling applied the term *sincerity* (Golomb, 1995). Sincerity, so understood, is synonymous with *true* and *honest*. But, whereas *sincerity* refers to congruity between inner convictions and overt behavior, *authenticity*, as explored by the existential writers, pertains to self-creation. It is to this that Golomb alluded by the "eclipse of 'truth' by 'truthfulness,' the transition from objective sincerity to personal authenticity" (p. 8). Surely, authenticity in this existential sense is the more profound and more complex phenomenon.

If we look to the writing of psychotherapists, the term *authenticity*, when applied to the psychotherapist, and as revealed by its kindred terms *self-congruence*, *genuineness*, *non-duplicity*, and *transparency*, is used mainly in the sense to which Lionel Trilling applied the term *sincerity*. It is authenticity-as-sincerity, for the most part, that is valued as a characteristic of the *person of the therapist*. When used in reference to the *person in therapy*, however, authenticity is sometimes used in its more profound existential sense. The very idea of self-actualization, or self-realization, begs for authenticity in this sense. But if this quest for authenticity, in its more profound sense, is an ongoing act of creation, it follows that blind acceptance of anything — an ideology, a system of values, a set of beliefs, even a moral code — is anathema. Therefore, for a true existential therapy, it is the act of self-creation that may best be modeled by the therapist. This is a far greater challenge for the therapist than simply being sincere.

From this existential perspective, what the therapist ultimately has to offer is exposure of her or his way of being, a way of being that is one of self-creation. This is a showing of one's personhood, the presenting of oneself as a possible model. As Heidegger (Golomb, 1995, p. 113) suggested, one's authenticity is a call to others to aspire to their own authenticity. Diminished authenticity in the therapist would, therefore, be a limitation not only in her or his being, but at the same time in her or his value to the person in therapy.

Others, too, have written in resonance with this idea that who the therapist is as a person is of a higher level of importance than what the therapist does. As viewed through a psychodynamic lens, Jung wrote that "an analyst can help his patient just so far as he himself has gone and not a step further" (The Practice of Psychotherapy, 1966,

p. 330). Continuing in the psychodynamic idiom, Jung believed that if the therapist suffers from a neurosis, that therapist will inevitably develop an unconscious identity with the person in therapy, a counter-transference if you will. But even in the absence of neurosis, an extensive area of unconsciousness in the analyst may lead to a mutual unconsciousness, constituting, again, a counter-transference. It is this state of unconscious identity that underlies the fact that the analyst can help the person in therapy only as far as he or she, the analyst, has gone in terms of personal development. Expressed more poignantly, Jung (Dunne, 2000) stated that "only the wounded physician heals and even he, in the last analysis, cannot heal beyond the extent to which he has healed himself" (p. 92).

Speaking from a position informed by Eastern spirituality, Ram Dass (1974) has written that "the only thing you have to offer to another human being, ever, is your own state of being" (p. 6). Again, the focus is on the *being* of the person who is the therapist. Eschewing the dichotomy of being and doing, he turned *doing* back on itself and thus into *being* by adding, "You are only doing your own being, you're only manifesting how evolved a consciousness you are" (p. 6). And this is, he proclaimed, using the phrase for the title of his book, *The Only Dance There Is* (p. 6)! The kinship of *consciousness*, as used by Ram Dass, and of *authenticity*, as the latter term was intended by the existential writers, is revealed by Ram Dass's statement that "the matter of consciousness is how quickly you give up a past model, so that you can be here and now" (p. 43). Borrowing a common but effective metaphor, he continued, "In other words, the deck has now been re-dealt" (p.6). Such a re-dealing of the deck sits well beside the existential notion of creating oneself in the moment by virtue of one's choices. To act authentically requires a willingness to move forward from past models, choosing, every step of the way.

Turning to the sacred writing of Taoism, we find in Chapter forty-seven of the *Tao Te Ching*, in the pithiness of Lao Tzu, the same point:

The way to do is to be [Bynner translation, 1962, p. 55].

Only slightly less pithy, in Chapter thirty-seven is the following:

The way to use life is to do nothing through acting.
The way to use life is to do everything through being [p. 48].

Part of the beauty of different translations of the ancient *Tao Te Ching* is the nuance that can be found in each, a whisper of difference that adds to understanding. Turning, then, to the translation by Gia-Fu Feng and Jane English (1972), Chapter thirty-seven begins:

> Tao abides in non-action.
> Yet nothing is left undone [no page number].

The latter translation, more mysterious if not esoteric, anchors being/non-doing firmly in the spiritual realm. It, too, assures us that in being/non-doing all will be done. In this we may be secure.

Exploring this notion, known in Taoism as *wu wei*, Huston Smith (1958) warned that it does not mean "a vacant attitude of passive abstention." It is rather a quality of being in harmony with the universe, a "creative quietude" which is constituted at once of "supreme activity and supreme relaxation" (p. 189). *Wu wei* offers release from the "law of reversed effort," which states that the harder one tries, the less the tried-for result ensues. In words hinting at the spiritual profundity of *wu wei*, Smith wrote that it "is the supreme action, the precious suppleness, simplicity, and freedom that flows from us, or rather through us, when our private egos and conscious efforts yield to a power not their own" (p. 189). "Never forcing, never under strain," this is the way of the Tao (p. 190).

Simple, but not necessarily easy, *being* with a person in therapy may be a daunting challenge for the therapist. This may be especially true for the less experienced therapist. Doubting that he or she has much of value to offer, he or she may fall back on the appearance of competence via techniques. Such technically based confidence may seem more robust, safer, and more easily defended to those entities falling under the rubric of third parties. For as Nietzsche warned in his own apophthegm:

> What a person *is* begins to betray itself when his talent
> decreases, — when he ceases to show what he *can do*. Talent
> is also an adornment; an adornment is also a concealment
> [p. 84].

With experience the therapist will perhaps lean less on technical acumen and stand with more self-support, having developed the confidence of personhood. This is not to say that techniques have no legitimate place. Rather it is as Charles Brooks (1974) proposed, that "the things we do become less and less *techniques* as one matures" (p. 18). To extrapolate only slightly, the things we do become more and more expressions of our person.

In a related discipline, that of pedagogy, and guided by a Quaker perspective, Mary Rose O'Reilley (1998) wrote enthusiastically of a path of being as opposed to a path of doing. She championed attention, which she elaborated as being *deep listening* or the openhearted, non-judgmental reception of the other. Through such attention, she believed that one can, as she phrased it, "listen someone into existence" (p. 21). With a most endearing and bucolic metaphor, O'Reilley described this deep listening that invites and intensifies the inner searching of the other as "listening like a cow" (p. 22)! For those readers who have experience with cows, pause and remember what it is like to linger in such bovine presence. Perhaps it was just this listening presence to which Henry Miller (1978) referred in a handwritten letter to *Voices*. Having been referred several persons by a physician friend, he recounted as follows: "I had quite a success with the 7 or 8 patients he sent me. My only method was to let them talk and between times have a nap. I have no idea what 'cured' them" (p. 22). The lesson is just to listen and to try to be present, radically present.

Radical presence, as thus presented by O'Reilley, surely bespeaks a powerful personal presence. And powerful personal presence is one of the qualities of a guru, according to Sheldon Kopp (1971). Considering the psychotherapist as today's guru, Kopp emphasized that we must understand that such a person is not simply a highly skilled technician. Once this is understood, a context is established in which her or his essential qualities become prominent. "To be a guru is to have grace of manner, powerful personal presence, a spirit of inner freedom, and an inspirationally creative imagination" (p. 10). Consider Kopp's words, each disposition, in turn. Perhaps Kopp has come closest to understanding the person of the therapist — grace, presence, inner freedom, creative imagination. It is, Kopp told us, the guru's own freedom that inspires others. Quoting Lipman and Pizzurro, Kopp wrote that "the apparent unpredictability of the [guru's] behavior and his seeming indifference to the most awesome obstacles and dangers" are a source of charisma (p. 7). It is, then, through *unpredictable arbitrariness*, combined with *naive fearlessness* that the spirit of inner freedom and creative imagination become manifest, a revelation of spontaneity. Before leaving Kopp, it will do well for us to be reminded that he warned that the guru-cum-therapist must "live with the greatest of all lusts, the continuing temptation to arrogance" (p. 8).

Let us now consider *grace* more carefully. Insofar as the dispositions that Kopp identified form a gestalt, we can expect that any alteration in one will affect all. Lack of grace, consequently, may decrease the power of personal presence. For grace, in this sense, means poise, it means balance, it means harmony. But what is the essence of grace in this meaning and in the context of psychotherapy? As I have previously written:

> It involves the skilled use of timing and intensity. Speaking too soon or too late reduces the impact of presence. Likewise, intervening with too little or too much intensity misses the mark. The too little or too much, the too soon or too late, constitute awkwardness. The right intensity at just the right time — that is grace [Smith, 1998, p. 50].

I find timing to be of special interest. Lending emphasis to the remarkable if not awesome quality that it can usher in, Laura Perls (1978) wrote that the "miracles [in psychotherapy] are a result not only of intuition, but of timing" (p. 36). Timing may, then, define grace in its moment-to-moment display and also in its manifestation in the larger time frame of a course in therapy. If the latter is touched upon by Laura Perls, it is the focus of the discussion offered by Henri Ellenberger (1967) in *Existence*. Psychotherapists, he wrote, have long known that there are times when a particular person in therapy is inwardly ready for a particular intervention and that this intervention will be successful at that time only. Before that time, the intervention would have been premature, hence ineffective; after that time, also, the intervention would be ineffective. According to Kielhloz, Ellenberger wrote, instances of such a critical and decisive point can be found in work with neurotic, psychopathic, and psychotic individuals. This critical point, this decisive point has been termed *kairos*.

If we consult the sacred Taoist literature, we find attention to timing, furnishing validation of its importance from this realm of the spiritual. In Chapter eight of the *Tao Te Ching*, Lao Tsu offered advice concerning dwelling place, meditation, dealing with others, speech, ruling, and business. And then, he said, "In action, watch the timing" (1972, no page number).

Still in the realm of sacred literature, but now in the robust if not raucous articulation of Odin, we find in the *Poetic Edda*, too, attention to timing. Using an earthy example, Odin speaks at once with literal situation and metaphor:

> Too late by far   to some feasts I came;
>   to others, all too soon;
> The beer was drunk,   or yet unbrewed:
>   Never hits it the hapless one right [p.24].

With this understanding of grace, we can return it to the gestalt of dispositions by which Kopp empowers the guru-cum-psychotherapist. Kopp's perspective is not, however, one that is hobbled by strictly pragmatic considerations. On the contrary, exceeding the limits of pragmatics, he has moved us deftly into an esthetic sphere. Grace itself is the bridge over which he invited us. Not only does grace, understood as exquisite timing, contribute significantly to efficacy in psychotherapy, but grace, understood as graceful, also offers an immediate felt sense of refinement and beauty.

Having thus entered an esthetic and, at the same time, spiritually informed domain, I want to suggest consideration of the Apollonian and Dionysian world views. These views have long been juxtaposed and explored in philosophy and in psychotherapy, as well as in the realm of spirituality, wherein they originated. For every psychotherapist, it is a choice to be made whether one adopts a more Apollonian or a more Dionysian world view, both in the moment and, as those moments of choice accumulate, in a more ongoing sense. The choice itself is best informed by esthetic and by spiritual considerations. The choice between these two emphases is so important in its implications and repercussions that I want to devote considerable space to its examination.

These two emphases, one on the control and insightful guidance of passion and desire and the other on the expression of passion itself, can be related to two alternative visions which appear across cultures. These competing world views have been labeled in various ways, but their elements are consistent. The first has been related to Apollo, Greek god of light, moderation, reason, truth, order, balance

and boundaries. The second vision has been related to the Greek god
of excess, fantasy and metamorphosis, Dionysus, the god of wine.

Dionysus seems the more complex figure, and the symbolism of
this god more mysterious. Even his origin offers complex and intriguing symbolism. Zeus was so madly in love with the Theban princess
Semele that he promised he would do anything she asked of him,
swearing by the river Styx, an oath unbreakable even for the supreme
god. Semele said she wanted above all to see Zeus in his full splendor as King of Heaven and Lord of the Thunderbolt. Knowing that
no mortal could behold him as such and survive, but being bound
by his oath, he appeared to Semele as she had asked. She perished in
the glory of burning light. As she died, Zeus snatched from her their
unborn child. He hid the child in his side until time for it to be born
so that Hera, wife and sister to him, would not know; it was she who,
in her jealousy, had put the fatal wish into the heart of Semele. When
Dionysus was born, Zeus entrusted his care to the nymphs of the
loveliest of the earth's valleys, a valley never seen by a mortal. These
nymphs are believed by some to be the stars which bring rain when
near the horizon, the Hyades. "So the God of the Vine was born of
fire and nursed by rain, the hard burning heat that ripens the grapes
and the water that keeps the plant alive" (Hamilton, 1942, p. 55).

Dionysus, as the only god not born of two divine parents, presents even in his origin a promise of mystery, perhaps even danger.
Just as he sprang from two sides, one divine and one mortal, he himself shows two sides. As God of wine, fantasy, and metamorphosis,
he inspires the freeing of the soul to dream, imagine, and to transform. Think of his vines themselves. In winter they are black and
withered and appear dead, but in spring they send forth their green
shoots, coming into a full verdant splendor with the summer, and
with summer and autumn are heavy with grapes. The metamorphosis
is striking and the symbolism powerful. In addition, the
grape–to–grape juice–to–wine transformation offers an equally striking and powerful symbolization of metamorphosis.

The other side of Dionysus is shown in his being the god of wine
and excess. Just as wine used in moderation can lift and inspire, used
immoderately it can lead to behavior of terrible excess. In one story,
Dionysus, who was on a ship, took the form of an angry lion, causing
the sailors to jump overboard (and to be transformed into dolphins).
In another, he drove a group of women mad, causing them to attack

and dismember the child of one of them (Hamilton, 1942). (This is still a problem today, as alcohol-abusing parents may terrorize their children, sometimes resulting in the children's *jumping ship*.)

The gods of Olympus tended to love order and beauty in their worship and in their temples, following the way of Apollo. But the followers of Dionysus had no temples, preferring to "worship under the open sky and the ecstasy of joy it brought in the wild beauty of the world" (Hamilton, p. 57). "Frenzied with wine ... they rushed through woods and mountains uttering sharp cries ..., swept away in a fierce ecstasy" (p. 56).

While Apollo remained for the Romans what he had been for the Greeks, Dionysus became the Roman god Bacchus and the side of excess came to be emphasized (Partridge, 1960). Sheldon Kopp (1971, p. 74) summarized the transition in this way: "Later, when this cult of the Mad God appeared in Rome, it became debased into celebration of orgies of debauchery, rather than simple revelry.... Bacchanalia." In the words of John Milton (Sabin, 1940), "Bacchus, that first from out the purple grape Crushed the sweet poison of mis-used wine" (p. 38). There is even a theory that the word tragedy may have its origin in "the goat-song" which was used in the worship of Bacchus. Only later, this theory purports, did the word become associated with drama (Sabin, 1940, p. 39).

The complexity of the two-sided nature of Dionysus is subtly yet powerfully revealed, again, in the mythopoesis. We are told (Hamilton, 1942) that Dionysus did not forget about his mother, though he never knew her, and he longed for her. Therefore, he dared the perilous journey to the netherworld in order to find her. Defying the power of Death to keep her, he won, and took her to Olympus. As mother of a god, although herself a mortal, she was allowed to dwell among the immortals.

I offer this interpretation: Dionysian ecstasy does not necessarily require the abandonment or forgetting of our human origins (or nature), even while inspiring us to great daring and noble deeds. And though mortal, we can be delivered to lofty heights. Our relationship with divine ecstasy can deliver us to a realm of divine-like existence, that is, the dwelling with the divine. Another interpretation is that it is a perilous and daring task for the male to seek out the feminine (which is part of him) within his depths. But, if he succeeds in this task, his feminine part becomes exalted, as if divine.

Put in terms most mundane, "Wine is bad as well as good. It cheers and warms men's hearts; it also makes them drunk" (Hamilton, 1942, p. 60). "The worship of Dionysus was centered in these two ideas so far apart — of freedom and ecstatic joy and of savage brutality. The God of Wine could give either to his worshipers" (p. 57). Consider this, as well. Liber, an ancient Italian deity of the vine also worshiped as a fertility god, came to be identified with Dionysus and his Roman counterpart, Bacchus (Funk and Wagnalls, 1984). It is from his name, Liber, that we derive such words as "liberty," "liberation," "liberal," and "libertine." So, again, we see freedom, being set free, not restricted, and licentiousness (indulging desires without restraint) as stemming from the same source.

Although we do not know a lot about the Greek mystery religions — the Eleusinian, the Orphic, the Dionysian — because they did remain mysteries (Campbell, 1990), we do have the mythic material concerning Dionysus. And, importantly, we have the expression of those two competing world views often referred to and so beautifully symbolized by Apollo and Dionysus.

Moving from the mythopoetic to the philosophical, Nietzsche placed himself clearly and strongly on the side of the Dionysian. In *Twilight of the Idols*, he declared himself boldly, "I, the last disciple of the philosopher Dionysus — I, the teacher of the eternal recurrence" (Kaufmann, 1982, p. 563). Nietzsche saw in the Dionysian the very core of the Greek veneration of life:

> For it is only in the Dionysian mysteries, in the psychology of the Dionysian state, that the *basic fact* of the Hellenic instinct finds expression — its "will to life." ... Saying Yes to life even in its strangest and hardest problems, the will to life rejoicing over its own inexhaustibility even in the very sacrifice of its highest types—*that* is what I call Dionysian [pp. 561–562].

Somewhat earlier, in speaking of the Hellenic instinct, Nietzsche referred to "that wonderful phenomenon which bears the name of Dionysus," and goes on to say that "it is explicable only in terms of an *excess* of force" (Kaufmann, 1982, p. 560).

Thus Spoke Zarathustra, Nietzsche's most popular book, is replete with examples of what Kaufmann terms "Dionysian exuberance" (Kaufmann, 1982, p. 107). (In fact a strong case could be made that this work is an account of a Dionysian epiphany.) As an example of his regard for passion, Zarathustra speaks the following: "And whether you came from the tribe of the choleric or of the voluptuous or of the fanatic or of the vengeful, in the end all your passions become virtues and all your devils, angels" (p. 148).

Joseph Campbell (1990) offered a noteworthy summary of the meaning of the Dionysian:

> The best discussion, in my opinion, of Dionysos [*sic*] and Apollo is in Nietzsche's *The Birth of Tragedy*, where they are shown in relation to the whole world of the classic arts. Nietzsche writes of Dionysos as the dynamic of time that rolls through all things, destroying old forms and bringing forth new with, what he terms is, an 'indifference to the differences.' In contrast to this is the light world of Apollo and its interest in the exquisite differences of forms, which Nietzsche calls the *principium individuationis*. The power of Dionysos is to ride on the full fury of the life force. That's what he represents. So, the essential message of the rites, apparently, is that of a realization in a properly prepared way of the dynamic of inexhaustible nature which pours its energy into the field of time and with which we are to be in harmony, both in its destructive and in its productive aspects. This is experience of the life power in its full career [p. 198].

Nietzsche himself, in his discourse "Toward a psychology of the artist" in *Twilight of the Idols* (Kaufmann, 1982), gives us an especially valuable perspective:

> If there is to be art, if there is to be any aesthetic doing and seeing, one physiological condition is indispensable: frenzy.... In this state one enriches everything out of one's own fullness.... A man in this state transforms things until they mirror his power — until they are reflections of his perfection. This *having to* transform into perfection is — art [p. 518].

(In reading these pieces which I have strung together, and in the following ones, consider psychotherapy as one of the arts, with the therapist and the person in therapy as co-creators. Add the *art of psychotherapy* to the arts which Nietzsche explicitly addresses — painting, sculpture, poetry, music, acting, dancing.) Nietzsche proceeds to distinguish the Apollonian and Dionysian forces in art:

> What is the meaning of the conceptual opposites which I have
> introduced into aesthetics, *Apollinian* [*sic*] and *Dionysian*,
> both conceived as kinds of frenzy? The Apollinian frenzy
> excites the eye above all, so that it gains the power of
> vision.... In the Dionysian state, on the other hand, the whole
> affective system is excited and enhanced: so that it discharges
> all its means of expression at once and drives forth simultane-
> ously the power of representation, imitation, transfiguration,
> transformation, and every kind of mimicking and acting. The
> essential feature here remains the ease of metamorphosis....
> It is impossible for the Dionysian type not to understand any
> suggestion; he does not overlook any sign of an affect; he
> possesses the instinct of understanding and guessing in the
> highest degree, just as he commands the art of communica-
> tion in the highest degree [p. 519–520].

Before departing Nietzsche (and keeping the art of psychotherapy still in mind), I want to call attention to one more of his insights.
That is, "all becoming and growing — all that guarantees a future —
involves pain" (Kaufmann, 1982, p. 562). Let us not lose sight of this
point in its brevity. *Nota bene: All becoming and growing involves
pain.*

In her discussion of the Apollonian and Dionysian in the context of psychotherapy, Karen Horney (Shostrom, 1968) identified the
former with mastery and molding, the latter with surrender and drift.
To her way of thinking, neither is better or worse, per se. They are
two natural human tendencies. No one is completely one or the other,
but rather we all lean more toward one or the other, sometimes preferring one, sometimes the other. When manifesting the Apollonian
leaning, the person will emphasize being in charge and in control,
making things happen as he or she wants, trying to change the environment to suit his or her will. In contrast, the Dionysian leaning
becomes manifest in an acceptance of and surrender to what is and
a *willingness* to be taken away, carried away, to flow with the river
that is life. That river may be halcyon or it may be tempestuous, but
it is most often arousing of passion.

At this point we can bridge into the thinking of Carl Jung (1970)
by mention of his discussion of the principles of *logos* and *eros*. The
logos principle is one of objective interest, putting aside emotional
and personal subjective considerations. Logos, being found both in

Greek and Latin, meant the word by which the inward thought is expressed, or the thought itself. It refers to the doctrine of reason or thought as the controlling principle of the universe; hence, *logic* and *logistic*. Eros, in contrast, comes from the name of the Greek god of love, Cupid for the Romans; hence, *erotic*, pertaining to or prompted by sexual desires, and *cupidity*. Therefore the eros principle is one of affective-cum-psychic relatedness, a subjectively emotional mode of experiencing the world. Jung noted that, in the Western view, this mode of psychic relatedness is usually seen as feminine, whereas the logos principle is more often identified with the masculine orientation. With origin in the collective unconscious, these archetypes evolved into the psychic structures of anima (the feminine within the man) and animus (the masculine within the woman).

Before leaving Jung's contribution to our understanding of the two world views, I want to offer a summary: The logos principle represents reason and objective interest, it is archetypally masculine, its structural representation in the psyche of woman is the animus, and the ectopsychic function most related to it is Thinking. The eros principle represents psychic, affectively based relatedness, it is archetypally feminine, its structural representation in the psyche of man is the anima, and the ectopsychic function most related to it is Feeling. The logos principle is Apollonian. The eros principle is Dionysian.

Writing for the popular audience, Sam Keen (1974) addressed the Apollonian and the Dionysian respectively as the *rational* view and the *cosmic* view. He emphasized work as valued above play in the rational view, and the opposite value in the cosmic. In addition to this difference in content, work versus play, Keen suggested that in the rational view efficiency is sought, whereas in the cosmic view it is ecstasy. The two world views can be summarized, as I understand Keen's position, as valuing efficient work (the rational or Apollonian view) or valuing ecstatic play (the cosmic or Dionysian view).

In his popular novel, *Zen and the Art of Motorcycle Maintenance*, Robert Pirsig (1974) also addressed the Apollonian and Dionysian world views, naming them respectively *classical understanding* and *romantic understanding*. His book is subtitled "an inquiry into values," and explores classical understanding and romantic understanding through what might well be seen as an allegory. The allegory involves riding and maintaining motorcycles on a long motorcycle journey. As he wrote, "Although motorcycle riding is romantic, motorcycle maintenance is purely classic" (p. 67). His exploration derives the following characterization of the classical understanding: fundamentally, the world is seen as underlying form. From this, the mode of classical understanding proceeds in an orderly fashion using reason and laws or principles. Facts take priority over esthetic considerations, as thought takes priority over feelings in the pursuit of control.

Romantic understanding, for Pirsig, is derived from seeing the world in terms of immediate experience. Thus the mode of romantic understanding tends to be inspirational, imaginative, creative, and intuitive. Feelings and esthetic considerations are given priority over thoughts and facts in the pursuit of experience and intuitive understanding.

Of particular importance for the understanding of the person of the therapist is an insight offered by Pirsig concerning misunderstandings. He suggested that because persons tend to orient themselves through one of these two modes of understanding, classical *or* romantic, they will have difficulty understanding or appreciating those who orient through the other mode.

Call them what you wish, keeping in mind that each pair of labels hints at a nuance of inflection: Apollonian-Dionysian, Logos-Eros, Rational-Cosmic, Classical-Romantic. These two world views are reflected, of course, in the person of the therapist. So, the Apollonian-Dionysian, Logos-Eros, Rational-Cosmic, Classical-Romantic world views and values are manifested in the microcosm of psychotherapy. I suggest that the therapist more inclined to the Apollonian view will tend toward insight-oriented approaches, whereas the more Dionysian therapist will tend to prefer expressive styles of therapy.

I have referred to the Apollonian-Dionysian as a polarity or dimension. Horney (Shostrom, 1968), as noted earlier, saw them as two natural human tendencies, with no person being all one or all the other. Any given therapist may lean more one way or the other, with the degree of leaning being somewhat changeable over time. But for heuristic purposes it is easier, at times, to speak of the poles, not the continuum between. Thus, I identify the Insight mode of therapy with the Apollonian world view, and the Expressive mode with the Dionysian. Additionally, therapists at the extreme of the

Apollonian pole may prefer the Action (Behavioral) mode of therapy. At the extreme of the other pole, beyond the Dionysian, lies the Bacchanalian. And so the Expressive mode, debased, is irresponsible and harmful, as some of us have witnessed, particularly in the excesses of the 1960s and 1970s. If the most extreme of the Expressive mode is Bacchanalian, with impulsive acting out and unbridled eros, what is the most extreme of the Action mode? It is dehumanization through the mechanical, dispassioned application of techniques. In the words of Paul Tillich (1962), "A self which has become a matter of calculation and management has ceased to be a self. It has become a thing" (p. 653).

"Nothing too much." This was pithy advice of the Sages of Ancient Greece (Kopp, 1971). Applied to our topic, this could suggest not too much Apollonian insight (meaning insight without expression), and not too much Dionysian expression (meaning expression without insight). This sage advice is echoed in Aristotle's Doctrine of the Mean, popularly referred to as the "Golden Mean" (Popkin & Stroll, 1956). For Aristotle, this is the way to happiness, acting so as to steer a path between the two extremes. These ancient sources are a call to a resolution of polarities.

Both world views offer something of value, both have their forte, as we have already seen. But that valued emphasis, that strong point, may also be a limitation. Through the character of Harry Haller, known as the Steppenwolf, Herman Hesse (1969) demonstrated clearly for us that "every strength may become a weakness (and under some circumstances must)" (p. 55).

We see, then, an emerging integration of Insight and Expression. Expression, the more liberal pole (that is, of Liber), animates and enlivens, celebrating aliveness. Insight, its guide, is the conservative pole, slowing the pace and lending security to each animated step. But, too much slowing of the pace may deaden, under the guise of security. "And you all know," Hecate (the lead witch in Shakespeare's *Macbeth*) reminds us, "security is mortal's chiefest enemy" (p. 935).

If we turn once again to the mythopoetic, trusting in its metaphorical epistemology, we can be instructed in the relationship of Insight and Expression. We learn in the *Prose Edda* (Sturluson, 1954) that two ravens sit on the shoulders of Odin. He sends them out every day to fly over the whole world and return to him, bringing him news of all they see and hear. Their names are Hugin and Munin, meaning

Thought and Memory. Thus are we told that Odin, active and passionate as he is, is informed by thought and memory. That is to say, Odin's Expression has benefit of Insight. Lee Hollander, in his translation of the *Poetic Edda* (1962), speaks of Hugin and Munin as "'Thought' and 'Remembrance,' Othin's [*sic*] ravens which bring him intelligence" (p. 57).

At another level of interpretation, we can look to the birds themselves. They are ravens, seen in the Viking world as birds of the battlefield. So, by virtue of the mental functions they stand for and the expressive activity they symbolize, they themselves are a metaphor for the bringing together of Insight and Expression.

Let us take the myth further. In the *Poetic Edda* we find the following: "The whole earth over, every day, hover Hugin and Munin; I dread lest Hugin droop in his flight, yet I fear me still more for Munin" (p. 57). Is Odin telling us that he fears the loss of thought, but he fears the loss of memory more? It appears that this is the case. This would then suggest that the more conservative function (memory) is of the greater importance in the constituting of guiding intelligence.

The Norse mythology, in summary, appears to offer us a clue to the reconciliation of the polarity of Insight and Expression, of the Apollonian and the Dionysian. To wit, action is best guided when informed by thought *and* memory. Action/Expression, being liberal benefits from the conservative influence of thought and memory/ Insight. Memory, being the more conservative, may be the more important component of Insight.

I have suggested elsewhere that the Gestalt approach is heavily imbued with a Dionysian world view (Smith, 1991). Perhaps the Dionysian core of the Gestalt approach is best reflected by Arnold Beisser (1970) in his expression of the "paradoxical theory of change" (p. 77). Briefly stated, "change occurs when one becomes what he is, not when he tries to become what he is not" (p. 77). There it is, not mastery and control, but rather *the surrender to one's nature*. Is this not the commitment to which Nietzsche was challenging us—*amor fati*?

Once again, the words of Lao Tzu seem apropos:

> A man acquiring life loses himself in it,
> Has less and less to bear in mind,
> Less and less to do,
> Because life, he finds, is well inclined,
> Including himself too [Bynner translation, 1962, p. 55].

We can embed the paradoxical theory of change in the broader base of the theory of Gestalt therapy, going back to a lecture that Fritz Perls (1979) delivered at the William Alanson White Institute in 1946 or 1947. In that lecture, "Planned Psychotherapy," Perls expressed his view that the neurotic individual "is a split and dissociated personality and that the cure has to be effected by a reintegration of personality and its interpersonal relations" (p. 7). Continuing, with a statement most pithy, "The reintegration of the dissociated parts of the personality is best undertaken by resensitizing and remobilizing the system[s] of orientation and manipulation" (p. 21). Contained within the very description of the neurotic individual is the conviction that the crux of the problem is a fragmentation of the personality, not that there is anything missing. It is not that new elements need be added, but rather that aspects of the person that have been disowned, denied, desecrated, need to be re-owned, accepted as parts of oneself, and brought into functional coordination with all other aspects. The manner of so doing is in re-sensitizing, that is, in facilitating awareness through the concentrated use of the sensoria, and in re-mobilizing expression through manipulation of the environment. More particularly, this is brought about by the abandonment of those psychological strategies whose purpose it is to desensitize, that is, any dulling of awareness by decreasing the acuity of a sensory modality. And it is brought about by avoiding expressive action. *Nota bene:* Re-sensitization and re-mobilization are not a matter of *doing* something, but rather a matter of *not-doing* something, not choosing to enact the strategies of desensitization or the blocking or inhibiting of expressive action. We have now entered the realm of the paradox and of the double negative, where natural sensory acuity and spontaneous expression can be negated by strategies of desensitization and immobilization; re-sensitization and re-mobilization are effected by negating the negation, simply by stopping the stopping! (Identifying this process as simple does not imply that it is necessarily easy, however.)

Perls (1979) suggested that the planning of a course of therapy, be that conscious or unconscious, is influenced by the *weltanschauung* of the therapist. Therapists he divided into those who interfere with the biological figure-background formation and those who facilitate it. (Perls is here referring to the natural process, based on the *wisdom of the organism*, whereby a need and those features of the

environment that are relevant to that need emerge from the perceptual background as figural.) The former group of therapists favor
deliberateness, the latter *spontaneity.* Notice that these words are from
the lexicons of Apollo and Dionysus, respectively.

We can understand what Perls was saying, then, in the context
of a Dionysian vision. He distinguished two types of person of the
therapist, one more Apollonian, the other more Dionysian. Not only
would these two elect a different style of manifesting their persons,
therapeutically speaking, but the more Dionysian person would res-
onate more surely with the perspective on psychopathology that Perls
articulated. (To delve more deeply into the theory of psychopathology set forth in Gestalt therapy at this point would, I believe, be a
divagation. Perls has offered expatiation throughout his several vol-
umes. For a succinct overview, I recommend my chapters "An Organismic Perspective on Personality Dynamics, " and "An Organismic
Perspective on Psychopathology" in *The Body in Psychotherapy*
[Smith, 1985]).

Shuttling once again from the world of psychotherapy to that
of the spiritual, we can find a parallel between the two types of therapists distinguished by Perls and the two approaches to spiritual
development found in Indian philosophy. Alan Watts (1974) has
related that in Indian philosophy, basic to both Hinduism and Buddhism, two ways are offered for letting go of attachment to the dis-
tractions from enlightenment. The first, known as *renunciation of
pleasure,* is the way of detachment and asceticism. Characterized by
deliberateness, this approach is bent on mastery over oneself. Thus,
for instance, through renunciation of food save for the most simple
and minimal amount required for sustaining life, an ascetic may
become master over former attachment to gluttony or epicurean taste.
Systematically clearing away the veil of such attachments, the person
can come to enlightenment.

The second way, less well known than the first, is called *Tantra,*
and is just the opposite of the way of renunciation. Rather than withdrawing from life, the person on the Tantric path plunges into life
with the "fullest possible acceptance of one's desires, feelings, and
situation" (Watts, 1974, p. 175). Full engagement with life is sought,
including food, drink, and sex. But this is not to be done with abandonment, and not "in the half-hearted and timid spirit of the ordinary pleasure seeker" (p. 175). For it is in full, and at the same time

mindful, engagement with life, experienced with keen awareness, that one may come to know oneself, and through this to know the divine.

Is it not this way of the Tantra to which William Blake (Schoen, 1994) lent his force, in writing his plentitude of aphorisms, "The Proverbs of Hell"? Consider but a sample.

> The road of excess leads to the palace of wisdom [p. 30].
> If the fool would persist in his folly he would become
>   wise [p. 32].

And, most succinctly put,

> Exuberance is beauty [p. 30].

The therapist who interferes with natural biological figure-ground formation and the therapist who facilitates it, to use Perls' idiom, are in harmony with the spiritual path of renunciation of pleasure and the path of Tantra, respectively. The latter therapist appreciates the therapeutic value of re-sensitization where the person in therapy is desensitized, and re-mobilization where that person is immobilized. The latter therapist is in resonance, too, with the paradoxical theory of change. The former therapist walks with Apollo, while the therapist on the Tantric path dances with Dionysus!

In these two spiritual paths and in these two parallel orientations to psychotherapy, we can discern a very basic difference: Is human inclination to be distrusted, and, therefore, at least at times, to be held in check and improved upon through intentional effort? Or is human inclination to be trusted, and, therefore, encouraged and surrendered to, with the belief that the *wisdom of the organism* will prevail?

The *person* who endorses the one orientation and the *person* who endorses the other are surely different. This should be apparent as their persons become manifest as therapists. But, it is not the issue of psychotherapeutic efficacy that is addressed by such consideration of personhood. Rather, and to reiterate what has been said earlier in the present chapter, in this realm of the philosophical-cum-anagogical, the issue is one of ethics or of esthetics. The issue is one of authenticity, the issue is one of beauty. Psychotherapy, so constructed, is sacred art.

————————— *Chapter 5* —————————

A Note
on the Development
of Personhood

> Only one thing matters: live a good life. Do your heart's
> bidding, even when it leads you on paths that timid souls
> would avoid. Even when life is a torment, don't let it harden
> you.
> — Wilhelm Reich (1948) in *Listen, Little Man* [p. 127]

With a literature on personality development already so plen-
teously supplied — theories of cognitive development, moral development, oral-aggressive development, psycho-sexual development,
spiritual development, and so forth — it may seem at first glance an
exercise in pleonasm to address the development of the person of the
therapist. A second and more meticulous look, however, reveals that
these existing theories either do not address *personhood* at the level
intended herein, or do not address *personhood of the therapist* as is
the present focus. In addition, many of the developmental theories
have relatively little to offer as to *how* development is fostered, particularly intentional and self-directed development.

*Personhood, as I wish to use this term, is in reference to depth and
richness of unique being.* I choose to ensconce my conceptualization

of the development of personhood within a spiritual framework. My conception of the development of the person of the therapist is more than just an epigenetic view. It is not just that personhood is not inherited; it is not just that it does not unfold from a natural and automatic psychobiological process. Rather, personhood is developed through experience. It accrues through learning. My conception of development of personhood takes, as suggested above, a hormic perspective, seeing the therapist as one who develops both in and through experience, with intentionality, nisus. My view must, therefore, unfold at three levels. First is the level of *spiritual inspiration*, then the level of *general guidelines*, and finally the level of *psychological processes*. In good Gestalt fashion, I will begin at the most general or holistic level and differentiate increasingly specific levels.

To begin, and to commence the construction of the spiritual framework, I accept that I exist, I live, life is. Life came into being. Whatever force, power, principle, or spirit that is involved I can call God, Brahman, Allah, Yahweh, Great Spirit, the Tao, or as Wilhelm Reich did, "primal cosmic energy," or any number of other names which have been suggested. This position does not require a belief in a personal God, that is, a God who is a person of any sort, nor does this position necessarily preclude such belief. Joseph Campbell, as well as Carl Jung, would indubitably want to remind us that the many names that have been used are but cultural inflections of the god archetype, a universal motif offered up at a particular time in a particular place. For its brevity and particular tradition, and without intending it in the narrow personal sense, I will use the word *God*.

God created life; God is life. This statement, bald as it is, is the foundation of my spiritual framework. Keep in mind that I do not mean, necessarily, a personal God, an entity, or any sort of quasi-personified being. I mean simply that power or energy or principle by which life came to be and is. As stated by Paul Williams (1973), succinctly and with a touch of the poetic, "Life is the self-creating energy creature we call God" (p. 148).

Therefore, to affirm life is to be in harmony with God. If life is from God, of God, Godly, and I am part of that, then to affirm life is in keeping with the Way of God. Ergo, not to affirm life or to disaffirm life is to a lesser or greater degree to be out of harmony with God. Non-affirmation of life can be seen, then, in degrees. In milder forms it may be mere passive failure to affirm, while in more extreme forms it is constituted of acts of disaffirmation or deadening. Speaking of deadening, Rollo May (1991) has expressed that "just as there are many gradations of Eros, so Thanatos includes many phases, including illness, fatigue, and all of what Paul Tillich called non-being" (p. 77).

Being in harmony with God may be thought of as *being in God's grace*, in the sense of being in God's favor. With God considered not as a personal God of judgment, but rather as a force or principle, this becomes clearer. If I live, for me to affirm life (that which I am) favors me and is in my favor, because it is consistent with God's creation.

Therefore, the ultimate worship of God is a life abundantly lived. What better way could there be to honor life and the source of life but to live fully? In his simple words and straightforward manner, Ernest Hemingway said, consistent with this perspective, that "life is short and the years run away and you must do everything you really want to" (Hotchner, 1983, p. 99); and continuing on a more personal note, added that he never regretted anything he ever did, only things he didn't do.

But be not deceived, the life lived abundantly is a life of pain as well as joy. So, too, then, must pain be experienced and not run from as if it were an evil. James Bugenthal (1971) included this idea in his statement of a "humanistic ethic" by making the valuing of non-hedonic emotion a tenet alongside the tenet of commitment to growth-oriented experiencing. By non-hedonic emotion he meant the emotions that are unpleasant, such as anger, fear, and grief. Even though they are unpleasant, they are an ineluctable and vital part of the experience of being human. To try to shun them, given their inevitability, is, then, only to impede the natural emergence of the experience of full humanness. So it is that Paul Williams (1973) stated that "the affirmation of one's life — the acceptance of one's destiny as it manifests itself in each moment — is the supreme act of faith" (p. 80). And, in a more exuberant tone, he continued with, "Open yourself to absolutely anything that gets thrown at you — including death, and life" (p. 119). In these statements we can hear the echo of Nietzsche —*amor fati!*

Theodore Roosevelt (1901) has been immortalized by these words:

> Far better it is to dare mighty things, to win glorious
> triumphs, even though checkered by failure, than to take

> rank with those poor spirits who neither enjoy much nor
> suffer much, because they live in the gray twilight that knows
> not victory nor defeat [no page number].

Such words as these may inspire one to a life of abundance. But
lest, with such zeal aroused, this appear all too easy, Fritz Perls (1969)
solemnly warned, "To suffer one's death and to be reborn is not easy"
(back cover). To be reborn to a life lived abundantly requires incred-
ible courage. Courage, as I consider it, is manifested in a willingness
to take reasonable risks, to experiment and try out new things, not
knowing what may ensue. It means to allow a natural rhythm of
expansion into the world and relaxation into self, avoiding neither
phase of the cycle. Courage, in the aspect of fortitude, includes being
undaunted by frustrations, delays, setbacks, and the lack of understanding or misunderstanding on the part of others. Misfortune must
not be cause for shrinking from life. The challenge offered by misfortune may be, as Perls (1969) admonished concerning the loss of
our status quo, "to *realize* that it's just an inconvenience, that it's not
a catastrophe, but just an unpleasantness, [and this] is part of coming into your own, part of waking up" (p. 33).

Therefore, the ultimate praise of God is to embrace life joyously.
If living life fully is the ultimate act of worship, then surely to embrace
life with alacrity is the ultimate of praise. Hugh Prather (1977)
reminded us that "there is another way to go through life besides
being pulled through it kicking and screaming" (no page number).
And that other way is, as Horace suggested, "Carpe diem." Putting
this in context and in translation,

> In the moment of our talking, envious time
>   has ebbed away,
> Seize the present, trust tomorrow e'en as little
>   as you may [Naranjo, 1970, p. 63].

Let us look, also, at this passage from Ovid's *Art of Love*:

> Seize the flower,
> for if you pluck it not 'twill fade and fall
>   [p. 64].

Centuries later, Goethe echoed Horace and Ovid when he stated,

He who seizes the moment is the right man [p. 66].

To these, add the words of King Solomon:

> A man hath no better thing under the sun, than to eat, and to drink, and to be merry [p. 62].

Following these leads, Claudio Naranjo wrote convincingly and at some length about an archetype consisting of present-centeredness, the view that the present is a gift of pleasure, and the awareness of death and decay. To embrace life with alacrity is none other than to embody this archetype and render it manifest.

Therefore, that which one does which diminishes one's own life (or that of others) constitutes sin. Anything one chooses which detracts from aliveness misses the mark. Clearly, then, we are, as Sheldon Kopp (1974) suggested, punished not *for* our sins, but *by* them! In *The Marriage of Heaven and Hell*, William Blake instructed us by saying, on the one hand,

> No bird soars too high, if he soars with his own wings [p. xviii].

Not to do so, on the other hand, would be a pity, a sin. As Blake put it,

> He who desires but acts not, breeds pestilence [p. xviii].

With greater acerbity, and equally to the point, he wrote,

> Sooner murder an infant in its cradle than nurse unacted desires [p. xx].

If, in pusillanimity, one fears acting the fool, Blake assured us that

> If the fool would persist in his folly he would become wise [p. xviii].

So, what of the *rules*? Saint Augustine, a man not unfamiliar with the lusty life, said, "Love God, and do what thou wilt!" Later, Martin Luther (using a different definition of the term from mine) declared, "Sin bravely" (Kopp, 1974, p. 48). Summarized by Sheldon

Kopp, we have the advice, "Never mind the rules! Forget conventional wisdom and morality if you would be healed, saved, made free!" (p. 48). In *Wandering in Eden*, Michael Adam (1976) suggested "deadliness as the origin of all other 'sins'" (p. 3). Consider this carefully.

Therefore, one's spiritual practice is to recognize and eschew whatever one does which is deadening and seek that which is enlivening. If deadening oneself is sin, then letting go of such is surely the highest of spiritual practices. By "practice" I mean consistent, disciplined, ongoing working on oneself. This means being self-vigilant, becoming aware of one's means of self-deadening, whatever those means may be, and actively changing from those patterns. Ram Dass (1974), reminded us, "So, you see that the only option is to work on yourself" (p. 41).

Most if not all psychotherapies would embrace aliveness as a value. Some, however, are more explicit in acknowledging this and even make it a focus. We see this especially in the tradition of the body-oriented therapies which have their philosophical origins in Nietzsche. Aliveness is a focus in the works of Wilhelm Reich, his student Fritz Perls, and their colleagues and professional descendants, the neo–Reichians and Gestalt therapists. It was this focus I wished to emphasize by my choice of *Sexual Aliveness: A Reichian Gestalt Perspective* for the title of my book on the psychology of human sexuality (Smith, 1987). And it is this focus which is reflected in Barry Stevens' (1970) paradoxical declaration that for her "it is more important … to bring someone to life than to be moral" (p. 231).

A theology based on the value of life itself, a bio-existential theology, can be a grounding for psychotherapy. It is for me. (It has become a ground out of which my therapy and most of my writing come.) And it is in the development of aliveness of the therapist herself or himself, the enthusiastic embracing of life, that the therapist is best prepared for the role. This was made clear by Ram Dass (1974). "Work on yourself, see, because your 'patients' will be as free as you are. That's why I come back to the statement that therapy is as high as the therapist is" (p.28). So, *affirming life, living life abundantly, embracing life joyously, eschewing all that diminishes life is the way of harmony, worship, praise and spiritual practice.* It is a way to be inspired, possessed by God —*en theos.*

Even if inspired by this framework within which *person*al growth may be understood anagogically, there is the further question of how to nurture such growth. The spiritual framework itself offers a hierarchical answer, namely, *affirm life, live abundantly, embrace life with alacrity, recognize and eschew all that is deadening.* This answer may be satisfying at the level that it addresses, but even though it is in itself hierarchical, there are yet other levels entirely. There is next the level of general guidelines. And so, to ask the question at this level, a level at once more specific and concrete, how does one go about inviting and encouraging growth in one's person?

The sages of ancient Greece offered as one of their three guiding principles the succinct charge "Know thyself." Prior to the time of Socrates, these words of Apollo were understood in a social sense, as in "know your station in life and the duties attending it and do not usurp a position not yours by right." But with Socrates, the meaning of "know thyself" was transformed to a looking inward, an examination of oneself (Allen, 1966). To know oneself in this latter sense is at once vital and difficult. This difficulty is well reflected in Blackham's (1959) rendering of Heidegger: "A man is possibility, he has the power to be. His existence is in his choice of the possibilities which are open to him, and since his choice is never final, once for all, his existence is indeterminate" (p. 88). He continued by explicating "two decisively opposed modes of being: authentic being rooted in the explicit sense of my situation ... and inauthentic being, moving automatically in the established ruts and routes of the organized world" (pp. 92–93). Perhaps the poet e.e. cummings has expressed this struggle to be oneself most poignantly:

> To be nobody-but-yourself—in a world which is doing its
> best, night and day, to make you everybody else—means to
> fight the hardest battle which any human being can fight; and
> never stop fighting [Letter, n.d.].

If authentic being is an ongoing enterprise, if existence is indeterminate, as Heidegger suggested (Blackham, 1959), then to know oneself is a continuing challenge. To know oneself is not a static goal, but rather a process of making oneself a focus of curiosity in an ongoing manner, for one is constantly creating oneself. The idea of ongoing self-creation is underscored in a bold if not shocking manner in the thought of Jean-Paul Sartre, even replacing the more traditional view of personality. In his lecture "L'Existentialisme Est un Humanisme," Sartre (Kaufmann, 1989) declared that "*existence* comes before *essence*"(p. 348), and expanded on this, saying that "there is no human nature," and that "man is nothing else but that which he makes of himself" (p. 349)! Predating Sartre's lecture by a few years, José Ortega y Gasset (Kaufman, 1989) wrote the following:

> The stone is given its existence; it need not fight for being what it is—a stone in the field. Man has to be himself in spite of unfavorable circumstances; that means he has to make his own existence at every single moment. He is given the abstract possibility of existing, but not the reality. This he has to conquer hour after hour [p. 153–154].

Summarizing this view, Ortega wrote, "*Man, in a word, has no nature; what he has is — history.* Expressed differently; what nature is to things, history ... is to man" (p. 157).

Perhaps this ongoing struggle of self-creation is best understood from the perspective of Martin Heidegger's modes of being-in-the-world. Eschewing systematization of his thought (as is true of existential writers as a group), Heidegger would no doubt object to my interpretation of his work that is to follow. In addition, his style of writing, almost legendary for its abstruse quality, leaves any interpretation vulnerable to the judgement of misinterpretation. If I may, I will nevertheless be so bold (or so foolish) as to offer the following. Although my understanding of Heidegger is heavily informed by the work of Jacob Golomb (1995) and by that of Clark Moustakas (1994), I take responsibility for my rendition.

Man alone *exists*, not rocks, trees, horses, angels, or God. They *are*, but they do not *exist* (Kaufmann, 1989, p. 272). That is to say, the mineral, the vegetable, the animal, and the metaphysical are limited in and by their non-existence. As Heidegger wrote, "The being that exists is man" (p. 272). What we are and how we are is *Being*. One's Being can be understood through the interpretation and understanding of *Dasein*, literally my *being-there*, including my knowing of myself and my world, my standing out, and my taking a stance. Existence is characterized by *being-in-the-world*, world referring to how one exists, to the medium in which one exists. There are three modes of world, namely *Umwelt, Mitwelt*, and *Eigenwelt*.

Umwelt, or the "around world" refers to the physical and biological world into which I am *thrown*. This, for Sartre is *facticité*, in which he included both physical and biological facticity and cultural/

historical facticity (class, family, tradition) (Golomb, 1995). As a personal example, I was born during World War II of middle-class white parents in the Midwest of the United States, with a certain array of genes. This I was thrown into, not having been given choice. The time in history, the geographical location, the socio-economic position, and the other multifarious circumstances into which we are born constitute our throwness. But this is not the full extent of our *throwness*. We continue to be susceptible to being thrown into circumstances beyond our control throughout our lives. Any sudden or dramatic change may throw us into a revised circumstance. Likewise, choices we make may have unforseen consequences. These, too, may throw us into a new situation.

Our throwness both opens possibilities and sets limits on our Being. To expand on my personal example, I was afforded opportunities for reasonably good health care and diet, a relatively safe environment in which to grow up, and an opportunity for education. It was soon apparent that I was smart. At the same time, I spent some early years without a father, he being a soldier and a prisoner of war; travel was restricted by tire and gasoline rationing and other war efforts at home; and in time it became apparent that I was not likely to have the opportunity to play professional basketball or football, regardless of the amount of practice given such pursuit. Even through these superficial examples, it is clear that my being has not been all of my choice. The failure to recognize the role of throwness can only nurture the view that is characteristic of a naive, if not puerile, belief that anyone can be anything that he or she desires. Unfortunately, this latter is a view that sometimes characterizes attempts at New Age popularization of humanistic psychology. An antidote to such a naive view is the fact of throwness as identified by Heidegger. I am free to choose, and as Sartre (Kaufmann,1989) stated poignantly, it is even that "what is not possible is not to choose.... [I]f I do not choose, that is still a choice" (p. 363). However, my choices are always bound by my throwness and take place within the context of my throwness. For Sartre, the challenge was to create ourselves through our choices within the limitations of the *facticité* of our heredity, history, and traditions (Golomb, 1995). The Umwelt into which I am thrown allows for the emergence of possible choices while precluding the possibility of others, often without my recognizing or even imagining the latter. Karl Marx, too, made this point, stating, "Men make their own history but not just as they wish; not under circumstances of their own choosing, but under the given and inherited circumstances that directly confront them" (Pletsch, 1999, p. 338).

We are thrown into the Umwelt, without choice. (Some New Age writers would take issue with this, believing that we choose our parents. I, however, prefer the existential position just stated.) Concerning the Mitwelt, or the "with world," the social world of relationships, the situation is different. In this mode of world, we have choice. The danger in this world with others, however, is *falling*. *Fallenness* into the world means being absorbed in *Being-with-one-another* (Golomb, 1995). In this state, as Heidegger wrote so poignantly, "Everyone is the other, and no one is himself" (Moustakas, 1994, p. 36). Sartre referred to this as *being-with-others*, and saw it as a basic negative attitude toward oneself. In being-with-others, one treats oneself as an *other*, not as one's self. This, for Sartre is a sort of *bad faith, mauvaise foi* (Golomb, 1995).

Just how does one fall then? Heidegger suggested that we do so through *idle talk*—insignificant, indifferent, and superficial communication. With such talk, there is no significant expression of values, beliefs, ideas or genuine emotions. Ergo, authentic meanings are covered up by inauthentic ones. Heidegger went so far as to suggest that the voice of conscience or the call to authenticity "discourses solely and constantly in the mode of keeping silent" (Golomb, 1995, p. 121). Also, through *curiosity* we may fall. Heidegger offered an unusual perspective here, as curiosity is usually given a favorable connotation. But in Heidegger's use of the term, curiosity invites continual absorption into things. Distracted, we may flit from thing to thing as if attention-deficit disordered, restless and distracted. Thirdly, we may fall because of *ambiguity*, our failure to be discerning of messages, thereby confusing genuineness and fakery (Moustakas, 1994).

Everyday routines and relationships constantly endanger authentic existence as they ratchet down one's experience to a level of average existence. Absorbed in such everydayness, one loses touch with uniqueness and is alienated from one's self. Consider, for a moment, a most mundane example, that of eating lunch because it is noon rather than eating because one is hungry. Eating on clock time is falling into everyday and public routine, and is thereby disrespectful of the wisdom of one's own organism.

Neither Heidegger nor Sartre could anticipate the impact of the *hot media* that emerged into prominence in the years following their deaths. The novelty of television evolved into a ubiquitous presence in industrialized countries and the gargantuan mainframe computers spawned personal computers in numbers which seem to have grown exponentially, served by a worldwide web on interconnectedness. I suggest that we can profit from defining hot media with reference to the Mitwelt and the concept of falling. Succinctly stated, hot media are those media that offer strong invitations to fall into the Mitwelt. They tend to seduce by eliciting the orienting reflex through rapidly changing sound, movement, and color. Additionally, they offer an array of options of incomprehensible size, such that at times this has been referred to as an information glut. Keep in mind, too, that television is first and foremost an advertising medium; entertainment and education, of secondary and tertiary importance, are but the material that fills the time between commercials. With programming driven by ratings, the goal is to appeal to the greatest number of people, thus resulting typically in the employment, by design, of the vocabulary of a twelve-year-old. Advertising is increasingly combined with the indiscriminate posting of information on the worldwide web to add further to the surfeit of material.

A few minutes of reflection make it clear that the hot media invite a fall into the averageness and leveling down of the Mitwelt. They call one to idle talk, to curiosity, and to ambiguity! The quintessence of these, in combination, is seen in channel surfing and surfing the Internet for hours. Chitchat, jumping from one thing to another, and indiscriminate exposure to information are their hallmarks. Relatively speaking, in contrast, are *cool media*, such as books, requiring sustained attention and a higher level of cognitive processing.

Moustakas (1974), in a description most revealing, has limned the falling into Mitwelt with emphasis on the disruption of authentic development:

> There is much in life to interfere with authentic development
> of the self — the humdrum of everyday living, drifting with
> convention, being stuck in rules and regulations instead of
> openly meeting life, yielding to pressures, compromising,
> doing the expected, and everything that passes for morality,
> particularly the superficial cliches and rules of convention and

propriety. Other forces that hinder the development of the self include playing a role, [and] doing one's duty [p. 44].

The world of relationship to one's self is, in Heidegger's word, the *Eigenwelt*. In this mode of world, when one is authentic, one is present to oneself and is aware of the meaning of things and events in relation to oneself. This mode is one of choice, choices through which one creates, to offer Sartre's term, a *transcendent ego*. The transcendent ego is analogous to a melody, in that intentional acts create, over time, a pattern that we perceive as personality or character, just as separate notes when played come to constitute a melody (Golomb, 1995, p. 137).

We see, then, the following analogy. *Throwness into Umwelt, Falling into Mitwelt, and Choice of Eigenwelt : Heidegger :: Facticité, Being-with-others, and Transcendence : Sartre.* Fullness of personhood implies a completeness and a balance among the Heideggerian modes of world. As suggested by Moustakas (1994), the modes of world are interrelated ways of structuring life; trouble begins when balance is lost, with one mode dominating. Compatible with Heidegger's view as expressed by Moustakas, Sartre suggested that failure to recognize the self both in its facticity and in its transcendence is an act of bad faith. That is, the individual who regards herself or himself as pure transcendence does not possess a situated freedom, existing as if beyond any biological, physical, and cultural/historical context. Conversely, the individual who treats oneself as an-*other* turns oneself into pure facticity. Furthermore, the individual who completely denies her or his transcendence slips into *l'esprit de sérieux*, a spirit of seriousness, therein viewing oneself as a thing, not a person (Golomb, 1995). These three negative attitudes toward the self reflect imbalance, and, consistent with a dominance of one mode of world, define an incompleteness of personhood.

As attractive as Heidegger's view and Sartre's view are in the search for an understanding of the development of personhood, they leave us with a pivotal question, that of motivation. On a more specific level, what is the urge that would account for a person's choosing to be absorbed into the crowd, to fall into the Mitwelt? Conversely, what is the urge that would describe the creation of personal meaning, a mode of Eigenwelt, a transcendent ego? And additionally, what is the urge that would describe the creation of balance among the modes of world? The answer may be revealed through the application of the theory of motivation that was explicated by Abraham Maslow (1969b). Well-known in the culture of humanistic psychology, the theory and model have undergone revisions, and so appear in somewhat different form in various sources. My understanding and my interpretation are as follows.

Maslow (Weiten & Lloyd, 1997) presented a model in which various motivations, based on and reflective of needs, are arranged in a hierarchy, graphically represented by a pyramid. In the lower part of the pyramid are found basic needs that, in their deficiency, motivate one to satisfy them. These are referred to as *deficiency needs* and are the bases for *deficiency motivation, D-motivation*. Beginning at the base are physiological needs such as the need for air, water, nutrients, and a particular temperature range. Next is the need for safety and security (stability and order), then belonging and love, then esteem (competence and recognition). This is the order of prepotency of these needs. Maslow suggested that as a need is reasonably well met, the need above it in the hierarchy becomes salient.

With these basic needs met, the *growth needs* or *being needs* emerge, with the attendant *growth motivation* or *being motivation, B-motivation*. Seeing the gratification of the basic needs as perhaps a necessary, but not a sufficient condition for *metamotivation*, Maslow (1969a) posed the question of under what conditions and by which people B-values are chosen. His answer was that B-values are "preferred by: (1) people who are more healthy, matured, (2) older, (3) stronger, more independent, (4) more courageous, (5) more educated, etc. The conditions which will increase the percentage of choice of B-values are: (a) absence of great social pressure, etc." (p. 80). (There is, I believe, a degree of circularity in Maslow's answer that weakens it by revealing that it is not the ultimate answer. Read through the next few paragraphs and this weakness will likely become more apparent.)

Although having earlier placed them in hierarchical order among themselves, Maslow (1969b) later put these *meta-needs*—cognitive needs (knowledge and understanding), esthetic needs (order and beauty), and self-actualization (realization of potential)—on the same plane, above the basic needs, and suggested that "in any given individual, they may be and often are hierarchically arranged according to idiosyncratic talents and constitutional differences.... Perhaps they form a unity of some sort, with each specific B-value being simply the whole seen from another angle" (pp. 178–179).

We now can unveil some answers to the questions posed above by applying Maslow's theory. First, as to why one may choose to be absorbed in the Mitwelt, we can suggest that a frustrated or insistent need for belonging and love may make Being-with-others appealing. Lacking a sense of belonging and love, this need would take priority, with an attendant vulnerability to role-playing and social conformity as tactics and strategies for meeting the felt deficiency. Even at the next level of Maslow's hierarchy, a frustrated desire for recognition could tempt one to conform to group values and expressions thereof in the interest of esteem through peer recognition. A rereading of the quotation from Moustakas describing the fall into Mitwelt helps to make this point clear. Maslow (1969b) himself suggested that persons motivated by the basic needs of "belongingness, affection, respect, and self-esteem" are prone to feel "anxiety-ridden, insecure, unsafe, … alone, ostracized, rootless, or isolated, … unlovable, rejected, or unwanted, … looked down upon, … deeply unworthy," inferior and worthless (p. 154).

"Self-actualizing individuals (more matured, more fully-human), by definition, already suitably gratified in their basic needs, are now motivated in other higher ways, to be called 'metamotivations'" (Maslow, 1969b, p. 153). I believe that the metamotivations imply an inclination to the Eigenwelt, or the transcendent self. Not inconsistent with Heidegger's idea that the mode of Eigenwelt involves the creation of meaning of things and events in relation to oneself, Maslow suggested that the self-actualizing person has become an enlarged self by means of transcending the self-and-not-self distinction because "he has incorporated into himself part of the world and defines himself thereby" (p. 166). *What* has been incorporated is an axiological question. That is to say, one assimilates that which passes the filters of one's esthetic and moral values, that which one deems worthy. (*Note bene:* I am distinguishing *assimilation* from *introjection*, that more-or-less indiscriminate form of incorporation.)

In addition to inclining one to the Eigenwelt, I believe the metamotivations incline one to a balance of the modes of world. I take as evidence a statement made by Maslow which reflects appreciation of the Umwelt. "Not only is man PART of nature, and it part of him, but also he must be at least minimally isomorphic with nature (similar to it) in order to be viable in it. It has evolved him" (Maslow, 1969b, p. 188). Further evidence that the metamotivations incline towards balance of the Heideggerian modes of world is found in the descriptions of self-actualized individuals. Maslow (Fadiman & Frager, 1994) listed the following:

1. More efficient perception of reality and more comfortable relations with it;
2. Acceptance (self, others, nature);
3. Spontaneity; simplicity; naturalness;
4. Problem centering (as opposed to being ego-centered);
5. The quality of detachment; the need for privacy;
6. Autonomy; independence of culture and environment;
7. Continued freshness of appreciation;
8. Mystic and peak experiences;
9. *Gemeinschaftsgefühl* (a feeling of kinship with others);
10. Deeper and more profound interpersonal relations;
11. The democratic character structure;
12. Discrimination between means and ends, between good and evil;
13. Philosophical, unhostile sense of humor;
14. Self-actualizing creativeness;
15. Resistance to enculturation; the transcendence of any particular culture [p. 473].

Consider these carefully in turn.

In spite of any circularity noted in the foregoing discussion, I believe that Maslow's hierarchical theory of motivation offers quite a useful perspective. It allows for a more comprehensive understanding of the Unwelt, the Mitwelt, the Eigenwelt, and their balance, or lack thereof, by introducing the psychological aspect of personal motivation.

The existential views of Heidegger and Sartre expressed above, and further elucidated, may be taken as a guidelines for the development of personhood. The complete person is present to herself or himself, finding meaning in things and events with reference to self; is in concerned contact with her or his fellow humans, but without being absorbed into them; and does all of this with awareness of her or his biological, physical, and cultural/historical context. In working on oneself, then, one may aspire to such authenticity.

If Heidegger and Sartre have provided us an erudite ontological

framework through which we may better understand the development of personhood, Nietzsche has proffered a view at once metaphorical in form and challenging in its provocation to action. In "On
Three Metamorphoses" Nietzsche, through the voice of Zarathustra,
spoke of how the spirit becomes a camel, the camel a lion, and the
lion, finally, a child. Zarathustra began by acknowledging that there
is much that is difficult for the spirit. The spirit that would bear much
takes on the most difficult things and, like the camel, speeds into the
desert. But in the loneliest desert the spirit can become the lion who
would be master of its own desert. The camel can become the lion if
it seeks out its last master and defeats him. But who is this last master? Zarathustra declared,

> "Thou shalt" is the name of the great dragon. But the spirit of
> the lion says, "I will." "Thou shalt" lies in his way, sparkling
> like gold, an animal covered with scales; and on every scale
> shines a golden 'thou shalt' [*The Portable Nietzsche*, 1982b,
> pp. 138–139].

The dragon, reflecting the values long ago created, and claiming to
be all created value, proclaims, verily, there shall be no more "I will."

Zarathustra posed the question of why there is need for the spirit
of the lion, why the reverent beast of burden is not enough. He then
answered,

> The creation of freedom for oneself and a sacred 'No' even to
> duty—for that ... the lion is needed.... He once loved 'thou
> shalt' as most sacred: now he must find illusion and caprice
> even in the most sacred, that freedom from his love may
> become his prey: the lion is needed for such prey [p. 139].

There is more, however. Even after the leonine "No!" to all of
the "thou shalts," there is something more that the child can do. "The
child is innocence and forgetting, a new beginning, a game, a self-
propelled wheel, a first movement, a sacred 'Yes'" (p. 139). It is only
through the sacred "Yes" that the spirit wills its own will and con-
quers its own world. Zarathustra told us that the game of creation
requires this sacred "Yes."

The traditional virtues, constituted of the "thou shalts," conse-
crate stereotyped mediocrity, but seduce with the offer of sound sleep.
As Zarathustra spoke,

> Now I understand clearly what was once sought above all
> when teachers of virtue were sought. Good sleep was sought,
> and opiate virtues for it. For all these much praised sages who
> were teachers of virtue, wisdom was the sleep without
> dreams: they know no better meaning of life [p. 142].

Thus are we warned: where sleep is the goal, life lacks meaning. And so the camel plods on through its desert.

Nietzsche's metaphor of "The Three Metamorphoses" both delineates stages of development of personhood and posits first rebelliousness, then a "yes" to life as requirements for the metamorphoses to take place. To put this in practical terms, Nietzsche's instruction is to rebel against the traditional virtues that are based on rigid commandments, if one wishes to evolve as a person. Then, once this stage of development is attained, and if one is to evolve further, one must say "yes" to one's own will. Nietzsche's metaphor thus can be taken quite pragmatically, as a general guideline in developing depth of one's person.

Let us not underestimate the role or importance of rebellion in the development of the person. Nietzsche's use of the lion to symbolize rebellion is surely apt in its reflection of the ferocity with which one's "No!" must be spit out if the introjected "thou shalts" are to be overcome. Perhaps influenced by Nietzsche's "The Three Metamorphoses," and well informed by her own clinical experience, Karen Horney (1950) devoted a chapter of *Neurosis and Human Growth: The Struggle Toward Self-Realization* to "The Tyranny of the Should." (Horney cites Nietzsche elsewhere in her volume.) By "tyranny of the should," she referred to inexorable inner dictates which comprise "all that the neurotic should be able to do, to be, to feel, to know — and taboos on how and what he should not be" (p. 65). These "shoulds" are characterized by a disregard for feasibility, a disregard for the conditions under which they could be fulfilled, and a disregard for the psychic condition of the person involved. These inner dictates are, in a word, blind. Resulting, she wrote, from both the feeling of necessity to become the ideal self and from the conviction that one is able to do so, the "shoulds" inevitably lead to a feeling of strain, strain to actualize the ideal image held of oneself, disturbances in relationships, often manifesting as hypersensitivity to criticism, and an impairment of spontaneity. Understood from Horney's perspective, we can better appreciate Nietzsche's choice to invoke the lion.

Noting the pervasiveness of rebellion throughout history, Camus went so far as to take its universality as proof of a human characteristic that underlies, and thus precedes, the rebellious attitude. He thereby rebutted Sartre's claim that "existence precedes essence" (Golomb,1995, p. 191). And, therein, he underscored its importance, making rebelliousness a core part of being fully human. What is the human essence, the nature of the human? Camus (Golomb, 1995) suggests pride, honor, respect, and dignity. It is these from which rebellion is born.

In rebellion, through that leonine roar, what is created? An authentic self. This is not, however, a goal to be attained only once. Rather, it is an ongoing challenge and an ongoing process. For, as Golomb has interpreted Kierkegaard, "authentic selves do not exist; there are only certain individuals who carry out authentic acts and live authentic modes of life, in contradistinction to persons ... who escape the responsibility and 'dizziness' of freedom into inauthentic ways of living" (1995, p. 54). Furthermore, "an act either is authentic or is not authentic. One cannot stipulate degrees of authenticity and progressive levels of its so-called realization. Hence there are no 'stages' of authenticity" (p. 54). There may be stages of development of personhood, as suggested by Nietzsche, and within a stage there may be authentic or inauthentic acts.

In considering the development of personhood, and the place of authenticity in that, it is worthwhile to consider, in their subtlety, the two seemingly contradictory models of authenticity that can be found in Nietzsche's thought. Golomb referred to these as deriving inspiration from a biological metaphor and deriving from art. It is the former that is more clearly found in the Gestalt literature. Consider Perls's rather matter-of-fact statement that "every individual, every plant, every animal has only one inborn goal — to actualize itself as it is" (Perls, 1969, p. 33). Expanding on this, he explicitly referred to the rose, the elephant, the kangaroo, and the bird, each actualizing into itself, and not into any other form of life. An example that I have used on occasion is that of the antelope and the elephant. Each in its actualizing form may be seen as beautiful, the antelope in its grace and speed, the elephant in its size and strength. To wax metaphorical, the person who is like the antelope can find meaning and a certain satisfaction in developing her or his *antelopeness*, the elephant her or his *elephantness*. If, however, the antelope resolves to pull as heavy a weight as the elephant, or the elephant to jump as high as the antelope, he or she will surely fail. In contrast to self-actualization, this is an attempt at *self-image actualization*, and a sure course to unhappiness born of perpetual frustration. Each person, then, is called upon to discover her or his nature, and if she or he is to self-actualize, to actualize that particular nature.

It is this biological model of authenticity that is implied in the *paradoxical theory of change* that was explicated by Arnold Beisser (1970) and that has become such an important guide for many Gestalt therapists. (In a 1975 recorded interview, Jim Simkin [Harman, 1992, p. 130] declared Beisser's chapter to be required reading for any well-rounded Gestalt therapist, indicating that if one understood this chapter, one would understand how to conceptualize existential theory in a Gestalt framework.) Briefly stated, the theory is "that change occurs when one becomes what he is, not when he tries to become what he is not" (p. 77). This paradoxical theory of change not only invites the person in question to genuine self-realization, but also precludes any coercive attempt by anyone else to bring about change in said person. Viewed in the acute time frame, self-actualization occurs, then, by fully entering into one's experience in the moment. Quoting Proust as an ally in this view, Beisser (1970) suggested that "to heal a suffering one must experience it to the full."

Nietzsche's other model of authenticity, that of the artist, emphasizes the awesome freedom of choice that one has in creating herself or himself. In contrast to the biological model of authenticity which seems to put the limiting factor of one's nature on a par with the opportunity for choice, the artistic model clearly highlights creative choice. To invoke Heidegger's view of the modes of world again, Nietzsche's biological model, with its attention to essence or inborn nature, takes the Umwelt as its starting place, making the choice of actualizing or not actualizing that essence the crux of authenticity. The artistic model seems aligned more with the Eigenwelt, oneself shaping oneself heroically, in spite of the forces of cultural conditioning, or Mitwelt.

So, to develop depth of personhood, one is well advised not only to actualize one's innate potentials, but to invoke the muses and rhapsodize on oneself, to create a singular self through a unique sequence of spontaneous choices. Putting this guidance in concrete and practical terms, Nietzsche suggested that one look back on one's life, asking what one has truly loved, what has drawn one's soul aloft. The answers may reveal one's created self. As a corollary, since we are free to choose our educators, our mentors, we may look back at those for whom we feel admiration, and through self-analyses recognize what we genuinely value (Golomb, 1995).

Continuing to explore guidelines for the development of personhood, we can well consider the following. Having identified the archetype constituted of present-centeredness, the view that the present is a gift of both pleasure and the awareness of death and decay, Naranjo (1970) further illuminated it through the "implicit moral injunctions of Gestalt therapy" (p. 49). Intended not as statements of duty, but rather as proclamations of truth, these injunctions may be taken as guides for working on oneself:

> "Live now." ("Be concerned with the present rather than the
> past or future.")
> "Live here." ("Deal with what is present rather than with
> what is absent.")

Taken together, these bring us to the phrase so commonly found in the Gestalt literature — here-and-now. *Hic et nunc.* As I interpret this, it does not mean to live impulsively, as if there will be no future, never planning, never preparing. On the other hand, it warns of the loss to the present that comes from dwelling on the past or dwelling on the future. The meaning is not to live *for the present*, but to live *in the present*. The past and the future are images. And so, to continue with Naranjo's injunctions,

> "Stop imagining." ("Experience the real.")
> "Stop unnecessary thinking."

Translated into psychoanalytic parlance, this is *intellectualization*, which is also, as I have suggested elsewhere, operationalized as the *super-reasonable* verbal stance and the *computer* non-verbal stance in Virginia Satir's communication model (Smith, 1996). In essence, it is the use of thinking in order to attenuate experiencing. Continuing once again:

> "Express rather than manipulate, explain, justify or judge."
> "Give in to unpleasantness and pain just as to pleasure."

"Accept no *should* or *ought* other than your own."
"Take full responsibility for your actions, feelings and
    thoughts."
"Surrender to being as you are" [Naranjo, 1970, pp. 49–50].

These specific moral injunctions were summarized by Naranjo under
three general principles, as follows:

"Valuation of actuality: temporal (present versus past or
    future), spatial (present versus absent), and substantial
    (act versus symbol)."
"Valuation of awareness and the acceptance of experience."
"Valuation of wholeness, or responsibility" [p. 50].

Consider the above injunctions and the general principles that
summarize them as a moral cadre. One's conduct could be guided by
such a framework, with the praxis constituting work on one's personal development.

In a tone and intent not unlike Naranjo's, Abraham Maslow
(Fadiman & Frager, 1994) described eight behaviors that are self-
actualizing:

(1) Experience "fully, vividly, selflessly, with full concentration
    and total absorption."
(2) When given the choice between growth and the safety of
    the familiar, make the growth choice.
(3) Become aware of one's own inner nature, and act in accord
    with that.
(4) Be honest rather than posing or trying to impress.
(5) Trust one's own judgement.

By following the five self-actualizing behaviors above, one prepares
oneself to make "better life choices." For, in Maslow's words, "One
cannot choose wisely for a life unless he dares to listen to himself,
his own self, at each moment in life."

(6) Using one's abilities and intelligence, strive to do well
    those things that one really wants to do.
(7) Be open to *peak experiences*, those transient moments of
    self-actualization characterized by ecstasy, rapture, bliss,
    great joy.

(8) Become aware of one's ego defenses, those mechanisms through which one denies or distorts one's image of oneself or the world, and abandon them [pp. 474–476].

Focusing on self-actualization, Maslow's guidelines may not be as systematic as the moral injunctions put forth by Naranjo. In their breadth, however, they offer clear direction for personal development.

I wish to include another set of guidelines, this set from the writings of Carlos Castaneda (1972). Setting aside the controversy concerning the fictive nature of Castaneda's work, I find the suggestions found therein to be both eminently practical and particularly intriguing. The context for these suggestions is the apprenticeship of Castaneda to don Juan, a Yaqui *brujo* (medicine man or sorcerer). To become a *man of knowledge*, Castaneda was told, he had to follow truthfully the hardships of learning, neither rushing nor faltering, and go as far as he could in unraveling the secrets of personal power. Well-being is to be groomed, the trick being in what one emphasizes—making oneself miserable or making oneself strong. Either option takes the same amount of work. Don Juan chastised Castaneda, telling him that his life was messy, and that he was a fool, adding that all of us are fools. The reasons that don Juan offered for the messiness of Castaneda's life were as follows:

He had too much feeling of importance.
He had too much personal history.
He did not take enough responsibility for his acts.
He did not use death as his advisor.
He was too accessible.

These five criticisms draw one's attention, with at least three of them — the second, the fourth, and the fifth — sounding rather cryptic. But, to be of practical use, these require explanation and elaboration. First, let us examine the issue of feeling too much importance. One can not truly appreciate the world, don Juan explained, as long as one feels that he or she is the most important thing in the world. Such self-importance must be dropped. The specific practice recommended by don Juan is to treat everything as one's equal by talking to everything, including animals, plants, and inanimate objects. If, for instance, one picks a plant to eat, talk to it and acknowledge that today it is food for you, but one day you will be food for the plants.

Implicit in this criticism and its resolution is the recognition and invitation to the felt meaning of being not better than, but part of, nature.

By personal history don Juan meant not what one knows of one's past, but what one tells others of one's past. Such recounting of one's past to others creates a personal history that may lead others then to have expectations of one. When someone else knows one's history, or, more accurately, when, by sharing memories of one's past with someone, the two people construct a history, the other person is most likely to attribute things to one based on that history. Thus, the other may attribute beliefs, values, attitudes, preferences, personal qualities, and so forth, leading to behavioral expectations. Personal history is perpetuated by the ongoing telling to others what one is doing in one's life. To the extent that one can erase personal history, one can become free from the encumbering thoughts of others. Others are then less likely to be disappointed or disillusioned with one's behavior. And, as one has less personal history even unto oneself, more space is created for a feeling of freshness and for acting with a greater degree of spontaneity.

The position that don Juan took with regard to responsibility is uncomplicated and yet intriguing in its extremity. He said simply that everything one does is one's decision and one's responsibility. As a corollary, he said one must know why one is doing something, and then to proceed with the chosen action without doubt or remorse. That is to say, don Juan championed intentionality and declined regret. These are especially important because we are here in this "marvelous world … in this marvelous time … and must make every act count, since [we] are going to be here for only a short while" (Castaneda, 1972, p. 92).

These last few words are a bridge to the next criticism imposed on Castaneda — not using death as his advisor. Death, don Juan explained, using a metaphor of animation if not personification, is our eternal companion, an arm's length away and always on our left. It is always watching, until the day it taps us. The only wise advisor we have, Death should be consulted whenever one feels impatient, or when one feels things are going wrong. To consult Death, don Juan instructed, one is to turn to the left and ask advice. If ever Death makes a gesture, if one catches a glimpse of it, or if one gets the felt sense that Death is watching, one will likely reassess things and drop any pettiness that is found! Once one accepts Death as an advisor, one has no time for petty thoughts or for foul moods. Furthermore, only those who believe that they are immortal can afford to regret or doubt decisions, or to procrastinate in acting on them. "In a world where death is the hunter, ... there is no time for regrets or doubts. There is only time for decisions" (Castaneda, 1972, p. 47). And this means that all decisions are decisions made in "the face of our inevitable death" (p. 51). So, once one knows that one's life will not last forever, why hesitate to do what one wants to do? Furthermore, one's acts take on quite different meaning when one considers each act as possibly one's last act on earth.

Perhaps the charge of being too accessible is the most enigmatic element of don Juan's reproach. With a decidedly poetic flavor, don Juan advised Castaneda, saying, "You must retrieve yourself from the middle of a trafficked way" (Castaneda, 1972, p. 76). Being too accessible means being too available to others, always within their reach, and thus vulnerable to exhausting oneself and exhausting others. In not being too accessible, one touches the world sparingly and with tenderness, not squeezing the world of people or the world of things, of plants, or of animals. One does not gorge oneself on anything. Now, in an unexpected turn, don Juan related worrying to becoming unwittingly accessible. With worry, one tends to cling to the person or thing one fears losing; with clinging one is most likely to become exhausted or to exhaust whomever or whatever it is to whom or to which one clings. The challenge is to become deliberately available and deliberately unavailable, touching the world only lightly, staying in touch only as long as one needs to, and then moving away leaving hardly a mark.

Although not part of his critique, don Juan offered Castaneda two more quite specific pieces of advice. One was to disrupt the routines of his life, making himself less predictable (Castaneda, 1972, p. 85). The other was to understand everything as a challenge, rather than judging everything, as the ordinary person tends to do, as either a curse or a blessing. Challenges are not either good or bad; they are simply challenges (Castaneda, 1974, p. 108–109). Taken together, these two suggestions encourage freshness and spontaneity in one's living, and in turn, the chance for deeper and richer experiencing.

Taken as etiological factors in a messy life, and enucleated from the structure of shamanic training, don Juan's criticisms may serve as directives on the path of development of the person of the therapist. Likewise, the two additional suggestions can be practiced intentionally as part of that path.

I find a certain axiological affinity among the moral injunctions and their summary by Naranjo, the self-actualizing behaviors of Maslow, and the challenges of don Juan. The core value that is held in common, as I understand it, seems to be one of *intending to full aliveness*, manifested by being in the here-and-now, with awareness of and acceptance of what is, taking full responsibility for oneself. Each illuminates from a particular perspective, and like three well-placed lamps in a room, together they provide an ambient light that gives us a clear view of personal development. In each case, the items put forth can be taken as specific and concrete guidelines, with the intentional use of these guidelines constituting one's personal practice.

Those who have read Joseph Campbell or watched his video-taped lectures or interviews are familiar with his advice to those seeking direction or the deepening of their experience in living. With the rhythm of mantra meditation and with deceptive simplicity he offered the words, "Follow your bliss!" If we are to understand this and be able to use it as yet another general guide to personal development, we would do well to dig below the surface level and find deeper meaning in this short imperative sentence. Campbell (1990) revealed this deeper meaning himself in discussing parallels between Egyptian symbology and the mystical philosophy of India. Although he did not explicitly relate this discussion to his oft-offered advice, the connection seems clear enough.

In Hinduism there is discussion of five sheaths that enclose the *Atman*—this being, of course, the part of Brahman (the supreme reality personified as Brahma the Creator, Vishnu the Preserver, and Shiva the Destroyer) found in each individual. *Anamayakosha*, the outermost sheath, is the body, made of food, and, in time, becoming food for other creatures. The second sheath, named *Prana-mayakosha*, is the sheath of breath that ignites the food, bringing heat and life. Next is the mental sheath, *Manamayakosha*. Oriented to the first two sheaths, it is happy when the body is satisfied, sad when the body is in pain. The fourth is *Janamayakosha*, the sheath of wisdom. This, the *wisdom body*, is spontaneous, with mentality riding upon it. It is through the wisdom of the body that one knows to breathe, how to digest food, when to sleep, and so forth. It is through this sheath that all vegetative processes are informed. Underneath all of these sheaths, surrounded by them, each in its turn, is the fifth, the sheath of *bliss*. *Anandamayakosha* it is called, and what it knows is that life is a manifestation of rapture (Campbell, 1990).

Therefore, when Campbell advised a student, saying, "Follow your bliss!", he was invoking the deepest level of personal knowing. Going below the levels of physical body, the enlivening of that body, the mind that reacts with judgement, and even the level of bodily wisdom, he was calling upon that which knows rapture. His advice was simple, but not to be mistaken as necessarily easy. It requires contact with one's deepest knowing, the knowing that can direct one to bliss. From this level, or sheath, one is best guided in one's decisions. Note that decisions coming from this level are profoundly personal, for only you can know yourself at this depth. One must, therefore, eschew secondhand answers from without, finding them rather from deep within. So, when in doubt, follow the path that leads to rapture, the direction that leads to bliss.

Let us now leave the realm of *general guidelines* for the development of depth and richness of personhood and go to another stratum where the question of *psychological process* emerges as the focus. My answer to the question of the specific and concrete psychological process involved in inviting and encouraging *person*al development can best be understood when guided by a particular theory. The theoretical cynosure is as follows. *Note bene:*

> *Growth takes place through here-and-now experience under conditions of heightened awareness.*

"This means that growth is a lived experience, entered into and actively participated in.... If not organismically experienced, the event does not become part of the person" (Smith, 1998, p. 10). Fritz Perls (1969) said simply, "Everything is grounded in *awareness*. *Awareness* is the only basis of knowledge" (p. 48). And, as Barry Stevens (1984) asked rhetorically, concerning the way to live creatively, "What is it but awareness and acting in accord with circumstances?" (p. 4). "Be aware, alert and sensing, living and moving in harmony" (p. 73). (Although not fully equivalent, *awareness* in Gestalt theory corresponds to *insight* in psychoanalytic theory. The two terms are analogous, in a nominative sense, as one can have an awareness in the same sense that one can have an insight. Awareness, however, carries not only this shared meaning, but also refers to the process by which the named awareness comes about. That is to say, awareness is both a product and a process; one becomes aware by being aware! Unless otherwise indicated, in the present context awareness will be used to refer to the process.) Implicated in this theory are both awareness and exposure qua experience. Not without directionality, awareness as process may be introversive or extratensive. That is to say, awareness or *mindfulness*, to add the Buddhist term, is attitudinal, whereas exposure, arising either from attention inward or attention outward, is content. If awareness is the *how* of all growth-filled experiences, then exposure is in reference to the *what*.

Oliver Wendell Holmes wrote that "a moment's insight is sometimes worth a life's experience" (Evans, 1968, p. 351). Not only does this quotation call attention to the two elements of awareness and exposure, it suggests that the former is the ascendant factor in the regulation of the potency of an experience. This idea is worth further exploration. When pushed, this exploration leads quickly to the spiritual, if not the mystical realm.

The Tao, according to Chuang-tzu, cannot be conveyed either by words or by silence. It is found, rather, in that state that is neither sound nor silence. Required for reaching that state is the cultivation of two things. First, one must cultivate the harmonic resonance of one's life energy, or *ch'i*. Second, and of greater pertinence to the present discussion, one must cultivate mindfulness. So, there it is—energy in harmony, and awareness—the requisites for true depth of being. Such cultivation is difficult, and is a lifelong process (Walker, 2001).

Pushed even further, and reflected in the words of Chuang-tzu's predecessor, Lao Tsu (sometimes spelled Lao Tzu), we find the following concerning exquisite awareness directed inward:

> Without going outside, you may know the whole world.
> Without looking through the window, you may see the ways
>   of heaven.
> ... Thus the sage knows without traveling [Feng & English
>   translation, 1972, Chapter 47].

Here, then, is the idea that depth can be found at home. But what is hinted at by this? What, really, is meant by not going outside? The

answer is revealed in another translation of the forty-seventh chapter of the *Tao Te Ching* (Bynner translation, 1962):

> There is no need to run outside
> For better seeing,
> Nor to peer from a window. Rather abide
> At the center of your being;
> For the more you leave it, the less you
> learn [p. 55].

There is the revelatory phrase, *abide at the center of your being.* This
is the key to awareness— to experience from the center of one's being.
The direction of awareness is here, again, inward, but not in the sense
of superficial introspection. Rather, like the Uroboros with its own
tail in its mouth, *awareness from the center of one's being is focused on
that center of one's being.* (Pray, do not demand that this phrase be
explicitly defined or too explicitly explained, for we are situating our
exploration in the realm of the mystical, not the realm of science
where precision is sought and accorded such high value. Allow yourself, instead, felt meaning.)

   Others, in an idiom more Western, have expressed the same perspective. Consider, for example, Franz Kafka's final aphorism (Schoen,
1994):

> You do not need to leave the room. Remain sitting at your
> table and listen. Do not even listen, simply wait. Do not even
> wait, be quite still and solitary. The world will freely offer
> itself to you to be unmasked, it has no choice, it will roll in
> ecstasy at your feet [p. 82].

Or, tersely and simply, as Rainer Maria Rilke advised a young poet,
"Go into yourself" (Schoen, 1994, p. 54).

   With apology, for search as I might, I have not been able to find
the reference and must rely only on my notes in one of my personal
journals, I offer a few lines from Robert Browning:

> There is an inmost center in us all, where truth abides in
> fullness and to know rather consists in opening out a way
> whence the imprisoned splendor may escape than in effecting
> entry for light supposed to be without.

In these various expressions of seeking enlightenment, the source of depth knowledge is taken to be one's self — the center, that is, of one's being. Therefore, it follows that if the source of knowledge is within, then the path is an introspective one, a profound focus of awareness from and on one's core. (I am indebted to George Moraitis [1999] for his discussion, in which he related various presumptions of the source of knowledge to the ways to get to those sources.)

Was it awareness, in this most profound sense, that William Blake had in mind when he wrote of his fourfold method of envisioning reality? It has been suggested by Milton Klonsky (1977) that Blake's fourfold method is a reflection of the fourfold hermeneutics devised by cabalists and biblical scholars. It was they who spoke of "the literal-historical, the allegorical, the tropological (or moral), and, finally, the anagogical (or spiritual) levels of meaning in Scripture [that] are successively revealed" (p. 11). (A brief clarification of the word "tropological" may be welcomed before going on to Blake's actual schema. Tropology refers to a figurative mode of speech or writing, or a method of interpretation in which emphasis is placed on the figurative use of the language.) Notice, now, the parallel. Single vision, for Blake, "occurs when we see with, not thro', our eyes" (pp. 10–11). This, as I understand it, is the relatively objective and consensual perception that is traditionally so highly valued in the natural sciences. Blake saw this exemplified by the sleep in which people had been entranced by Newtonian science. With twofold vision, the outward eye can see that which is consensual, but the inward eye discerns something else. Herein is the recognition not only of the extroversive, but also the introversive world. Threefold vision is annealed by passion, and is of the "erotic realm of the creative unconscious" (p. 10). The word "annealed" is interesting in its implication of heat — herein the heat of passion — as well as in its denotation of toughening and rendering less brittle. This denotation is an interesting one, in both of its parts, when applied to vision qua perception. It is with fourfold vision that "the phenomenal world has been transcended by the Divine Imagination and reunited with Spirit" (p. 11). Blake, of course, was a champion of Imagination, seeing it as of a higher order than Reason, for Reason, as he saw it, is passive and limited by the five senses. Imagination, in contrast, he saw as active and more fruitful of Truth. The Reasoners he also called

Devourers; those of Imagination he identified as Creators or the Prolific.

Put in the context of his fourfold method of envisioning reality, it now becomes clearer what Blake meant by his enigmatic proclamation,

> If the doors of perception were cleansed every thing would appear to man as it is, Infinite. For man has closed himself up, till he sees all things thro' narrow chinks of his cavern [1975 edition, p. xxii].

Only the level of heightened awareness that attends fourfold vision allows for the perception of the Infinite. And, as is implied by the second sentence, this level of awareness, this fourfold vision, is natural, but for most has been lost. But, if one will cleanse the doors of perception, Blake would say, one may come

> To see a World in a Grain of Sand
> And a Heaven in a Wild Flower,
> Hold Infinity in the palm of your hand
> And Eternity in an hour [Klonsky, 1977, p. 8].

So, it is not simply what one has or has not been exposed to that in and of itself predicts depth and richness of personhood. It is also the degree of awareness which one brings to experience, be that experience in the private world of one's center or the public world out there. Although not in words that correspond exactly, the gist of this idea was nicely captured by Aldous Huxley when he wrote the following:

> Experience is not a matter of having actually swum the Hellespont, or danced with the dervishes, or slept in a dosshouse. It is a matter of sensibility and intuition, of seeing and hearing the significant things, of paying attention at the right moment, of understanding and co-ordinating. Experience is not what happens to a man; it is what a man does with what happens to him [Quotation in *Voices*, p. 42].

Having given awareness its rightful place of pre-eminence, we can, nevertheless, look more carefully at the allusion found in the final words of Huxley's statement. To the extent that what happens to a person is directly or indirectly by choice, surely it behooves one to consider that some happenings may have greater potential for personal growth than others. James Bugenthal (1971) took this into account when he fashioned his statement of a humanistic ethic. Acknowledging that such an ethic of growth is not a fixed creed, but rather an evolving attitudinal set, his statement is perhaps best regarded as a prolegomenon to a humanistic ethic. Although only one of the five points is of direct relevance to the present discussion, I will mention the other four in the interest of forming the gestalt of the ethical statement, adding brief parenthetical explanations.

> Centered responsibility for one's own life. (Recognizing that the influences of contingency, social pressure, and concern for others do not displace one from the position of mediating all such influences.)
> Mutuality in relationship. (Recognition and honoring of the subjecthood of the other, allowing genuine encounter.)
> Here-and-now perspective. (One always lives in the present moment.)
> Acceptance of non-hedonic emotions. (Recognition that unpleasant emotions are parts of the human experience, and therefore to be valued.)
> Growth-oriented experiencing. (The seeking for experiences that facilitate personal growth.) [pp. 12–21].

The gestalt so formed is one of the autonomy and dignity of the individual, seeking to be authentic. As a thread woven into place in a fabric, a commitment to growth-oriented experiencing finds place in this gestalt.

One who is intent on working on her or his personal growth would, thereby, be committed to growth-oriented experiencing; ergo, would seek out opportunity for experiences that hold the greatest promise for this. Many paths are possible, both in the literal sense of a path and the metaphorical. Taken in the metaphorical sense, there are a multitude of formal paths, formal practices. These are time-honored and time-proven methods that, when practiced with dedication and discipline (that is, being a disciple of the method), hold great potential for growth. Severin Peterson (1971), in an admirable attempt to survey the landscape of personal growth, offered up a catalog of more than forty such paths that one could follow. His list ranged from Aikido and Alexander Technique to various forms of yoga, from meditation and prayer to Sensory Awareness and Theater Games. Seeing these as auxiliaries, Peterson emphasized that each person *is* her or his own way of growth, and the methods must be used in the proper ways.

Whether following one of the formal paths or traversing the path of life, the commitment of the growth-oriented person is to experience from a position of heightened awareness. With phrasing most pleasing as well as apt, Michael Adam (1976) wrote of the Hindu value of fulfillment at one's particular level of development: "A man should grow to maturity by way of experiences that left no dark corners in him" (p. 18). The formal paths, by design, bring illumination to those dark corners. It is through the experience that one then is able to move on, traveling farther down the given path.

But which path is to be taken up, which path to be followed? This is a most personal decision, the rightness of which only the one who has chosen can judge. We can turn, once again, to the guidance of don Juan (Castaneda, 1968). Explaining that there are a million paths, don Juan emphasized to Carlos Castaneda that a path is only a path, and that one should never stay with a path that is not right for one. Only if one lives a disciplined life can one discern if a path is right, only then can one know in one's heart what to do. This decision, to stay on a path or leave it, must be made neither out of fear nor out of ambition. The question to ask, said don Juan, is this:

> Does this path have a heart? ... If it does, the path is good;
> if it doesn't, it is of no use. Both paths lead nowhere; but one
> has a heart, the other doesn't.... One makes for a joyful
> journey.... The other will make you curse your life [p. 106].

With a turn more personal, and a decidedly inspirational tone, don Juan said further,

> For me there is only the traveling on paths that have heart....
> There I travel, and the only worthwhile challenge is to traverse
> its full length.
> And there I travel looking, looking,
> breathlessly [no page].

The guidance offered by don Juan makes reference to the need for each person to find the path that is right for her or him. Implicit in this is the idea of the individualized path, the path made individual by selection of formal systems, or not.

In Joseph Campbell's (1990) interpretation, the Grail legend and the Arthurian romances represent the assimilation of the Near Eastern Christian tradition of valued membership in the community with the heroic tradition of the Germanic and Celtic people in which the individual path was more highly valued. As evidence of the higher value of the individual path in the latter tradition, Campbell cites the Old French text, *La Queste del Saint Graal.* Therein it was written that, after King Arthur's nephew Gawain proposed to the knights a quest of the Grail,

> They agreed that all would go on this quest, but they thought it would be a disgrace to go forth in a group, so each entered the forest at a point that he, himself, had chosen, where it was darkest and there was no path [p. 211].

What beautiful symbolism — "to go forth in a group" would be a disgrace. Each knight should enter the forest of adventure at a point self-chosen, a point where it was "darkest and there was no path." What is called for is the individual path into the unknown. And therein is another hint. The quest that takes one into the darkness, into the unknown, holds greater potential for growth than does the known path, common and well-trodden.

This idea finds further expression in the mythopoetic world. Perhaps this was hinted at when Beowulf spoke, saying "strong men should seek fame in far-off lands" (Crossley-Holland translation, p. 99). Could not "far-off lands" symbolize the same thing as the dark woods where there is no marked path? The poet of this epic moral commentary may have been reflecting on the richness of experience that could ensue from seeking fame in far-off lands when uttering the following. "Whoever lives long on earth, endures the unrest of these times, will be involved in much good and much evil" (p. 76). The sober tone of this trenchant line surely reflects the gravity of the journey, as much as the content implies the richness of experience.

Placing the development of personhood, again, in the context of the journey, and this time with reference to astuteness of social judgement as outcome, the *Poetic Edda* offers the following:

Only he is aware   who hath wandered much,
          and far hath been afield,
what manner of man   be he whom he meets,
          if himself be not wanting in wit
               [Hollander translation, p. 17].

Perhaps we can see "wit" as the faculty of awareness, thus linking experience with heightened awareness as the formula that I have earlier stated for personal growth.

Still within the Nordic mythology, as set forth in the *Poetic Edda* and the *Prose Edda* (Sturluson, 1954), there is offered an intricate cosmography of nine worlds. It is a tricentric structure, with three worlds on each of three levels, and rising vertically through the three levels is Yggdrasill, the World Tree. At the uppermost level are the worlds of the warrior gods and goddesses, the fertility gods and goddesses, and the light elves. On the middle plane are the worlds of humankind, the giants, and the dark elves or dwarfs. And on the lowest level are the worlds of fire, of ice, and of the dead who did not earn the right to dwell with the gods and goddesses. The lays tell of travels among the worlds, whereby gods and goddesses, giants, light elves, dark elves, and humans mingle. Taken concretely, the stories are accounts of fanciful journeys and adventures, pure fantasy, products of the *mundus imaginalis*. Taken metaphorically, however, the journeys are internal ones, the exploration of one's own psyche. These introspective journeys are at once psychological and anagogical, a potential for deepening and broadening one's being. In order to understand the aspects of being that are reflected by each of the worlds, one has only to read the stories while assuming a metaphorical attitude and note the qualities made manifest by the sentient beings of each world (and in the case of the world of ice and that of fire, the energetic dimension of cold, dark, quiet, and still versus heat, light, sound, and movement).

The Eddic stories may be taken, then, as a call to, and a guide to, the inward journey. For example, to travel to the land of the giants is to explore one's power to destroy. Destructive power can be positive in the sense of breaking old patterns, dismantling old structures, in order to make room for new creation. On the other hand, it may be manifest in the bringing about of chaos and confusion. One may be instructed in this dimension of destruction (de-structuring) by reading of the giants, trusting in the mythopoetic wisdom contained therein, and thus guided into self-exploration. Within the stories, too, one can find the sacred technology for entering into deep journeying through an altered state of consciousness. From the world of the warrior gods and goddesses, we find Odin undergoing a shamanic initiation through fasting, dehydration, social isolation, un-grounding by means of suspension from a tree, and the pain and blood loss resulting from a self-inflicted wound. (Note that each of these methods is a known technique for altering consciousness, found in various combinations among various peoples in their pursuit of spiritual growth or enlightenment.) And, so it is with each of the nine worlds.

This brief discussion of Odin's shamanic initiation has, no doubt, for many readers brought to mind the shamanic journey. Mircea Eliade, in his erudite and classic work first published in 1951, *Le Chamanisme et les Techniques Archaiques de l'Extase*, addressed the methods used by shamans:

> The pre-eminently shamanic technique is the passage from one cosmic region to another — from earth to the sky or from earth to the underworld. The shaman knows the mystery of the break-through in plane. This communication among the cosmic zones is made possible by the very structure of the universe…. The universe in general is conceived as having three levels — sky, earth, underworld — connected by a central axis [1964, p. 259].

As Eliade went on to explain, "What for the rest of the community remains a cosmological ideogram, for the shamans (and the heroes, etc.) becomes a mystical itinerary" (p. 265).

The archetype of the three-level universe, the empyrean trilogy, finds expression in many cultures, but in each case with particular cultural inflections. It may be interesting to consider the manifestation of this archetype in contemporary times, within the culture of psychotherapy, more specifically psychodynamic theory. With his publication of *The Ego and the Id* in 1923, Sigmund Freud introduced his structural model of the psyche. In his structural model, the id stands as the underworld, the ego as the middle world where we live our conscious lives, and the superego as the upper world.

> The core activity of Freud's "depth" psychology is to explore the lower region (and less often the upper region) in order

> better to understand existence on the conscious plane of the
> ego and to reconcile the intrapsychic conflicts. It is these
> conflicts among the three "worlds" which constitute "psycho-
> dynamics." To paraphrase Freud, where id was, then there
> shall ego be [Smith 2001, p. 26].

So where is the "dark wood," within or without? Perhaps it is
both. It is the unknown places out in the world, and it is the unconscious world within. And, may I suggest, the external journey is of
value in personal growth only insofar as it calls up the journey to the
inner world. It is when the introcosmic journey is called upon in resonance with the exposure to a novel external world that the latter may
be growth filled.

But what of the apparent contradiction introduced in the pre-
ceding pages, the championing of awareness and the championing of
exposure as the well of personal growth? My proposal is that the resolution of this apparent contradiction lies in a *calculus of growth*,
constituted of three variables. The formula for growth must take into
account awareness, the journey within, and the journey without. It
must set awareness at a critical level as a necessary but not sufficient
condition, necessary in order for the inner and outer journeys to be
assimilated, but not sufficient by itself because of its always having
to be an awareness of something. Becoming aware, as process,
requires a focus, a content. The content, then, is also a necessary but
not sufficient condition for growth to be realized. But, if the focus of
awareness is the external world, there must be resonance of such
awareness internally, the interior must be engaged. Some experiences
in the outside world are more likely to lead to growth because they
are more inviting of internal resonance, and one factor pertaining to
the intensity of invitation is novelty. Novelty may be from newness
of an event per se, or it may be from the complexity of the event, or
of a depth within simplicity, allowing for repetition without rou-
tinizing. (Of course, strictly speaking, no event can ever be repeated
exactly, for if nothing else, the fact that one has experienced the event
once means that on the second encounter of that event one is
approaching it having a history with it!) For example, practicing
Aikido is complex, and practicing an emptying meditation is simple,
but allowing of depth.

It may be interesting to consider personal growth as taking place,

in a sense, through a *personal dialectic*. That is to say, the self-as-con-
stituted-now (thesis) encounters the non-self, or that which is not
encompassed by the self (antithesis), choosing to assimilate the
latter (synthesis). The self-as-constituted-before [the encounter], by
virtue of the synthesis with the non-self, has become the new self-
as-constituted-now.

Erving and Miriam Polster (1973) offered a perspective that is
compatible with this idea of a personal dialectic. In their view, each
person has an "I-boundary," a boundary of what is permitted con-
tactfulness. This "defines those actions, ideas, people, values, settings,
images, memories ... in which he is willing and comparatively free
to engage fully with both the world outside himself and the rever-
berations within himself that this engagement may awaken" (p. 108).
Astutely, they noted that most people, out of a wish to be able to predict the results of their actions, do not easily risk trying new behaviors. And, they added, it is in this realm of new behavior that the
greatest opportunities exist. *Within* the I-boundary, contact is relatively easy and carried out gracefully. The risk is greater *at* the I-
boundary, and *outside* the I-boundary contact becomes very difficult.
Growth is defined, thereby, as expansion of the I-boundary, as a larger
definition of permissible experience.

If, as most theorists in humanistic psychology agree, the motivation to personal growth is innate, and if experience is an element
in the formula for growth, then it follows that the longing for experience is a natural part of all of us. Claudio Naranjo (1980), in writing about this thirst for experience, added what I believe to be a
crucial refinement. Noting that often the need for depth is replaced
by a craving for more, he suggested that if one is frustrated in the
intuitive seeking of depth or fullness of awareness, one may, as a substitute, seek environmental stimulation. Such "arousal-from-with-
out" is a form of environmental support, a seeking of stimulation
from the outside world by one who has become desensitized. In
keeping with his interpretation of the Gestalt approach, Naranjo
looks to sensitization, to "arousal-from-within" as of greater value.
The less aware one is, the more intense the environmental stimulation must be in order to give respite from that longing for depth of
experience. Naranjo pointed out the vicious cycle of more and more
intensity — hotter spices, riskier sports, more intense competition,
greater tragedies on the screen. They miss the point and the cycle

is self-perpetuating, until such time as the desensitized person is re-sensitized through exquisite awareness.

Let us distinguish among *depth of experience, breadth of experience,* and *intensity of experience.* Depth of experience is largely a function of awareness, and requires an openness to experience, a certain permeability of the self, or of the I-boundary. Breadth of experience refers to how widely one has experienced the inner and outer worlds. The greater the breadth of experience, the greater is the potential for personal growth. Being exquisitely aware and seeking wide exposure both reflect self-support. In contrast, intensity of experience, as used here, reflects a reliance on environmental support, and refers to a craving for increasing levels of stimulation.

And so, to reiterate:

> *Personal growth takes place through experience under conditions of heightened awareness.*

And, to expand this:

> *Experience may be of the inner world, or it may be of the outer world, but only if the latter activates a resonant experience within does it hold potential for growth. Thus, a geographical journey, if it is to usher in growth, must be accompanied by and potentiated by a corresponding introspective journey.*

If inspiration is sought for choosing the journey, and if one will not take offense at the gendered personification, surely the inspiration will be found in the words of Tom Robbins (1985):

> Upon those travelers who make their way without maps or guides, there breaks a wave of exhilaration with each unexpected change of plans. This exhilaration is not a whore who can be bought with money nor a neighborhood beauty who may be wooed. She ... is a wild and sea-eyed undine, the darling daughter of adventure, the sister of risk, and it is for her rare and always ephemeral embrace, the temporary pressure she exerts on the membrane of ecstasy, that many men leave home [p. 34].

In reading this, I am reminded of something that Carl Jung (1963) wrote in his autobiography concerning passion:

A man who has not passed through the inferno of his passions has never overcome them.... Whenever we give up, leave behind, and forget too much, there is always the danger that the things we have neglected will return with added force [p. 277].

So, here again, is the idea that in one's journey of growth, one should leave no corners unilluminated, no stones unturned, no lives unlived.

Now, let us continue to explore awareness. Having established, and reiterated, the pre-eminent position of awareness in the calculus of personal growth, it seems important to me to consider how one heightens awareness. What does one do to increase awareness? Immediately, in approaching this question, a fascinating paradox emerges. What one does is nothing, for awareness is enhanced not so much by doing as by non-doing. *Exquisite awareness ensues when one stops doing the things that cloud awareness.* Awareness is enhanced when one stops stopping it! Awareness is embedded in the orienting reflex, the latter being, of course, innate. We are born with an orienting reflex, and awareness is born of that reflex.

If increasing awareness is a matter of non-doing, then what are the things that one does that interfere with sharp and crisp awareness? Awareness may be clouded by several tactics used singly or in synergistic combination. The two subsets of *clouded awareness* that I have suggested are *confused awareness* and *dulled awareness* (Smith, 1985, 1987). Awareness may be *confused* through *introjection, projection,* or *confluence*:

In the case of introjection, I believe something is mine when it really is yours. That is, I have taken in your idea, value, belief, moral guideline, whatever, and act on it without having examined it thoroughly and decided if I really wanted to incorporate it.... Projection is the opposite process in that I attribute something (idea, belief, value, feeling ...) to you when it really is mine. Confluence involves a blurring of the ego boundary so that I do not differentiate "you" and "me," and recognize only "us" [1985, p. 39].

The issue in confused awareness is one of agency. It is a question of who is responsible for the idea, the value, the belief, the perspective.

Awareness may be *dulled* by means of *deflection* or by means of *desensitization.*

> Deflection is a maneuver for turning aside from direct contact
> with another person ... by circumlocution, by excessive
> language, by laughing off what one says, by not looking at the
> person one is talking to, by being abstract rather than specific,
> by not getting the point, by coming up with bad examples or
> none at all, by politeness instead of directness, by stereotyped
> language instead of original language, by substituting mild
> emotions for intense ones, by talking *about* rather than
> talking to, and by shrugging off the importance of what one
> has just said [Polster & Polster, 1973, p. 89].

I wish to add that deflection is not limited to contact with people;
one may deflect with anything by turning away from direct contact.

Desensitization refers to any dulling of awareness by means of
decreasing the acuity of a sensory modality. This can be effected by
removing corrective lenses, removing a hearing aid, smoking, fatigue
born of neglect of needed sleep, by surfeit of alcohol, drugs or food,
or by the very use of certain chemical substances.

In the Gestalt therapy literature, these methods of clouding
awareness are sometimes referred to as *contact boundary disturbances*.
Although introjection and projection are part of the psychoanalytic
lexicon, they refer, there, to defense mechanisms of the ego. The
nuance of difference in denotation is important, for these two, along
with confluence, deflection, and desensitization, are importantly recognized in the Gestalt approach as methods that have the effect of
decreasing the degree of contact between the person employing them
and her or his environment. Used individually or in synergistic combinations, they cloud awareness, creating a diminished exposure to
the world. Regardless of the richness of the world that one is exposed
to, the potential growth in personhood that could be experienced is
but a shadow when filtered through the haze of clouded awareness.
When one releases attachment to these methods, awareness can be
exquisite, with contact more vivid and lively, and the journey to personhood more yielding of richness.

Earlier in the present chapter, I indicated that by *personhood* I
refer to *depth and richness of unique being*. In addition to all that I
have already discussed, something more is needed in order to flesh
out an understanding of this definition. It is perhaps the most elusive and subtle quality of all. To quote Friedrich Nietzsche, "*One
thing is needful*. 'Giving style' to one's character — a great and rare

art!" (1982a, p. 98). To give style to one's person, or, as Nietzsche wrote, one's character, one must recognize all of one's strengths and weaknesses, and then "comprehend them in an artistic plan until everything appears as art and reason and even weakness delights the eye" (p. 98). With words that invoke the image of a sculptor or a painter, he described the process as follows:

> Here a large mass of second nature has been added; there
> a piece of original nature has been removed: both by long
> practice and daily labor. Here the ugly which could not be
> removed is hidden; there it has been reinterpreted and made
> sublime [p. 99].

Note that not only did Nietzsche use the metaphor of art to describe the process of creation of personhood; this we have encountered earlier in his exploration of authenticity. But, in addition, with the phrases "appears as art," and "delights the eye," he invoked an esthetic criterion for personhood. He continued his discussion, writing that it is needful that each person realize self-satisfaction, by whatever poetry and art that appeal to him or her.

Sheldon Kopp (1971) identified, in passing, one of the personal attributes that may appear as art and that qualifies as a delight to the eye. Identifying the psychotherapist as today's guru, he characterized the guru as having "grace of manner, powerful personal presence, a spirit of inner freedom, and an inspirationally creative imagination" (p. 10). The first of these is, of course, the one to which I allude. Kopp did not define "grace of manner" or offer any elaboration. My own understanding of grace of manner is as gracefulness. Being graceful has to do with intensity and with timing. It means acting with an intensity of emotion and action that is appropriate to the situation. And, it means action, be it proactive or reactive, that is manifested at an appropriate moment. Gracefulness is, then, acting in a manner that is not too much, not too little, and is not too soon, not too late. The person of the therapist, as an artistic creation, may be viewed along a dimension of gracefulness, and it is this very dimension that may be the polish, the refinement that lends elegance to personhood.

The journey of personal growth, if chosen, may be long; for many it stretches through a lifetime. It may require considerable discipline, and certainly an honesty of encounter with the things met both internally and externally. What is gained is therefore at a cost.

And there is a paradox in this in that the richness and depth that accrue along the way are constituted of simple things. Ernest Hemingway (Hotchner, 1983), in wistful tone, wrote something that captures this well.

> There are some things which cannot be learned quickly, and time, which is all we have, must be paid heavily for their acquiring. They are the very simplest things, and because it takes a man's life to know them the little new that each man gets from life is very costly ... [no page].

Chapter 6

A Political Note

By way of completing the present expatiation of the person of the therapist, I think it appropriate to consider certain topics that, for lack of a better label, are political in nature. They are political in the broadest sense of the term. They are political in that they have to do with the governance of the psychotherapist — mainly governance from within, but influenced by governance from without. Let us turn, now, to those several topics.

Consider, first, the training of the psychotherapist. There is some consensus as to the academic content and practical experience that is needed, or at least useful, in the training of the psychotherapist, and so by virtue of a relatively standardized psychotherapy curriculum the training is defined. There is, of course, a degree of variation in the training offered by each of the several professions involved in such training—clinical psychology, clinical social work, counseling psychology, pastoral counseling, psychiatry, psychiatric nursing, and so forth. Each of these professions is, in a sense, a subculture and, as such, gives its own inflection to the relatively standardized psychotherapy curriculum, an inflection that is an expression of the home in which it was born and nurtured. Each subculture extends the curriculum that is strictly psychotherapy with courses that are peculiar to that subculture, thus creating a unique total curriculum. Clinical psychology is a subculture that has traditionally been nurtured in colleges of the liberal arts or arts and sciences. (The frequent

147

choice of a hospital setting for the mandatory internship allows for a degree of hybridization between liberal arts and medicine.) Although programs in professional psychology are proliferating at free-standing schools (non-university affiliated), for the most part they continue the culture of psychology as coming from the liberal arts and sciences. Psychotherapy as clinical social work has quite a different history, emanating from case work and a tradition of dedicated schools of social work. Counseling psychology was spawned in colleges of education with the educational system as backdrop for the work. The work itself embraces several arenas of counseling — academic, career, personal (psychotherapy). Religion, of course, is the context for pastoral counseling. Psychiatry and psychiatric nursing are of the medical subculture, each having a subculture even within that. So each — medical school, school of nursing, seminary, college of education, school of social work, college of liberal arts and sciences — adds its distinctive perspective, special emphasis, and peculiar language to the broader common perspective, emphasis, and language of the psychotherapy culture.

With these subcultural variations in mind, it is only appropriate to note, once again, that the efficacy of psychotherapy is not a function of the subculture from which the therapist came or with which the therapist identifies. These subcultures do become prominent, however, when one considers the politics of psychotherapy, insofar as each of them has established parenting organizations and licensure. With parenting organizations come the power of *ethical* sanctions; with licensure, the power of *legal* sanctions. Licensure is, of course, intimately related to curriculum. The granting of each license is contingent on the successful completion of the curriculum required by the particular parenting organization, that curriculum containing both elements common to all psychotherapy training and elements peculiar to the training deemed appropriate by the parenting organization. Thus the subcultures of psychotherapy enter the realm of politics. They constitute the governance of psychotherapy from without.

In addition to the respective inflections of psychotherapy training offered by the several subcultures, some variations occur among the academic departments within each of these professions. Each department, by virtue of the particular faculty that constitute it, has its own theoretical orientation or combination of orientations, its own focus in terms of populations of clients, and other marks of specialization. Post-degree institutes (institutes of Adlerian therapy, cognitive therapy, existential therapy, Gestalt therapy, Jungian analysis, psychoanalysis, and so forth) add further variation of training based on specific and specialized interests. But, in spite of all of these differences, there is a core of academic and technical knowledge that is held in common in psychotherapy training. So it is that psychotherapists, even from the different subcultures and from the various professional degree programs and post-degree institutes, can converse, for they have learned to speak the same basic language of psychotherapy. Even with all the diversity of training, there is a common core.

Continuing to look at this context of control of the enterprise of psychotherapy from without, I want to comment from my own observations on the recent evolution of professional psychotherapy. Having sat down with my first client in the middle of the 1960s, my perspective on professional psychotherapy is one that fast approaches forty years. Informed by these years of experience, and by the secondhand knowledge that has come from those psychotherapists to whom I have listened and whose writings I have read, I have discerned a pattern in the evolution of psychotherapy as a profession.

The most obvious change that I have seen in the profession is the tremendous proliferation of the numbers of psychotherapists. With this enlargement of numbers have come various nomothetic means of handling therapists. That is, there has developed an increasing reliance on general rules and principles and on routine procedures, as opposed to the idiographic means that are more respectful of individual circumstances and individuality itself. There has been a veritable explosion of credentials, boards for issuing these licenses and certificates of specialization, laws to govern practice, an ever-growing list of enforceable ethical standards and aspirational ethical principles, boards and committees for the interpretation of these ethics, and sometimes the issuing of sanctions against those deemed to have violated the code. With increased numbers of therapists have come, too, more organizations and more complexity within those organizations. The practice of psychotherapy has become increasingly controlled through rigid, formal measures, increasingly monitored by an officialdom. What all of this reflects is *relentless bureaucratization* of the practice of psychotherapy.

At the same time that the practice of psychotherapy has become increasingly bureaucratized, it has become increasingly business oriented. Evidence for this can easily be gleaned from the list of workshops and presentations offered at professional conventions over the years. Hardly a convention is held in the field now that does not offer multiple workshops on "how to generate more referrals"; "how to computerize your recordkeeping," "your billing," and "your reports," all in the interest of greater efficiency-cum-profit; "how to market your practice"; and "how to insure your future."

With increased bureaucratization and increased business orientation in the profession, it is not surprising to find that many psychotherapists have become more image conscious. This tendency toward an image of prestige and respectability is evidenced in many of the numerous newsletters published by the various professional organizations. Not long ago, comments on "how a psychotherapist should dress" graced the pages of a major psychotherapy newsletter!

Certainly, there are positive effects of the evolution that I have just sketched. I do, however, believe that *the increased emphasis on bureaucratizing the practice of psychotherapy, on making it a better business and creating an image of prestige and respectability for it, has distracted from the core of that profession — the development of the therapist and the practice of the art.* The many workshops, newsletter articles, and, dare I say, even journal articles on these appurtenances reflect a *de facto* de-emphasis on matters that are, I maintain, more fundamental and more important.

I suggest that there is a curvilinear relationship between commitment to personal development and competence in the art of psychotherapy on the one hand and commitment to the appurtenances on the other hand. A total lack of interest in the art, or an extremely high level of interest in the accouterments, of psychotherapy probably accompanies a lesser development of personhood and therapeutic skill. I believe that neither belonging to many organizations and serving on many committees, nor having an M.B.A., nor wearing a business suit with wing tips or high heels makes one a better therapist. Time and energy placed in the service of the former are time and energy that cannot be devoted to the latter. Beyond this simple pragmatic consideration, I suggest that the values that support efforts at bureaucratization, at making a better business of psychotherapy, and at creating a more prestigious and respectable image are anathema to the values of personal growth and psychotherapeutic wisdom. *The ethic of bureaucracy, the ethic of business, and the ethic of image management, compatible as they are one to the other, are antithetical to the ethic of personal development and the ethic of psychotherapy.*

In considering the threat posed to psychotherapy by the ethics of bureaucracy, business, and image management, consider the following. History informs us that in every society there has been a creative minority whose task was to lead and guide the other members of that society through the maze of life as it is experienced. This minority represented the most creatively extraordinary of the populace. Its members have been called shaman, priest, witch doctor, magician, sorcerer, brujo, Zaddik, Master, sage, oracle, prophet, magus, wizard, counselor, and recently, psychotherapist. In each case the helper, healer, guide arose to meet a need that was recognized by members of the society and existed as a marginal person in that society, empowered by an unconventional perspective. That unconventional perspective, sometimes called wisdom, is spontaneous and is given expression only through the person of that individual. But with each of the above named, the creative *personal*, unconventional perspective was apprenticed, emulated, copied and eventually institutionalized. In time, by being institutionalized, that perspective became stale and rigid. Diminished now as a creative guide to life, it had become conventional. Its life was sapped. (For the seed of these ideas, I credit Sheldon Kopp's work, *Guru* [1971]).

The lesson from history is clear. If one chooses to grease the slide toward a moribund state for psychotherapy, one need only be conventional. Wear the uniform of the businessman, support ever-increasing regulation and standardization of the art, and avoid thinking or doing anything out of the ordinary. All of the institutionalized expedients of the business ethic, the narrow definitions of *treatment of choice*, and all further attempts at standardization of the practice of psychotherapy are impediments to the person-centered, creative art that is psychotherapy. Freud was a radical, and look at what he started! So, too, it was with Jung, Reich, Horney, Laing, and Perls. Wild persons all, they refused to be tamed.

Before leaving this critique of the evolution of the profession of psychotherapy as I see it, I must claim my right to critique it. In the interest of prolepsis, should the reader assume that my view is jaundiced, I will simply state my credentials. I have been licensed in two states to practice psychology; am certified as a Diplomate by the American Board of Professional Psychology (ABPP); have been elected a Fellow of the American Psychological Association (through three divisions), a Fellow of the Academy of Clinical Psychology, a Fellow of my state psychological association; have served on a divisional board of the American Psychological Association; and have chaired a standing committee of the American Academy of Psychotherapists. For eighteen years, I conducted a full-time independent practice of psychotherapy in a major metropolitan area, with additional years of part-time practice in both urban and rural settings. This is to say that my critique is based on an inside perspective on the profession. Oh, and yes, I own a pair of wing-tip shoes and sometimes even wear a necktie.

Having presented my observations and critique of the changes that I have seen in the organization of the profession of psychotherapy, I would like now to turn attention to changes in the core of psychotherapy — theory and techniques. Many theoretical orientations have arisen, persisted, and then faded, as if the theories themselves were watched over in turn by Brahma, Vishnu, and Shiva, the respective Hindu gods of creation, preservation, and destruction. Some of them have enjoyed resurgence. In some cases the prefix *neo-* has acknowledged the second wave of interest, as in neo–Freudian and neo–Reichian. In other cases, a new name has accompanied the rebirth and reflected a specific refinement of the earlier position. An example of this is object relations theory, growing out of psychoanalysis. An interesting feature of this movement in time is a cycle of waxing and waning of interest in the theories. For some theories the time has been too short to discern any pattern. Some may have had their moment. For others, it was a season. And, for others, those that might be termed major theories, there has been a cycle of waxing and waning prominence.

The originators of each position offered a philosophy, a theory, and a procedure that was fresh, radical enough to be noticed, but not so radical as to be dismissed summarily. Each position, then, offered something more or less effective for a given context, a given time, place, and consciousness. But, with the passage of time, the freshness and creative radicalness is lost, as second- and third-generation practitioners increasingly institutionalize the system. As they popularize and, inevitably, dilute the original position, they tend to trivialize it and rob it of its liveliness. In time, if it still holds wisdom, and if that wisdom is recognized, it may be born again with the help of an energetic and creative midwife. Some aspect of that nascent wisdom is elaborated, restated in a terminology more current, brought to the fore, and once again there is a position that speaks for a time, a place, and an attendant level of consciousness.

Two graphic models have been used to understand evolution such as that described above. One is that of the pendulum, the other the circle. The pendulum model speaks to the trend, swinging from one extreme to the other. Often we see the move from liberal to moderate to conservative attitudes, then back to moderate and then to liberal attitudes again.

Using the physical analogy of the pendulum, one can predict that when the extreme of either liberalism or conservatism is reached, a move back towards the other extreme will soon commence.

The circle model is but another graphic analogy for repeatability. We can think of various theoretical and procedural issues of psychotherapy. It seems that we keep coming back to these issues. They are like points on the circumference of the circle: As we move around the circle, we return to the same points again and again. A variation on the circle model is that of the spiral. The opening of the circle in this manner allows a depiction of movement through time. Now, as we move around the cylindrical spiral, we return to the same points (as seen in the two-dimensional projection of the spiral, i.e., the circle), but at different points in time. So, as the saying goes, "what goes around, comes around," but it is never quite the same. It is the same issue, but at a new point in time, and with, therefore, the benefit of the wisdom gained in each other instance of addressing the issue. The same point is reached, but at a new level.

Fritjof Capra (1984) has shown that the circle phenomenon and the pendulum phenomenon can be related as follows: Turn the circle so that its edge is toward the observer and shine a light on it. A point moving around the circle will then project onto a screen as a point oscillating between two extremes, appearing as a swinging pendulum. I suggest the conversion of the circle into a spiral, thus acknowledging the evolving through time. The projection of that spiral now becomes a wave. This wave model, I believe, may be of use in describing and understanding the evolution of the theory and practice of psychotherapy. It combines the analogies of the circle and that of the pendulum, while also taking the dimension of time into account. It is, then, in a sense, a historical, dynamic model for the evolution of psychotherapy, its values, attitudes, theoretical interests, and procedural trends. It is a graphic resolution of the paradoxical relationship between the following two statements: "History repeats itself," and "Nothing stays the same." So it is that both statements are true, in the evolution of psychotherapy. The consistency of psychotherapy and the constant change of psychotherapy become understandable, by analogy, with the consideration of the spiral-projection wave model.

This concept of change, as expressed in the spiral-projection wave, is one that is found in the mystical traditions. Consider the following from the *Tao Te Ching* (Bynner translation, 1962).

> Life on its way returns into a mist,
> Its quickness is its quietness again [p. 51].

To the mystic, all developments of the world, both the physical world and the social world, proceed in cyclic patterns. The world is one of continuous flow and change. And, as so well expressed by the Taoists, all change arises as a manifestation of the dynamic interplay of polar opposites. Thus, in speaking of the Tao,

> Being great, it flows.
> It flows far away.
> Having gone far, it returns
>   [Feng & English translation, 1972,
>   chapter 25, no page number].

This describes the swing of the pendulum, the turn of the circle. It is the spiral-projection wave form. And, in chapter forty of the *Tao Te Ching* (1972),

> Returning is the motion of the Tao.
> Yielding is the way of the Tao.
> The ten thousand things are born of being.
> Being is born of not being [no page number].

Perhaps we can better understand where psychotherapy has been and where it is going by seeing it as a dynamic interplay of opposites—opposites of attitude, value, theory, technique. Yielding and returning. The ten thousand things of psychotherapy.

It seems, then, that there is *control of psychotherapy imposed from without,* control by an establishment that has become highly bureaucratic, has adopted a large measure of business orientation, and has come to be quite concerned with image. Each psychotherapist has the choice of the degree to which he or she wants to conform to this triumvirate. Herein, in this choice, dwells at least in part the essence of *the control of the activity of psychotherapy from within.* But with the above consideration of *the swing of the pendulum* and *the turn of the spiral,* the distinction between control of the practice of psychotherapy from without and control of the same from within tends to blur. If the mystics are correct, the underlying pattern that is reflected in these two graphic metaphors is a configuration that is prescribed by nature. Insofar as we psychotherapists are part of nature, then we, on one level, make this configuration manifest, while, on another level, we choose our degree of participation in this configuration as it is manifest. Considering, then, both the agents of control (persons considered collectively as a professional organization, and persons considered as individuals) and the areas of control (professionalism, and core theory and technique) we can see a complex polity. The governance of psychotherapy is from without and from within, and touches both the art itself and the professional form that this art assumes.

At this point I wish to explore a further aspect of the control of the practice of psychotherapy from within. This aspect concerns the depth and pattern of self-selected training that the therapist undertakes throughout her or his career. I approach this from the perspective of stages of the therapeutic craft.

Allow me to explain the background of the discussion that will follow. Some time ago, I sat with dozen or so other members of the American Academy of Psychotherapists in a small room in an out-of-the-way hotel a few miles north of Ensenada, in Mexico. A couple of doors down the walkway, Steve Mc Queen had spent some of his last days, seeking assistance from a drug not legally available in his homeland. We talked about him, and, as we became more and more comfortable with each other, we began to be more disclosing of ourselves. Our self-disclosures soon came to focus on how we came to be psychotherapists. Two trends became apparent as we conversed long into the night. The first was reflected in the number of us who were firstborn or only children. The second was reflected in the number of us who had at least one psychologically suffering parent. The pattern for many of us was to have taken a responsible and helping role early in life vis-à-vis a psychologically needy parent. Most of us had been placed in the role of helper, to help the troubled parent or parents. Later, I walked alone along the high cliffs overlooking the Pacific Ocean. I pondered the conversation of the evening as I walked in mist and dampness, in foreign, and yet familiar, land.

I am sure, for myself, and I believe it is true for most others who do not merely dabble in psychotherapy but give long-term devotion to its pursuit, that the first stage in the therapist's development is a *setting of the stage*. Being the only child, as was my case, or a first-born child, and having a parent looking to one for help, sets the stage for one to become a therapist. Childhood, then, is the unrecognized internship. Much longer and much more intense it is than the recognized internship to be formally entered into many years later. If not overwhelmed or burned out by the familial internship, the child has set the stage, waiting until, grown and formally trained, the adult child can step upon it to enact the role of psychotherapist. The residues and continuations of the familial internship often form the bulk of the budding therapist's personal therapy.

Following that evening at the hotel near Ensenada, and for several months, I thought about the stages of the adult therapist's growth in the craft of psychotherapy. The major question with which I wrestled was this: What are the steps gone through as one plays out the role for which the stage was long ago set? The steps emerged as *stages of the therapeutic craft*, my thinking guided in part by autobiographical whispers (Smith, 1988).

Indulge me as I reiterate what is by now obvious, but worthy of a reminder because of its immeasurable importance. The therapist's development includes both personal growth and technical growth. That is, the therapist grows both in fullness of personhood and in skills of therapeutic technique. So, the therapist's development is two-faceted. The relationship between these two facets is an interesting one. Techniques that are not brought to life through the deeply developed personhood of the therapist lack humanness and tend to be mechanical. Such a therapist is a therapeutic technician, performing certain practiced maneuvers from a set repertoire. At best, he or she is shallow and fades as the novelty of those gimmicks is lost through over-use. At worst, out of self-serving ends, such a therapist is manipulative. The therapist who is lacking in technical skills, on the other hand, tends not to be very potent. He or she may be a good human being, compassionate and understanding, even a deep person. Yet, without effective procedures through which to relate to a person in therapy, this therapist may have little to offer in the facilitation of the growth process of another. In a highly functioning therapist, of course, techniques flow out of her or his person in such a way that it is difficult to differentiate *who the person is* from *what the person does*. He or she knows *how to be* and *what to do* in the authentic enactment of the therapeutic role.

This integrated growth in personhood and in technical skill takes time, much time; years. The path to mastery requires decades to traverse. I have found the *classical learning curve* to be a useful model for describing and understanding this path to mastery. For readers whose roots do not include experimental psychology or educational psychology, a brief description of the nature of the learning curve will be helpful.

The classical learning curve is derived in approximate form by the data generated in a simple learning task such as those traditionally studied in experimental psychology (e.g., maze running, memorization of nonsense syllables, reaction times, motor coordination tasks, and discriminate learning). Conventionally plotted with number of trials or time spent in practice on the horizontal axis and number of correct performance units on the vertical axis, the curve shows negative acceleration with an asymptote. That is, the curve becomes less steep across trials or amount of time of practice (negative acceleration) and reaches a point after which the amount of practice required for an increment of improvement in performance becomes much greater than before (the asymptote). In the vernacular, this is "the point of diminishing returns." In actual practice, the learning curves generated in the laboratory are not smooth, but show the ups and downs of erratic performance. An actual learning curve looks more like a curved saw blade, teeth pointing up. Oftentimes these cycles of progression and regression in learning tasks are the result of factors extraneous to the learning task *per se* (e.g., an environmental distraction, anxiety, loss of sleep, preoccupation with something else), so the curve is mathematically smoothed by averaging adjacent peaks and valleys.

Now, to relate this model to the growth and development of the therapist, picture a horizontal axis representing time and a vertical axis representing level of performance. Imagine a growth curve as described above, reflecting the improvement of performance over time. On the curve imagine five points, designated 0, 1, 2, 3, and 4, as I define their positions and the meaning of the areas of the curve between each pair of consecutive numbers.

The point where the vertical and horizontal axes meet, designated 0, represents a beginning point of professional investment, no time yet invested and no professional development in evidence.

The area under the curve from point 0 to point 1 represents the stage of the *neophyte therapist*. The curve is very steep here, which means that there is a rapid rate of growth during this stage. Beginning at a zero point, the neophyte enjoys a large return of learning for the time invested. This rapid rate of growth is usually exhilarating, lending the novice a strong sense of accomplishment. What is most likely learned during this stage are the essentials of a therapy system: basic vocabulary, basic concepts, and basic therapeutic procedures. Much of this learning of the basics is more through introjection than through assimilation. In other words, it is as if this new material were swallowed more or less whole, rather than having been chewed thoroughly and digested. Therefore, the new material is within the neophyte therapist, but it is not a part of her or him. It has not been assimilated, mentally speaking. The telltale indications of this introjection are that the therapist is prone to confusion (mental indigestion), and to rote behaviors copied from reading or imitated from mentors (mental regurgitation). Having introjected this material, the neophyte often either lacks confidence or has a false sense of confidence. The danger at this stage of development is that the novice does not know how much he or she does not know.

The second stage, that of the *journeyman therapist*, is represented by the area under the learning curve between points 1 and 2. Here the curve continues to be steep, although not as steep as it is in the neophyte stage. This reflects the fact that learning continues to be fairly rapid. The journeyman stage is the stage of the therapist's development in which the basics of the system, introjected during the neophyte stage, are ruminated on and thus made assimilable. By re-experiencing the basic vocabulary, concepts, and techniques again and again, and contemplating their meaning, they get assimilated.

They become part of the substance of the therapist. Having assimilated the basics, the journeyman therapist is afforded a certain clarity. The danger for the journeyman therapist is that the clarity thus gained may give rise to an illusion of expertise. At this stage of development the therapist has enough experience to have some genuine understanding of the therapy process, but not enough experience to have a seasoned perspective. The journeyman therapist has seen the basic elements, the usual manifestations of her or his therapy craft, but not yet those rare elements, those more unusual manifestations of the system.

Most therapists, I have come to believe, do not develop beyond the journeyman stage. Many do not even reach the journeyman stage, but spend their professional careers at the stage of the neophyte. This is the case of the *dilettante therapist*. Moving from one therapy system to another, without ever investing enough time in any one system to reach the stage of journeyman, the dilettante therapist is full of unassimilated material from many sources. Remember that the type of learning that characterizes the neophyte stage is introjection, and the content is limited to the basic features of the system. So the dilettante knows, in the sense of introjection, the basics of several systems, but lacks the genuine understanding that is afforded in the journeyman stage. In order for integration of material from different systems to be possible, the material from each individual system must first be assimilated, truly understood. Only then can the elements be connected in a manner that yields something new in the blend. By analogy, certain chemical elements may join to form compounds, while other combinations of elements, not having valence or affinity for each other, remain only mixtures. A neophyte chemist can mix chemicals together, but a journeyman chemist, one who understands valence (oxidation states), can create compounds.

The dilettante therapist is the product of a rampant and indiscriminate eclecticism. He or she chooses breadth of exposure over depth of exposure. There are, I believe, two factors that illuminate this choice and make it understandable. The first factor involves the dynamic of introjection. Remember, with introjection it is as if one swallowed material whole, not really getting one's teeth into that material. Without benefit of mastication, the material cannot be assimilated, cannot be made part of one. Not only does this result in mental indigestion, as discussed above, but it leaves an unmet hunger.

Impatient, the introjector does not get filled, then, in any satisfying and lasting way. So the dilettante therapist, rather than ruminating, in the best sense of the word, keeps moving on to new material in response to her or his hunger, only to introject again. And, continuing with the metaphor of mental food, the material of greatest substance requires the most chewing. It is the pap and the flummery that are easily taken in, as they demand little or no chewing. Therefore, the dilettante therapist is often attracted to oversimplifications and superficialities.

The second factor that makes dilettantism understandable is found in the nature of the learning curve that we have been using as our model. As we saw, the learning curve is steepest at the beginning. Learning is at a faster pace and is more exciting during this phase of the curve than at any other. Perhaps this is part of the reason that youth is such an exciting time of life; there is a continual beginning of new growth curves. Each facet of life presents another start on a course of growth and learning. The dilettante therapist seems to abandon the further pursuit of a therapy system when the excitement of the steep initial phase of the learning curve begins to wane. He or she then moves on to start learning another system, to feel once again the excitement of a beginning. So, out of a chronic hunger to know, coupled with a fondness for the excitement of beginnings, the dilettante therapist moves lambently from system to system, a candidate for the next therapy fad.

There is a Hindu story that trenchantly captures, by way of metaphor, this issue of uncritical eclecticism. Retold from the Kerala regional legends by D. K. M. Kartha (2001), it is a story about an unusual family in which the father was a very high caste Brahmana, the mother was a Pariah of very low social status, and their twelve children each belonged to a different caste. One day, the son Perumthachan, a master carpenter, went to visit his brother Agnihotri. The latter was of a priestly caste even higher than that of their father. When Perumthachan arrived at his brother's house, he waited in the courtyard, as was demanded by custom. A servant told him that Agnihotri was worshiping Ganesha in the family shrine. While he waited for his priest-brother, Perumthachan dug a hole in the courtyard. Time passed. The servant returned and said that Agnihotri was now worshiping Shiva. So Perumthachan dug another hole. Time passed. When the servant returned, he told Perumthachan that

Agnihotri was worshiping the Mother Goddess. Perumthachan dug a third hole. These events were repeated as Agnihotri continued his worship — Vishnu as Lion-man, Rama, and Krishna. Then came regional gods, then the Sun, Moon, and Planets, followed by snake deities, rivers, and mountains. Still worshiping, Agnihotri addressed the souls of sages and ancestors and more. During all of this considerable time, Perumthachan continued to dig holes.

When, finally, Agnihotri completed his worship and approached his brother in the courtyard, he found a host of holes. He asked, of course, why Perumthachan had dug these. Perumthachan answered that he had been digging for water. Astonished, Agnihotri exclaimed that if his brother had dug only one hole, had concentrated his efforts on one hole, surely he would have hit water by now. What he had done was foolish. Perumthachan replied, "Yes, it is very foolish. But it is no more foolish than worshiping hundreds of gods instead of worshiping just one with intense devotion" (p. 85). And with that, the two brothers laughed, a laugh that shook the house.

Entertained and enlightened by the Hindu story, let us return to the developing psychotherapist. Other therapists, somewhat more patient with rumination than is the dilettante, but still preferring breadth of perspective to profound depth of perspective, reach the journeyman level before moving on to learn another therapy system. Thereby, the *generalist therapist* is born. The generalist is a journeyman therapist several times over. Whereas the dilettante is eclectic in a superficial sense, the generalist is eclectic with a true understanding, developed through rumination and assimilation. As a journeyman, he or she is less likely to combine incompatible elements of different therapy systems into mere mixtures. Recognizing, and therefore not struggling with, those elements that are immiscible, the generalist may actually make some creative and workable compounds.

Those therapists who crave great depth of understanding of a therapy system continue their development into that stage which is represented by the area under the learning curve between points 2 and 3. I am labeling such a person an *expert therapist*. The slope of the curve is less steep now, a reflection of the fact that further growth for the expert therapist is much slower than it was for her or him at the journeyman stage. Much time and practice are required for experiencing the less common events of the craft. This is the stage of advanced growth, the growth into expertise. With the attainment of such expertise, the therapist has much to offer as a teacher or mentor of neophyte and journeyman therapists. The temptation for the expert therapist is to become arrogant. Sometimes the expert therapist, out of the experience of her or his very real power and understanding, may become haughty. This temptation can be offset by self-discipline, which may then provide passage to the last stage of growth.

The point on the learning curve designated by the 3 is the asymptote. Beyond this point, growth is very slow, with much time and experience being required for the realization of further increments of growth in the craft. The therapist may never stop growing, but the yield from additional experience from this point on is preciously small. During this stage it is the truly esoteric elements of the therapy system that are learned. I have named this stage, from point 3 to point 4, the stage of the *master therapist*. The master therapist is stopped from further growth as a therapist only by her or his death (point 4). It is these master therapists who sometimes are known for developing therapy systems. It is they who are the true luminaries of the craft of psychotherapy.

The growth curve can represent the entire lifetime of the master therapist. For others, there may be two or three or separate growth curves, each ending somewhere short of the master stage, the expert stage, or, as we have seen in the case of the dilettante, even the journeyman stage. If the master therapists develop the systems of psychotherapy and train the trainers, and the expert therapists train the journeyman therapists, it is the journeyman therapists who deliver most of the good psychotherapy to non-therapist clients. But keep in mind that the neophyte stage is a necessary, even desirable one. At this stage, the tyro therapist may wish to be exposed to several therapy systems, sampling and introjecting the rudiments of each system until he or she recognizes a personal fit. Recognizing a fit means recognizing a system that is ego-syntonic. That system may then be learned to a journeyman level, or perhaps even beyond. The problem, as I have suggested, arises if the neophyte therapist remains a perpetual novice by moving too quickly from one system to the next, without ever investing in the hard rumination that is necessary if one is to assimilate the material and thereby enter the realm of the journeyman.

These, then, are the stages as I see them —*neophyte, journey-man, expert,* and *master.* An eclectic therapist may be a neophyte many times over, and thus a *dilettante,* or a journeyman several times over, and thus a *generalist.* By virtue of the time required, it is very rare for an eclectic therapist to be an expert in more than one system, and almost by definition, there are no eclectic masters. Of course, it is possible to be an expert or even a master in a system and to have neophyte or even journeyman knowledge in another. (The evaluations that experts and masters sometimes offer of other systems bespeak their neophyte status relative to those other systems. Their remarks may lack the depth of understanding that character-izes assimilated material, and evidence, instead, an introjected cor-pus of basics.)

The model that I have presented, even in its simplification of such a complex topic, seems to me to be of interest and of use. In the same vein of simplification, but in the medium of poetry, Delacroix wrote the following (Smith, 1988, p. 55):

> To be a poet at twenty
>   is to be twenty.
> But to be a poet at forty
>   is to be a poet.

And, as I have paraphrased this,

> To be a therapist at thirty
>   is to be an imitator of technique.
> But to be a therapist at fifty
>   is to be a therapist [p. 55].

Although not necessarily tied to any particular stage of devel-opment in the therapeutic craft, there is a pitfall which any thera-pist may encounter, more commonly therapists in their earlier stages of development. For want of a label, I have referred to it as the "psy-chotherapist's disease" and have defined it in terms of its outstand-ing feature, the "pathologization of life" (Smith, 1995). The symptom is that of viewing life through a filter of psychopathology. How does this "disease" come about? I find a morality poem, taken from Alexander Pope's *An Essay on Man II,* to point in the direction of an answer.

Vice is a monster of so frightful mien
As to be hated needs but to be seen;
Yet seen too oft, familiar with her face,
We first endure, then pity, then embrace
[Ward edition, 1930, p. 206].

As I ponder this quatrain, the levels of meaning continue to unfold for me. To paraphrase the poem, psychopathology, when first clearly seen, is recognized as something wrong. But with continued exposure the psychotherapist may move through stages of accepting and tolerating psychopathology, to feeling sorry for it, to enjoying its presence, even. It may come to be embraced, taken to one's bosom. This succession surely deserves closer examination.

At the beginning, *craziness* is looked upon as strange, as alien. Depending on how extreme its nature and how florid its manifestation, it is seen as something negative. Here I am referring not to the benign *madness* of the free spirit or the creatively eccentric, but craziness in its early meaning. The archaic meaning of to *craze* was to break, to shatter, weaken, and destroy, as pertaining to health. Such dementia, when seen, alarms and strongly bids one to take careful notice.

But, with further exposure, the alarm may be muted. Quieted, no longer demanding careful notice, craziness may be accepted. One grows more comfortable in its presence. As the behavior therapists have demonstrated, continued exposure can lead to desensitization.

Following a period of comfort may come pity. Not to be confused with pity for the person afflicted with craziness, this is a pity with mercy toward the pathological phenomenon itself. At this point one would enter into a ruthful relationship with the craziness.

With continued and deepened familiarity, one may actually come to enjoy the presence of craziness. Having lost at this point its "frightful mien," no longer having a face that brings alarm and no longer even a call for sympathy or compassion, craziness may be embraced.

One of the dangers attendant on this change of perspective on psychopathology is the loss of recognition of the seriousness and awfulness of it. I am reminded of a passage in Nietzsche's *Twilight of the Idols* in which he warns of the danger of a "morality of sympathy," or a "morality of pity." The danger is in the lack of recognition of the extremes. In his words, "The strength to withstand tension, the width of the tensions between extremes, becomes even smaller today; finally, the extremes themselves become blurred to the point of similarity" (*The Portable Nietzsche*, 1982, p. 540). Without venturing into his complex line of reasoning or the evidence that he offered, let us hold his conclusion in mind. That is, sympathy or pity may reduce the perceived distance between extremes. In the case of psychopathology, the pity for it that may well follow from a certain degree of familiarity may lead one to look upon it as being closer to psychic health than is wise or is useful.

This phenomenon, just discussed, is captured in what might be called the first axiom of interpersonal medical dynamics. Simply stated, a physician is less afraid of treating a patient than the patient is of being treated. So obvious that it seems almost a truism, this axiom can be dismissed easily, and its importance trivialized. Taking surgery as a prime example, the surgeon, exposed over and over to a procedure, may come to regard it lightly compared to the gravity with which the surgical intervention is appraised by the patient. This is to say, the thing that was once regarded by the surgeon to be of "frightful mien" has come readily to be embraced, if not minimized, and perhaps even trivialized. I suggest that there is a parallel in psychotherapy. The psychotherapist is less afraid of doing psychotherapy than the person in therapy is of receiving it. Desensitized to the frightening aspects of psychotherapy through her or his extensive exposure, *a therapist may forget or overlook how threatening psychotherapy can be to the person in therapy. It is likewise the case for the psychopathology that has brought the person to therapy.*

As one becomes increasingly conversant with psychopathology, it may assume a more and more prominent place in one's thinking. Consider this. Perception is now recognized as an active and selective process in which a person organizes and interprets sensory data according to certain internal structures, at least some of which are learned. Thus, when the vocabulary and concepts of psychopathology have been learned, they can become an internal structure for organizing and interpreting one's experience. Psychopathology, then, can act as an overlay, a filter through which the world is viewed.

Ideally, the template of pathology is chosen when it is useful, when it helps to clarify understanding. A problem is created, however, when this filter of psychopathology is misused or overused. When psychopathology is well understood, there is no problem. But clear understanding of such complex material requires considerable mental work. It demands mental mastication and assimilation. It requires that one see and hear clearly, then ruminate on the material as long as necessary until it can be digested mentally and thus made part of one. Otherwise, unchewed or under chewed, the material will remain mentally indigestible. Such undigested material, swallowed whole or nearly so, if you will, is introjected and results in mental indigestion. The most dramatic symptom of mental indigestion is a regurgitation of the undigested material. Not being assimilated into oneself, it is vomited, thrown up, projected outward, as in the recitation of a poem learned by memorization without benefit of understanding. Not assimilated into the system as a whole, such material, introjected as it is, remains too prominent. It remains outside the larger context of that which has been assimilated into the person.

An introjected language and concept of psychopathology can be problematic in two ways. First, one can pathologize by externalizing a template of psychopathology, using this filter rigidly, even when it does not serve to clarify or when it is irrelevant. The opposite of looking at the world through rose-colored glasses, this is a case of viewing the world through glass stained with the pathological. Secondly, one can pathologize by being so sensitive to signs of pathology when it indeed exists that one magnifies the slightest hint into the dominant feature. This latter form of pathologization can be seen as an error of overinterpretation.

This psychotherapist's disease is fostered, I believe, as, in the course of continued and extensive exposure to psychopathology, one relies more and more heavily on this familiar and comfortable framework rather than developing a larger integrated framework. Equipped with the vocabulary and the concepts, the psychotherapist has a filter through which to pass information and a sensitization to the symptoms of psychopathology. If, however, he or she has not assimilated the essence-in-context, this material may function as a rigidly applied diagnostic framework evoked by minimal hints of psychopathology or by an inconsequential simulacrum.

To summarize, *pathologization of life takes place when the template of psychopathology is introjected rather than integrated into a larger conceptual-perceptual context and is then projected either as a rigid interpretive filter or as a hypersensitivity that leads to over-inter-*

preting the data. In the first case, psychopathology is seen where it does not exist; in the other, it may be seen in exaggerated form where it does exist.

What I have labeled as psychotherapist's disease has certainly been recognized elsewhere. I remember hearing in graduate school that Walter Klopfer, one of the pioneers of the Rorschach test, warned against having a "maladjustment bias" when analyzing test materials. I heard, too, that Timothy Leary, during that part of his career in which he was engaged in psychological assessment, cautioned against an overinterpretation of psychopathology, labeling this the "pathology error." Even earlier, in an abnormal psychology class, I heard of something called "medical student's disease." Medical student's disease refers to the not infrequent tendency of the novice medical student to diagnose in herself or himself each new disease studied. The difference is that in the case of medical student's disease the act is one of self-pathologizing, whereas in the case of psychotherapist's disease the act of pathologizing is other-directed.

Allow me to offer an anecdote, one that I believe would be instructive at this point. Some time ago, I chanced upon an acquaintance at a professional meeting. After we had exchanged greetings and caught up on the circumstances of our families, she inquired as to which workshops and events I had attended or planned to attend. I replied that the main thing that I wanted to do was to participate in a Native-American sweat lodge ceremony. Reacting quickly, she pronounced, "You're really getting addicted to those!" I was shocked at her words. The fact was that this would be only my second sweat lodge, my first having been two years earlier. (She knew that I had attended the earlier one.) She interpreted my behavior in a framework of pathology, specifically as an addiction.

The maladjustment bias can be identified whenever natural or adaptive behavior is conceptualized or labeled in pathological terms. The possibilities are myriad. Sadness (as experienced in the grieving of a loss) may be labeled "depression," and attention to detail (as in accurate measurement or recordkeeping) may be diagnosed "obsessive-compulsive." The energetic, extroverted child who protests being confined to a hard chair and solitary tasks for hours may be called "hyperactive," and the introverted child diagnosed "avoidant" or even "schizoid." A ravenous hunger may be labeled "bulimia," and any loss of appetite "anorexia nervosa." A lack of gullibility (as in skepticism about public statements made by politicians, especially during election campaigns) may be seen as "paranoia." Energetic exuberance may be called "mania," and any variation in mood "bipolar disorder." Excitement may be diagnosed as "anxiety," and discomfort with certain objects or circumstances may be labeled "phobia." Every pain can evoke a label of "psychogenic," or be taken as evidence of a "somatization disorder." And, if one is concerned about the pain, "hypochondriasis" may be suspected; if one is not concerned about the pain, suspicion may be raised of "denial" or "la belle indifference." Difficulty with a new living or working situation may be diagnosed as an "adjustment disorder," and many variations of personality can raise suspicion of a "personality disorder." If not already so, to continue the list would surely be tedious.

The maladjustment bias can be recognized sometimes by the gross use of a label, that is to say, by the use of a label in such a manner that it fails to respect degrees and to differentiate the common and ordinary from the problematic. Frequent examples of such use attend the terms "co-dependent," "survivor," "addiction," and "abuse." So, it may be that the aiding of a spouse who is sick or otherwise in need of support is labeled co-dependent behavior. One who has a history of distress or difficult circumstances is termed a survivor. Anything that someone does with regularity, be it something of negative, positive, or neutral impact on that person, is called an addiction. And, finally, any act of impoliteness, rudeness, or harshness comes to be called abuse. With such a degree of over-inclusiveness, the utility of these terms is lost. They become meaningless when they are applied so generally that they fail to differentiate between common behavior and experience, on the one hand, and that which is truly a pathological problem, on the other hand. Worse than this, they may be seriously misleading, introducing error and confusion where accuracy and clarity are sorely needed. The gross application of the label may create, in fact, its own iatrogenic problem. Diagnosed with one of these labels by an expert, one could surely find evidence in one's history to support the diagnosis, and thus arrive at a false and misleading self-understanding.

As is apparent from the above discussion, the pathology error has a trivializing effect. When the differentiation between pathology and non-pathology is obscured, the referent words and concepts become vapid. This problem may be understood with greater depth through the application of theory offered by Fritz Perls, based on that of Kurt Goldstein (Smith, 1997). Goldstein viewed behavior along a dimension from concrete to abstract. Concrete behavior is a direct, automatic reaction to the situation that one perceives; thus it is rigid. In contrast, abstract behavior is flexible. It involves thinking about what one perceives—what does it mean, what are its conceptual properties, what is its relation to other conceptual patterns—and acting on the conclusions of one's thinking. When one does not abstract and classify, one limits one's orientation and action, a phenomenon that Goldstein termed a "loss of categorical thinking." Building upon this theory, Perls placed great importance on care in speaking. He emphasized the value of using words that express the precise meaning that one wants to convey. In order to avoid what he termed a "frigidity of the palate," he encouraged the learning of the value of each word, an appreciation of the power hidden in the logos. We could, then, conceive of the pathology error as a case of frigidity of the palate, as a limitation of one's orientation and action through rigid, concrete thinking.

As the articulation of a Third Force, humanistic psychology has been an explicit attempt to avoid the maladjustment bias. Born out of dissatisfaction with the limitations of the pathological emphasis of psychoanalysis and the mechanistic, atomistic model of behaviorism (the first and second forces), humanistic psychology has sought to affirm an additional dimension of psychology (Krippner, 1991). Appreciative of the extensive vocabulary and syntax of psychopathology that was created by the psychoanalytic movement, humanistic psychology has primarily focused instead on the development of language and concepts that describe and facilitate an understanding of creativity, self-actualization, intentionality, natural experience, and spirituality. The model that it offers is one of growth rather than one of pathology.

Being fluent in the Third Force, humanistic psychology, as well as in the other two forces in psychology, allows for a broad perspective. It is a way of maintaining a larger context and therefore not succumbing so easily to the limitations of an overly prominent or rigid template of psychopathology. Having several conceptual filters and the flexibility to shift among them as each seems the most appropriate for a given situation is a corrective for the introjection and subsequent projection of the filter of psychopathology.

Thus, gazing too long through a lens of psychopathology has obvious dangers. Poignancy is added by consideration of Nietzsche's apophthegm,

> And if thou gaze long into an abyss,
> The abyss will also gaze into thee
> [*Beyond Good and Evil*, p.87].

So, the stages of the therapeutic craft are delineated, a guide for the politics of personal development as a therapist. And with this, the tocsin is rung, warning of the pathologization of life — the maladjustment bias, the pathology error — symptom of the psychotherapist's disease. If the tone of these discussions has been that of exhortation, my hope is that they will be taken kindly, while being taken to heart. To continue in that same vein, I want to add advice put forth by James Dublin (1992) in Undelivered Commencement Address. Founder and for many years the director of a psychotherapy training institute, Dublin penned, though never delivered, a passionate message to those who completed his training program. I will abbreviate and paraphrase his address.

With strong strokes, go against the backwards current. At first, in silence, look into the darkness. Without intent or definition, feel the uncertainty. Turn loose of all support and stand alone. Stand with your curiosity. And do not conform. Walk alone in the night, and write a song. After the dark night will come the mist of morning. Look carefully at the shapes in the mist and beware of crippling labels, calendars booked full with therapy appointments, uniforms, and quick cures. Get on the edge and be ready; light a match, even if your fingers get burned. Don't be too tough; see the needs of others. Don't be afraid when the creative energy comes. Do not seek power or domination. Do not offer yourself as a sacrifice. See each person freshly. Take care of your body and keep it together with your mind and your spirit. Ride the wind out. Know that you cannot create a better world. Skip to work and play hopscotch on your lunch break. Listen to the children — they know. Do what you will on weekends. Wherever you go, make music.

Because my paraphrasing constitutes an injustice to Dublin's intimacy with the logos, I add now the close of his address, in his own words.

Since a very tall tree is one way out of a very deep hole, learn to climb. Become a monkey if you have to. Climb to the sun. There's water there for the thirst, and rest, and peace. But not until you journey into the sky where the homeless wind lives. And, oh yeah, one last thing. Set the alarm, get up, and go to work like all the rest of us do [Dublin, 1992, p. 244].

---------------- *Chapter 7* ----------------

A Concluding Note

> The denominator relatively common to qualified psychother-
> apists is academic background and training. This can be rea-
> sonably defined. What is not definable and in need of definition
> is the voice through which the therapist applies his skills.
> Through the versatility of his human voice ... he can achieve
> an artistic talent that maximizes his effectiveness.

Originally appearing in 1965 in the inaugural issue of *Voices*, and
quoted thirty-four years later, this was written by Jules Baron (1999,
p. 77). I mention the year with wonder and with appreciation of the
fact that even though written over a third of a century ago, this piece
is equally valid today, and, save for the gender-biased pronouns,
sounds quite contemporary.

In the above passage, Baron chose a clever phrase, "the voice
through which the therapist applies his skills." This phrase acknowledges the techniques and methods that can be taught, while at the
same time giving just recognition to the *person*, with implied ubiquity, yet elusive of definition. Artistic talent recoils from any attempt
at definition through curriculum; personhood demands to be enigmatic and extracurricular.

Skills can be learned, but personhood must be *developed*.
Addressing this very distinction, Sheldon Kopp (1971) wrote the following:

> So it is that the most important aspects of the development
> of a psychotherapist occur outside the context of his pro-
> fessional school training, having more to do with his own
> personal sufferings, pleasures, risks, and adventures. In
> solitude, and later in the company of one who is already a
> guru, he must struggle with his own demons and must dare
> to free himself from them.... He must struggle alone, as well
> as in the company of others, with the joys and the agonies of
> his own personal life [p. 13].

In the present volume, having first created a *contextual* container for the enterprise of psychotherapy, and having searched the
literature available to me, I discussed *theories* of the person of the
therapist, and then reviewed the *research* pertaining thereto. Expanding beyond the traditional and arbitrary boundaries of psychology, I
then explored *philosophical and spiritual* aspects of personhood. The
existential writers offered the most from a philosophical perspective;
spiritual insights were found in abundance, cutting across many
sacred traditions. Next, I wrestled with the *development* of personhood. This was the most challenging of the several tasks, and, I
believe, the most important. It was in this wrestling, and I choose
this word advisedly, that I tried to address the development of the
"voice" of which Baron wrote, the "struggle" named by Kopp.

Ensconced in a spiritual framework in which richness and fullness of individualized being are sacredly regarded and most highly
treasured, guidelines were offered, based on the work of several careful thinkers, for working on oneself. Shifting from the levels of the
spiritual framework and the more specific guidelines, I moved to the
level of the psychological process of personal development, and introduced a calculus of personal growth. The formula is constituted of
three variables, those being awareness, experience within oneself, and
experience out in the world that is given resonance within. For *growth
takes place through here-and-now experience under conditions of heightened awareness.* I offered then a careful consideration of the means
whereby one can interfere with natural awareness, converting what
otherwise may be an exquisite awareness to one clouded by *confusion* or *dulling.*

It is not so much that there is one type of personality that makes
the best therapist. Rather, a good therapist is one who has and is
developing depth and richness of individual being. *It is this richness*

and depth of personhood, born of richness and depth of living, that is the most basic and the most potent qualification for facilitating growth in another. The final touch is a quality of style in one's being, a grace in one's manner. Perhaps indefinable in any ultimate sense, and open to debate, subject to one's particular taste, style and grace are surely of importance.

Finally, I approached the personal politics of psychotherapy. These *political* notes looped back to and became wrapped in the issue, once again, of the development of personhood.

The challenge, then, is to work on oneself, if one is to be a therapist. Better still, live fully, if one is to be a therapist. The rest you can learn.

Having written the present book, I have a better understanding of the meaning of the phrase *the person of the therapist*. My biases, at several levels, have been exposed. I also have new questions. I have learned to love these questions themselves, and it is to them that my heart now quickens.

References

Chapter 1

Bean, O. (1971). *Me and the Orgone*. New York: St. Martin's Press.

Bugental, J. F. T. (1987). *The Art of the Psychotherapist*. New York: Norton.

Colby, K. M. (1951). *A Primer for Psychotherapists*. New York: Ronald.

Frank, J. (1961). *Persuasion and Healing*. Baltimore: Johns Hopkins Press.

Harper, R. A. (1959). *Psychoanalysis & Psychotherapy: 36 Systems*. Englewood Cliffs: Prentice-Hall.

Jung, C. G. (1966). *The Practice of Psychotherapy: Volume 16 of The Collected Works of C. G. Jung* (2nd ed.). Princeton: Princeton University Press.

Lambert, M. J. (2001). "The Effectiveness of Psychotherapy: What Has a Century of Research Taught Us About the Effects of Treatment?" *Georgia Psychologist, 55*(2), 9–11.

Lambert, M. J., & Bergin, A. E. (1994). "The Effectiveness of Psychotherapy." In A. E. Bergin & S. L. Garfield (Eds.), *Handbook of Psychotherapy and Behavior Change* (4th ed., pp. 143–189). New York: Wiley.

Leland, T. W. (1965). "Voices: Nine Years A-Borning." *Voices, 1*(1), 5–6.

Levitsky, A. (1997). "Combining Hypnosis with Gestalt Therapy." In E. W. L. Smith (Ed.), *The Growing Edge of Gestalt Therapy* (pp. 111–123). Highland, N.Y.: Gestalt Journal Press.

London, P. (1964). *The Modes and Morals of Psychotherapy*. New York: Holt, Rinehart, and Winston.

Noll, R. (1997). *The Jung Cult: Origins of a Charismatic Movement*. New York: Free Press.

Rieff, P. (1966). *The Triumph of the Therapeutic: Uses of Faith After Freud.* New York: Harper & Row.

Rosenthal, S. G. (1999). [untitled]. *Voices, 35*(4), p. 7.

Seligman, M. P. (1995). "The Effectiveness of Psychotherapy: The *Consumer Reports* Study." *American Psychologist, 50,* 965–974.

Sharf, R. S. (2000). *Theories of Psychotherapy & Counseling* (2nd ed.). Belmont, Calif.: Wadsworth

Smith, E. W. L. (1975). "Altered States of Consciousness in Gestalt Therapy." *Journal of Contemporary Psychotherapy, 7*(1), 35–40.

Smith, E. W. L. (1978). "The Impasse Phenomenon: A Gestalt Therapy Experience Involving an Altered State of Consciousness." *The Gestalt Journal, 1*(1), 88–93.

Smith, E. W. L. (1985). *The Body in Psychotherapy.* Jefferson, N.C.: McFarland.

Smith, E. W. L. (2001). "Awe and Terror in the Living of the Resolution of the Polarity of Insight and Expression." *The Psychotherapy Patient, 11*(3/4), 99–121.

Chapter 2

Baker, E. F. (1967). *Man in the Trap.* New York: Collier.

Baumgardner, P. (1975). *Gifts from Lake Cowichan.* Palo Alto: Science and Behavior Books.

Berlin, I. (1953). *The Hedgehog and the Fox: An Essay on Tolstoy's View of History.* Chicago: Ivan R. Dee.

Bradford, K. (2001). "Therapeutic Courage." *Voices, 37*(2), 4–11.

Brothers, B. J. (1991). Introduction. *Journal of Couples Therapy, 2*(1/2), 1–10.

Brown, E. C. (1982). Preface to K. Malone, T. Malone, R. Kuckleburg, R. Cox, J. Barnett & D. Barstow, *Experiential Psychotherapy: Basic Principles, Part I. Pilgrimage, 10*(1), 25–26.

Colby, K. M. (1951). *A Primer for Psychotherapists.* New York: Ronald.

Dublin, J. E. (1971). "A Further Motive for Psychotherapists: Communicative Intimacy." *Psychiatry: Journal for the Study of Interpersonal Processes, 34,* 401–409.

Enelow, A. J., & Adler, L. M. (1965). Forward. In L. B. Fierman (Ed.), *Effective Psychotherapy: The Contribution of Hellmuth Kaiser* (pp. vii–xxvi). New York: Free Press.

Fagan, J. (1970). "The Tasks of the Therapist." In J. Fagan & I. L. Shepherd (Eds.), *Gestalt Therapy Now* (pp. 88–106). Palo Alto: Science and Behavior Books.

Felder, R. E., & Weiss, A. G. (1991). *Experiential Psychotherapy: A Symphony of Selves.* Lanham, Md.: University Press of America.

Fierman, L. B. (Ed.). (1965). *Effective Psychotherapy: The Contribution of Hellmuth Kaiser*. New York: Free Press.

Jung, C. G. (1966). *The Practice of Psychotherapy: Volume 16 of the Collected Works of C.G. Jung* (2nd ed.). Princeton: Princeton University Press.

Kaiser, H. (1965). "The Universal Symptom of the Psychoneuroses." In L. B. Fierman (Ed.), *Effective Psychotherapy: The Contribution of Hellmuth Kaiser* (pp. 14–171). New York: Free Press.

Klein, F. L. (2001). Experiential Psychotherapy — The Relationship Cure. *Voices, 37*(1), 13–16.

Kopp, S. B. (1971). *Guru: Metaphors from a Psychotherapist*. Palo Alto: Science and Behavior Books.

Lambert, M. J., & Bergin, A. E. (1994). "The Effectiveness of Psychotherapy." In A. E. Bergin & S. L. Garfield (Eds.), *Handbook of Psychotherapy and Behavior Change* (4th ed., pp. 143–189). New York: Wiley.

Levitsky, A., & Perls, F. S. (1970). "The Rules and Games of Gestalt Therapy." In J. Fagan & I. L. Shepherd (Eds.), *Gestalt Therapy Now* (pp. 140–149). Palo Alto: Science and Behavior Books.

Levy, L. H. (1963). *Psychological Interpretation*. New York: Holt, Rinehart and Winston.

Malone, K., Malone, T., Kuckleberg, R., Cox, R., Barnett, J., & Barstow, D. (1982). "Experiential Psychotherapy: Basic Principles, Part III." *Pilgrimage, 10*(3), 152–168.

Mendel, B. D. (1964). "On Therapist-Watching." *Psychiatry: Journal for the Study of Interpersonal Processes, 27*, 59–68.

Polster, E., & Polster, M. (1973). *Gestalt Therapy Integrated: Contours of Theory and Practice*. New York: Brunner/Mazel.

Reich, W. (1949). *Character-Analysis*. New York: Orgone Institute Press.

Reich, W. (1974). *Listen, Little Man!* New York: Noonday Press (Original work published 1948).

Rychlak, J. F. (1965). "The Motives to Psychotherapy." *Psychotherapy, 2*, 151–157.

Satir, V. (2000). "The Personhood of the Therapist: Effect on Systems." *Journal of Couples Therapy, 9*(3/4), 1–14.

Shepherd, I. L. (1992). "Teaching Therapy Through the Lives of the Masters: A Personal Statement." In E. W. L. Smith (Ed.), *Gestalt Voices* (pp. 239–240). Norwood, N.J.: Ablex.

Smith, E. W. L. (1984). Comment. In J. A. Travers (Ed.), *Psychotherapy and the Uncommitted Patient* (pp. 48–49). New York: Haworth.

Smith, E. W. L. (1985). *The Body in Psychotherapy*. Jefferson, N.C.: McFarland.

Smith, E. W. L. (2000). "Toward the Meaning of 'The Person of the Therapist.'" In B. J. Brothers (Ed.), *The Personhood of the Therapist* (pp. 43–49). New York: Haworth.

Smith, E. W. L. (2001). "The Person of the Therapist: Research Findings." *Voices, 37*(2), 73–79.

Stevens, B. (1970). *Don't Push the River*. Moab, Utah: Real People Press.

Weiss, A. G. (2001). "Between a Tabula Rasa and the Transparent Self: The 'Therapist's Use of Self' Revisited." *Voices, 37*(1), 4–12.

Welling, H. (2000). "On the Therapeutic Potency of Kaiser's Techniques: Some Misunderstandings?" *Psychotherapy, 37*(1), 57–63.

Whitaker, C. A., & Malone, T. P. (1953). *The Roots of Psychotherapy*. New York: Blakiston.

Chapter 3

Ackerman, S. J., & Hilsenroth, M. J. (2001). "A Review of Therapist Characteristics and Techniques Negatively Impacting the Therapeutic Alliance." *Psychotherapy, 38*(2), 171–185.

Beutler, L. E., Machado, P. P. P., & Neufeldt, S. A. (1994). "Therapist Variables." In A. E. Bergin & S. L. Garfield (Eds.), *Handbook of Psychotherapy and Behavior Change* (4th ed., pp. 229–269). New York: Wiley.

Conway, C. B. (1974). *Performance on the Myers-Briggs Type Indicator and Direction of Lateral Eye Movement as a Function of Performance on the A-B Scale*. Unpublished master's thesis, Georgia State University, Atlanta.

Dupont, D. G. (1976). *The Ability to Interpret Graphic and Tactile Communication of Emotion as a Function of A-B Character Type*. Unpublished master's thesis, Georgia State University, Atlanta.

Heffler, J. B. (1973). *The A-B Dimension of Personality and the Use of Metaphorical Language in Psychotherapy*. Unpublished doctoral dissertation, Georgia State University, Atlanta.

Kerr, D. R. (2000). *Becoming a Therapist: A Workbook for Personal Exploration*. Prospect Heights, Ill.: Waveland.

Lambert, M. J., & Bergin, A. E. (1994). "The Effectiveness of Psychotherapy." In A. E. Bergin & S. L. Garfield (Eds.), *Handbook of Psychotherapy and Behavior Change* (pp. 143–189). New York: Wiley.

Norcross, J. C. (2000). "Empirically Supported Therapeutic Relationships: A Division 29 Task Force." *Psychotherapy Bulletin, 35*(2), 2–4.

Schoen, S. (1994). *Presence of Mind: Literary and Philosophical Roots of a Wise Psychotherapy*. Highland, N.Y.: Gestalt Journal Press.

Smith, E. W. L. (1972). "Postural and Gestural Communication of A and B 'Therapist Types' During Dyadic Interviews." *Journal of Consulting and Clinical Psychology, 39*(1), 29–36.

Warkentin, J. (1965). "Dedication to Hungry Therapists." *Voices, 1*(1), 4.

Chapter 4

The Analects of Confucius (Chichung Huang, Trans.). (1997). New York: Oxford.

Bhagavad-Gita. (Swami Prabhavananda & C. Isherwood, Trans.). (1951). New York: Mentor.

Beisser, A. R. (1970). "The Paradoxical Theory of Change." In J. Fagan & I. L. Shepherd (Eds.), *Gestalt Therapy Now* (pp. 77–80). Palo Alto: Science and Behavior Books.

The Book of the Dead. (E. A. Wallis Budge, Trans.). (1960). New Hyde Park, N.Y.: University Books.

Brinton, C., Christopher, J. B., & Wolff, R. L. (1958). *A History of Civilization: Volume I: Prehistory to 1715*. Englewood Cliffs: Prentice-Hall.

Brooks, Charles V. W. (1974). *Sensory Awareness: The Rediscovery of Experiencing*. New York: Viking.

Campbell, J. (1988a). *The Power of Myth* (with Bill Moyers) [Public Broadcasting Service interview, Episode 2, "The Message of the Myth"]. New York: Mystic Fire Video.

Campbell, J. (1988b). *The Power of Myth* (with Bill Moyers). New York: Doubleday.

Campbell, J. (1990). *Transformations of Myth Through Time*. New York: Harper & Row.

Chaucer, G. *The Canterbury Tales* (N. Coghill, Trans.). (1960). Baltimore: Penguin.

Chuang Tsu. *Inner Chapters* (G. Feng & J. English, Trans.). (1974). New York: Random House.

Dante Alighieri. *The Divine Comedy: Hell* (D. Sayers, Trans.). (1960). Baltimore: Penguin.

Dunne, C. (2000). *Carl Jung: Wounded Healer of the Soul*. New York: Parabola.

Ellenberger, H. F. (1967). "A Clinical Introduction to Psychiatric Phenomenology and Existential Analysis." In R. May, E. Angel & H. F. Ellenberger (Eds.), *Existence* (pp. 92–124). New York: Clarion.

Evans, B. (Ed.). (1968). *Dictionary of Quotations*. New York: Avenel.

Funk & Wagnalls Standard Dictionary of Folklore, Mythology, and Legend. (1984). New York: Harper & Row.

Golomb, J. (1995). *In Search of Authenticity: From Kierkegaard to Camus*. New York: Routledge.

Golomb, J. (1999). Introductory Essay: "Nietzsche's 'New Psychology.'" In J. Golomb, W. Santaniello & R. L. Lehrer (Eds.), *Nietzsche and Depth Psychology* (pp. 1–19). Albany: State University of New York Press.

Hamilton, E. (1942). *Mythology*. New York: Mentor.

Hesse, H. (1969). *The Steppenwolf*. New York: Bantam. (Original work published 1927).

The *Holy Bible* (King James Version). (n.d.). Cleveland: World.

Jourard, S. M. (1964). *The Transparent Self: Self-Disclosure and Well-Being.* Princeton: Van Nostrand.

Jung, C. G. (1966). *The Practice of Psychotherapy: Volume 16 of the Collected Works of C. G. Jung* (2nd ed.). Princeton: Princeton University Press.

Jung, C. G. (1970). *Civilization in Transition.* Princeton: Princeton University Press.

Kaufmann, W. (Ed.). (1982). *The Portable Nietzsche.* New York: Viking Penguin.

Keen, S. (1974). "The Cosmic versus the Rational." *Psychology Today, 8*(2), 56–59.

Kopp, S. B. (1971). *Guru: Metapors from a Psychotherapist.* Palo Alto: Science and Behavior Books.

Lander, N. R., & Nahon, D. (2000). "Personhood of the Therapist in Couples Therapy: An Integrity Therapy Perspective." In B. J. Brothers (Ed.), *The Personhood of the Therapist* (pp. 29–42). New York: Haworth.

Lao Tsu. *Tao te ching* (Gia-Fu Feng & J. English, Trans.). (1972). New York: Vintage.

Lao Tzu. *Tao te ching* (W. Bynner, Trans.). (1962). New York: Capricorn.

Leitner, L. M. (2001). "The Role of Awe in Experiential Personal Construct Psychology." In R. B. Marchesani & E. M. Stern (Eds.), *Frightful Stages: From the Primitive to the Therapeutic* (p. 149–162). New York: Haworth.

The Meaning of the Glorious Koran (M. M. Pickthall, Trans.). (1961). New York: Mentor.

Miller, H. (1978). [Letter] *Voices, 14*(3), 21–22.

Montaigne, M. de. *The Essays: A Selection* (M. A. Screech, Trans.). (1993). New York: Penguin. (Original work published 1580).

Nietzsche, F. (n.d.). *Beyond Good and Evil.* New York: Carlton House.

O'Reilley, M. R. (1998). *Radical Presence: Teaching as Contemplative Practice.* Portsmouth, N.H.: Boynton/Cook.

Partridge, B. (1960). *A History of Orgies.* New York: Bonanza.

Perls, F. S. (1969). *Gestalt Therapy Verbatim.* Moab, Utah: Real People Press.

Perls, F. S. (1979). "Planned Psychotherapy." [Edited and with footnote commentary by Laura Perls]. *The Gestalt Journal, II*(2), 4–23.

Perls, F. S. (1998). "The Manipulator: A Session of Gestalt Therapy with Dr. Frederick Perls and Group." *The Gestalt Journal, 21*(2), 75–90.

Perls, L. (1978). Concepts and Misconceptions of Gestalt Therapy. *Voices, 14*(3), 31–36.

Pirsig, R. (1974). *Zen and the Art of Motorcycle Maintenance.* New York: William Morrow.

Poetic Edda. (L. M. Hollander, Trans.). (2nd ed., 1962). Austin: University of Texas Press.

Popkin, R. & Stroll, A. (1956). *Philosophy Made Simple*. Garden City: Doubleday.

Ram Dass. (1974). *The Only Dance There Is*. Garden City: Anchor.

Raskin, N. J. (1974). "Studies of Psychotherapeutic Orientation: Ideology and Practice." *Research Monograph of the American Academy of Psychotherapists, 1.*

Sabin, F. (1940). *Classical Myths That Live Today*. New York: Silver Burdett.

Schoen, S. (1994). *Presence of Mind: Literary and Philosophical Roots of a Wise Psychotherapy*. Highland, N.Y.: The Gestalt Journal Press.

Shakespeare, W. (n.d.). *Hamlet*. In *The Complete Works of William Shakespeare* (pp. 945–980). Cleveland: World Syndicate.

Shakespeare, W. (n.d.). *Macbeth*. In *The Complete Works of William Shakespeare* (pp. 922–944). Cleveland: World Syndicate.

Shostrom, E. L. (1968). *Man, the Manipulator: The Inner Journey from Manipulation to Actualization*. New York: Bantam.

Smith, E. W. L. (1985). *The Body in Psychotherapy*. Jefferson, N.C.: McFarland.

Smith, E. W. L. (1991). "Gestalt, a Dionysian Path." *The Gestalt Journal, 14*(2), 61–69.

Smith, E. W. L. (1998). "A Taxonomy and Ethics of Touch in Psychotherapy." In E. W. L. Smith, P. R. Clance & S. Imes (Eds.), *Touch in Psychotherapy: Theory, Research, and Practice.* (pp. 36–51). New York: Guilford.

Smith, H. (1958). *The Religions of Man*. New York: Mentor.

Sturluson, S. *Prose Edda.* (Jean Young, Trans.). (1954). Berkeley: University of California Press.

Tillich, P. (1962). "The Courage to Be." In W. Barrett & H. Aiken (Eds.), *Philosophy in the Twentieth Century* (pp. 652–687). New York: Random House.

Watts, A. (1974). *Cloud-Hidden, Whereabouts Unknown*. New York: Vintage.

Chapter 5

Adam, M. (1976). *Wandering in Eden*. New York: Alfred A. Knopf.

Allen, R. E. (Ed.). (1966). *Greek Philosophy: Thales to Aristotle*. New York: Free Press.

Beisser, A. R. (1970). "The Paradoxical Theory of Change." In J. Fagan & I. L. Shepherd (Eds.), *Gestalt Therapy Now* (pp. 77–80). Palo Alto: Science and Behavior Books.

Beowulf. (K. Crossley-Holland, Trans.). (1987). Suffolk, England: Boydell.

Blackham, H. J. (1959). *Six Existentialist Thinkers*. New York: Harper Torchbooks.

Blake, W. (1975). *The Marriage of Heaven and Hell*. Oxford: Oxford University Press. (Original work published 1789).

Bugenthal, J. F. T. (1971). "The Humanistic Ethic—The Individual in Psychotherapy as a Societal Change Agent." *The Journal of Humanistic Psychology, 11*(1), 11–25.

Campbell, J. (1990). *Transformations of Myth Through Time*. New York: Harper & Row.

Castaneda, C. (1968). *The Teachings of Don Juan: A Yaqui Way of Knowledge*. Berkeley: University of California Press.

Castaneda, C. (1972). *Journey to Ixtlan*. New York: Simon and Schuster.

Castaneda, C. (1974). *Tales of Power*. New York: Simon and Schuster.

cummings, e. e. (n.d.). Letter. Retrieved March 18, 2002, from http://www.erowid.org/culture/poetry.

Eliade, M. (1964). *Shamanism: Archaic Techniques of Ecstasy*. Princeton: Princeton University Press.

Evans, B. (Ed.). (1968). *Dictionary of Quotations*. New York: Avenel.

Fadiman, J., & Frager, R. (1994). *Personality and Personal Growth* (5th ed.). New York: Harper Collins.

Freud, S. (1960). *The Ego and the Id*. New York: Norton. (Original work published 1923)

Golomb, J. (1995). *In Search of Authenticity: From Kierkegaard to Camus*. New York: Routledge.

Harman, R. L. (1992). "Gestalt Therapy Discussed: An Interview with James E. Simkin." In E. W. L. Smith (Ed.), *Gestalt Voices* (pp. 124–133). Norwood, N.J.: Ablex.

Horney, K. (1950). *Neurosis and Human Growth: The Struggle Toward Self-Realization*. New York: Norton.

Hotchner, A. E. (1983). *Papa Hemingway*. New York: Quill.

Huxley, A. (2001). [quotation]. *Voices, 37*(1), 42.

Jung, C. G. (1963). *Memories, Dreams, Reflections*. New York: Vintage.

Kaufmann, W. (1989). *Existentialism from Dostoevsky to Sartre*. New York: Meridian.

Klonsky, M. (1977). *William Blake: The Seer and His Visions*. New York: Harmony Books.

Kopp, S. B. (1971). *Guru: Metaphors from a Psychotherapist*. Palo Alto: Science and Behavior Books.

Kopp, S. B. (1974). *The Hanged Man*. Palo Alto, CA: Science and Behavior Books.

Lao Tsu. *Tao te ching* (Gia-Fu Feng & J. English, Trans.). (1972). New York: Vintage.

Lao Tzu. *Tao te ching* (W. Bynner, Trans.). (1962). New York: Capricorn.

Maslow, A. H. (1969a). "Notes on Being-Psychology." In A. J. Sutich & M. A. Vich (Eds.), *Readings in Humanistic Psychology* (pp. 51–80). New York: Free Press.

Maslow, A. H. (1969b). "A Theory of Metamotivation: The Biological Rooting of the Value-Life." In A. J. Sutich & M. A. Vich (Eds.), *Readings in Humanistic Psychology* (pp. 153–199). New York: Free Press.

May, R. (1991). *The Cry for Myth*. New York: Delta.

Moraitis, G. (1999). "Nietzsche's Readers and Their 'Will to Ignorance.'" In J. Golomb, W. Santaniello & R. Lehrer (Eds.), *Nietzsche and Depth Psychology* (pp. 317–330). Albany: State University of New York Press.

Moustakas, C. (1974). *Finding Yourself, Finding Others*. Englewood Cliffs: Prentice-Hall.

Moustakas, C. (1994). *Existential Psychotherapy and the Interpretation of Dreams*. Northvale, N.J.: Jason Aronson.

Naranjo, C. (1970). "Present-Centeredness: Technique, Prescription, and Ideal." In J. Fagan & I. L. Shepherd (Eds.), *Gestalt Therapy Now* (pp. 47–69). Palo Alto: Science and Behavior Books.

Naranjo, C. (1980). *The Techniques of Gestalt Therapy*. Highland, NY: Gestalt Journal Press.

Nietzsche, F. (1982a). *The Gay Science*. In W. Kaufmann (Ed.), *The Portable Nietzsche* (pp. 93–102). New York: Viking Penguin.

Nietzsche, F. (1982b). *Thus Spoke Zarathustra*. In W. Kaufmann (Ed.), *The Portable Nietzsche* (pp. 103–439). New York: Viking Penguin.

Perls, F. S. (1969). *Gestalt Therapy Verbatim*. Moab, Utah: Real People Press.

Petersen, S. (1971). *A Catalog of the Ways People Grow*. New York: Ballantine.

Pletsch, C. (1999). "Nietzsche's Striving." In J. Golomb, W. Santaniello & R. Lehrer (Eds.), *Nietzsche and Depth Psychology* (pp. 331–341). Albany: State University of New York Press.

Poetic Edda. (L. M. Hollander, Trans.). (2nd ed., 1962). Austin: University of Texas Press.

Polster, E., & Polster, M. (1973). *Gestalt Therapy Integrated: Contours of Theory and Practice*. New York: Brunner/Mazel.

Prather, H. (1977). *Notes on Love and Courage*. Garden City: Doubleday.

Ram Dass (1974). *The Only Dance There Is*. Garden City: Anchor.

Reich, W. (1974). *Listen, Little Man!* New York: Noonday Press. (Original work published 1948)

Robbins, T. (1985). *Jitterbug Perfume*. New York: Bantam.

Roosevelt, T. (1901). *The Strenuous Life*. New York: Century.

Schoen, S. (1994). *Presence of Mind: Literary and Philosophical Roots of a Wise Psychotherapy*. Highland, N.Y.: Gestalt Journal Press.

Smith, E. W. L. (1985). *The Body in Psychotherapy*. Jefferson, N.C.: McFarland.

Smith, E. W. L. (1987). *Sexual Aliveness: A Reichian Gestalt Perspective*. Jefferson, N.C.: McFarland.

Smith, E. W. L. (1996). "Relating the Couple and the Logos." In B. J. Brothers

(Ed.), *Couples and the Tao of Congruence* (pp. 27–33). New York: Haworth.

Smith, E. W. L. (1998). "At the Cusp of Being and Becoming: The Growing Edge Phenomenon." *The Gestalt Journal, XXI*(2), 9–19.

Smith, E. W. L. (2001). "Shamanism, Psychoanalysis, and Gestalt Therapy: An Integrative Paradigm." *Georgia Psychologist, 55*(1), 26–27.

Stevens, B. (1970). *Don't Push the River.* Moab, Utah: Real People Press.

Stevens, B. (1984). *Burst Out Laughing.* Berkeley: Celestial Arts.

Sturluson, S. *Prose Edda.* (Jean Young, Trans.). (1954). Berkeley: University of California Press.

Walker, J. L. (2001). "The Alchemy of the Teapot." *Parabola, 26*(3), 79–84.

Weiten, W., & Lloyd, M. A. (1997). *Psychology Applied to Modern Life: Adjustment in the 90's* (5th ed.). Pacific Grove, Calif.: Brooks/Cole.

Williams, P. (1973). *Das Energi.* New York: Warner.

Chapter 6

Capra, F. (1984). *The Tao of Physics.* New York: Bantam.

Dublin, J. E. (1992). Undelivered Commencement Address. In E. W. L. Smith (Ed.), *Gestalt Voices* (pp. 241–244). Norwood, N.J.: Ablex.

Kartha, D. K. M. (2001). "One God or Many Gods?" *Parabola, 26* (3), 85–86.

Kopp, S. B. (1971). *Guru: Metaphors from a Psychotherapist.* Palo Alto: Science and Behavior Books.

Krippner, S. (1991). Forward. In C. M. Aanstoos (Ed.), *Studies in Humanistic Psychology* (pp. vi–viii). Carrollton: West Georgia College Press.

Lao Tsu. *Tao te ching* (Gia-Fu Feng & J. English, Trans.). (1972). New York: Vintage.

Lao Tzu. *Tao te ching* (W. Bynner, Trans.). (1962). New York: Capricorn.

Nietzsche, F. (n.d.). *Beyond Good and Evil.* New York: Carlton House.

Nietzsche, F. (1982). *Twilight of the Idols.* In W. Kaufmann (Ed.), *The Portable Nietzsche* (pp. 463–563). New York: Viking Penguin.

Pope, A. (1930). *An Essay on Man II.* In A. W. Ward (Ed.), *The Poetical Works of Alexander Pope* (p. 206). London: MacMillan.

Smith, E. W. L. (1988). "Stages of the Therapeutic Craft." *Voices, 23*(4), 49–55.

Smith, E. W. L. (1995). "On the Pathologization of Life: Psychotherapist's Disease." In M. B. Sussman (Ed.), *A Perilous Calling: The Hazards of Psychotherapy Practice* (pp. 81–88). New York: Wiley.

Smith, E. W. L. (1997). "The Roots of Gestalt Therapy." In E. W. L. Smith, (Ed.), *The Growing Edge of Gestalt Therapy* (pp. 3–36). Highland, N.Y.: Gestalt Journal Press.

Chapter 7

Baron, J. (1999). [quotation] *Voices*, *35*(4), 77.

Kopp, S. B. (1971). *Guru: Metaphors from a Psychotherapist*. Palo Alto: Science and Behavior Books.

Index

abstract behavior 169
accurate empathy 25, 57
Ackerman, S. 60, 61
action therapy 9
Adam, M. 110, 136
Adler, L. 30
Adlerian stage 37
affective model 10
age, impact on therapy 52
analysis of context 30
analysis of duplicity 30
analysis of resistance 30
Apollonian world view 95–103
Aristotle 11, 99
art, therapy as 14, 15, 28, 93, 103
Atlanta Psychiatric Clinic 9, 12, 31
authenticity 69–71, 79, 84–87, 114, 115, 122, 123, 135
aware presence 27
awareness 130–134, 138–144

B-motivation 117
B-values 117, 118
Baker, E. 45
Barnett, J. 32, 33
Baron, J. 173
Barstow, D. 32, 33
Baumgardner, P. 41, 42
behavioral model 10

being motivation *see* B-motivation
being-in-the-world 112
being needs 117
being-with-others 114, 116, 118
Beisser, A. 100, 123
Bell's Graphic Emotions Index 54
Bergin, A. 17, 24, 26, 51, 59, 65, 67, 68
Berlin, I. 42, 43
Beutler, L. 52, 56–59
Binswanger, L. 47
Blake, W. 133, 134
Boss, M. 47
Bradford, K. 46
breadth of experience 142
Brooks, C. 89
Brothers, B. 35, 36
Brown, E. 33
Browning, R. 132
Buddhism 77, 102
Bugenthal, J. 48, 107, 135
Burber, M. 38, 39, 47
bureaucratization, of psychotherapy 149–151, 155

calculus of growth 140
Campbell, J. 70, 71, 95, 106, 129–130, 137
Camus, A. 122
Capra, F. 153

Carkhuff, R. 24, 25
Carkhuff Accurate Empathy Scale 54
Castaneda, C. 126–128, 136
character analysis 30
characteristics, of the therapist 67
Christian, views on truth 80–84
Chuang-tzu 131
classical learning curve 157–163
classical understanding 97, 98
classification, of therapy 7
Client Centered Therapy 24
client variable 25
clouded awareness 143; see also awareness
cognitive differential 40
cognitive model 10
Colby, K. 7
communication: intimacy 47, 48; non-verbal 54
computer non-verbal stance 124
concrete behavior 169
confession 36, 37, 73
confluence 143, 144
Confucianism, views on truth 84
Confucius 74–75
confused awareness 143; see also awareness
consistent resistance analysis 30
Constructive Personality Change 25, 26, 27
Consumer Reports 17
contact boundary disturbances 144
Conway, C. 54
cool media 115
core conditions 25
cosmic view 97
courage 108
covering therapy 7
Cox, R. 32, 33
curative motive 47

D-motivation 117
Dasein 112
Dass, R. 87, 110
defense analysis 30
deficiency motivation see D-motivation
deficiency needs 117
deflection 143, 144
delusion of fusion 29

depth of experience 142
Depth of Interpersonal Exploration 25
desensitization to pathology 143, 144, 164–169
dilettante therapist 159–161, 163
Dionysian world view 95–103
directive therapy 9
Don Juan 126–128, 136
Dublin, J. 47, 170
dulled awareness 143; see also awareness
duplicity analysis 30
Dupont, D. 54

education: in Jung's theory 36–37; of therapist 147–149
efficacy: of therapy 17, 18; of therapist 24, 26, 148
ego 139, 140, 144
Egyptian, truth 84
Eigenwelt 112, 116, 118, 119, 123
Eliade, M. 139
Ellenberger, H. 71, 90
Ellis, A. 11
elucidation 36, 37
emotional plaque 44–45; manifestations of 45
Enelow, A. 30
English, J. 75
enlightenment 131–133
equality 39–41; personal 38; in therapy 36
Ericksonian hypnosis 15, 16
Erksine, R. 10, 11
eros 96, 97
ethics 13, 14, 47, 68, 72–74, 79, 103
ethnicity, impact on therapy 53
evocative therapy 9
evolution, of psychotherapy 149–155
existential psychotherapy 47, 84–87
existential theory 123
Experiential Psychotherapy 9, 12, 33, 34
expert therapist 161–163
Expressive Mode 98–100
expressive therapies 10

facticité 112, 116
Fagan, J. 40–42
fallenness 114, 116

fear, in therapy 40
Fedler, R. 9, 33, 35
Feng, G. 75
Fierman, L. 28, 29
Frank, J. 9
Freud, S. 8, 30, 37, 47, 139, 151
Freudian stage 37

gender, impact on therapy 53, 56
generalist therapist 161, 163
God 106–108
Goethe, J. 108, 109
Goldstein, K. 169
Golomb, J. 85, 112, 122
grace 89–91
Grail, legend of 70, 71, 137
growth motivation *see* B-motivation
growth needs *see* being needs
growth of person in therapy 68
growth of therapist 150, 156–160

Harper, R. 5, 8
Heffler, J. 54
Heidegger, M. 71, 86, 111–116, 118, 119, 123
Hemingway, E. 107, 146
Hesse, H. 99
Hilsenroth, M. 60, 61
Hinduism 76, 84, 102, 129, 136, 160
Holmes, O. 131
honesty 33, 70, 72, 86, 145; *see also* authenticity
Horace 108
Horney, K. 96, 98, 121, 151
hot media 115
human condition 29
humanness, in therapy 41
Husley, A. 134
hypnosis, in therapy 15, 16

I-boundary 141, 142
I-Thou relationship 68
id 139
illusion of fusion 29
inequality, in therapy 36
insight 130
Insight Mode 98–100
insight therapy 9
Integrity Therapy 69
intensity of experience 142

Interpersonal Discrimination Test 55
interpersonal medical dynamics 165
interventions, purpose of 30
introjection 143
irrational therapy 8, 9
Islamic, views on truth 80, 81, 84

James, W. 21
Janov, A. 11
Johnson, R. 47
Jourard, S. 69
journeyman therapist 158, 159, 161–163
Judaism, views on truth 80, 81, 84
Jung, C. 7, 8, 20, 36–38, 72, 86, 87, 96, 97, 106, 142, 151
Jungian dimensions 53, 55

Kafka, F. 132
kairos 90
Kaiser, H. 12, 28–31
Keen, S. 97
Kempler, W. 47
Kerr, D. 51
Kierkegaard 122
Klein, F. 32–34
Klonsky, M. 133
Klopfer, W. 167
Kopp, S. 43, 44, 89, 91, 109, 110, 145, 151, 173, 174
Kuckleberg, R. 32, 33

Laing 151
Lambert, M. 16, 17, 24, 26, 51, 59, 60, 65
Lander, N. 69, 70
language, in psychotherapy 168, 169
Leary, T. 167
Leitner, L. 68, 69
LeLand, T. 14
Levy, L. 39, 40
logos 96, 97
London, P. 9, 10

Machado, P. 52, 56–59
Mahrer, A. 9
major psychotherapy 7, 8
maladjustment bias 167–169; *see also* psychotherapist's disease
Malone, K. 32, 33

Malone, T. 9, 31–35
Maslow, A. 117–119, 125, 126, 129
master therapist 162, 163
May, R. 107
Mendel, B. 42, 43
meta needs 117
metamotivations 118, 119
Miller, H. 89
minor psychotherapy 7
Mitwelt 112, 114–116, 118, 119, 123
models of therapy 7, 10
Montaigne, M. 73, 74
Moreno, J. 16
Moustakas, C. 112, 115, 116, 118
Mowrer, O. 69, 70
Myers-Briggs Type Indicator 53–55

Nahon, D. 69, 70
Naranjo, C. 109, 124–126, 129, 141
The Negative Confession 73
negative outcomes of therapy see out-
     comes of therapy
neophyte therapist 158, 162, 163
Neufeldt, S. 52, 56–59
neurotic 30; duplicity of 30, personal
     responsibility of 30
Nietzsche, F. 85, 88, 94, 95, 96, 100,
     107, 110, 120–123, 144, 145, 164,
     170
Noll, R. 20
Norcross, J. 59, 60
Nordic mythology 78–80, 100, 137–139:
     truth 84

O'Reilley, M. 89
Ortega, J. 112
outcomes of therapy: negative and
     positive 26, 27, 55–58, 68
Ovid 108

paradoxical theory of change 123
pathologization of life 163–168, 170
patient-vectors 34
patterning 41
perceptual differential 40
Perls, F. 38, 101, 102, 108, 110, 122, 130,
     151, 169
Perls, L. 90
person of the therapist 51, 61–65, 86
personal dialectic 141

personal equality 38
personal responsibility 30
personal therapy 38
personality characteristics 26, 27, 31
personhood 12, 25, 28, 31, 35, 36, 42
     86, 88, 105–130, 139, 140, 144, 156,
     173
Peterson, S. 135, 136
philosophy, of therapy 6
phoric differential 40
Pirsig, R. 97, 98
Plato 11
Poetic Edda 138, 139
Polster, E. 39, 141
Polster, M. 39, 141
Pope, A. 163
positive outcomes of therapy see out-
     comes of therapy
potency, in therapy 41
Prather, H. 108
pre–Freudian stage 37
Primal Therapy 11
projection 143
Prose Edda 138, 139
psychodrama 16
psychotherapist's disease 163–170; see
     also maladjustment bias
psychotherapy: approaches to 47;
     bureaucratization of 149–151, 155;
     defined by Dublin 47; evolution of
     149–155; teaching of 28

Rational Emotive Therapy 11
rational therapy 8, 9
rational view 97
rebellion 120–122
Reich, W. 30, 44–46, 110, 151
relationship oriented 31
relationships see therapeutic relation-
     ships
religion, in therapy 9, 20
renunciation of pleasure 102, 103
resistance analysis 30
reverence, in therapy 68
Rieff, P. 9, 20
right man theory 23, 48
Rilke, R. 49, 61, 132
Robbins, T. 142
Rogers, C. 24, 25, 28, 47, 57
romantic understanding 97–98

Roosevelt, T. 107
Rosenthal, S. 14
Ruitenbeek, H. 47, 48
Rychlak, J. 47

Sartre J. 29, 30, 111–116, 119, 122
Satir, V. 35, 36, 124
scholarly motive 47
scientific therapies 9
self-actualization 119, 122, 123, 125, 126, 129
self-awareness *see* awareness
self-disclosure 48, 69, 70, 155, 156
self-image actualization 122
Seligman, M. 17
Sergeant, E. 72
sex *see* gender
Sharf, R. 19
Shepard, I. 28, 39, 40
Shostrom, E. 72
Simkin, J. 39, 123
Smith, H. 80, 86
socio-culture, of therapy 7
Socrates 111
spirituality in therapy 69
stages of the therapeutic craft 156
Stevens, B. 23, 27, 48, 110, 130
Strong Vocational Interest Blank 53
superego 139
super-reasonable verbal stance 124
Systematic Desensitization 11

Tantra 102, 103
Tao Te Ching 154
Taoism 87, 88; truth 84
tasks of the therapist 40
teaching: psychotherapy 28; technique 35, 173; *see also* education
technical eclecticism 18
technique-oriented 31
technique, therapeutic 6, 11–13, 18, 23, 24, 35, 27, 53–55, 88, 89, 152, 156, 157, 173
theoretical eclecticism 19
theory, of therapy 6
therapeutic conditions: function of change 25
therapeutic relationships 11–13, 69; Atlanta Psychiatric Clinic's view on 31; characteristics of 32, 57; I-It 38;

I-Thou 38; importance of 32, 55; Kaiser's view on 31; in therapy 27, 47, 60, 61
therapist behaviors *see* therapist variables
therapist factor: in treatment outcome 24, 51
therapist self-congruence 25, 57
therapist variables: effect of 25, 51, 52, 60; "use of self" as 33–35
therapists-vectors 34
therapy, as art 93, 103
Third Force 169
throwness 113, 116
timing: in Nordic literature 91; in Taoist literature 90; in therapy 90
transcendence 116, 118
transcendent ego 116
transformation 36, 38
transparent self 69
transtheoretical integration 19
Trilling, L. 86
tropology 133
Truax, C. 24–26, 28, 57
truth 74–76, 77–84, 86; *see also* honesty and authenticity
Tsu, C. 75, 76
Tsu, L. 75, 87, 90, 91, 100, 131
Tzu, L. *see* Tsu, L.

Umwelt 112–114, 116, 118, 119, 123
Unconditional Positive Regard 25, 57
uncovering therapy 7
universal psychopathology 29
universal symptom 29
universal therapy 29
universal triad 29
use of self, therapist's 33, 35, 36

variables of therapy 25, 26

Warkentin, J. 8, 9
Watts, A. 102
Weiss, A. 33–35
Welling, H. 30
Whitaker, C. 9, 31, 34, 35
Williams, P. 107
Wolpe, J. 11, 47
wu wei 88